Barry E. O'Meara

Napoleon in Exile

Or, a voice from St. Helena. The opinions and reflections of Napoleon on the most important events of his life and government, in his own words. Vol. 2

Barry E. O'Meara

Napoleon in Exile

Or, a voice from St. Helena. The opinions and reflections of Napoleon on the most important events of his life and government, in his own words. Vol. 2

ISBN/EAN: 9783337350345

Printed in Europe, USA, Canada, Australia, Japan

Cover: Foto ©ninafisch / pixelio.de

More available books at **www.hansebooks.com**

NAPOLEON IN EXILE;

OR,

A VOICE FROM ST. HELENA

THE

OPINIONS AND REFLECTIONS OF NAPOLEON

ON THE

MOST IMPORTANT EVENTS IN HIS LIFE AND GOVERNMENT
IN HIS OWN WORDS.

BY BARRY E. O'MEARA, ESQ.,
HIS LATE SURGEON.

IN TWO VOLUMES.—VOL. II.

NEW YORK.
PETER ECKLER, PUBLISHER,
No. 35 Fulton Street.

NAPOLEON IN EXILE;

OR,

A VOICE FROM ST. HELENA.

7th.—Napoleon very particular in inquiring about Captain Meynell, whose death he observed would grieve him, as he had *l'air d'un brave homme.** Had some more conversation with him relative to the prisoners made at the commencement of the war. I said, that I believed he had demanded that the ships as well as the prisoners made in them should be given up in exchange for those detained in France. He replied, that he did not recollect that he had demanded the ships. "The only reason," added he, "that your government would give as a right for detaining them as prisoners was, that they *had always done so in preceding wars*, and that it would be lessening to the dignity of the government to give them up, or to consider as prisoners of war those who had been detained by me in France. To this I answered, that they had always done so, because they had to deal with *imbéciles*, and people who knew not how to act vigorously, and were afraid to retaliate. As to the exchange of prisoners, I offered to effect it in the following manner, viz. to send three thousand men, consisting of two thousand Spaniards and Portuguese, and one thousand English to a certain place, there to be exchanged for three thousand French, and so on until all were exchanged. Your government would not consent to this, but required that all the Eng-

---

* The appearance of a brave man.

lish should be exchanged at first; though the others were your allies, and were taken fighting by your side. As soon as the French prisoners in England heard of this proposal, they wrote over the strongest letters possible, protesting against and praying me not to consent to such terms, alleging, that as soon as your ministers had got all the English prisoners, amounting I believe to ten thousand, they would under some pretext break off the exchange;[*] and that they (the French prisoners) who were already treated badly enough, would then be subjected to every species of brutality and ill-treatment, as the English would no longer be afraid of reprisals. What I most regret," added he, "and am most to blame for is, that during my reign I had not caused the English prisoners to be put on board of *pontons*, and treated exactly as you treated mine in England. Indeed I had given orders to have it done, and to place them in ships in the Scheldt. Décres, the minister of marine, though he hated you as much as a man could do, opposed it on the ground of the expense, the difficulty of effecting it, and other reasons. There were numbers of reports also from your transport board, testifying the good treatment which the prisoners enjoyed, which imposed upon me for a time; but, as I found out from the prisoners themselves afterwards, they were filled with lies, like the reports that are sent from this island. I was also so much occupied with affairs of a more important nature, that I forgot it." I took the liberty of observing, that I hoped he did not credit what he saw in Pillet's libel. "No, no," replied Napoleon. "I believe no exaggerated statement of the kind. I reason from the testimonies of the prisoners themselves and from the circumstances. In the first place, it was *le comble du barbarie*[†] to put any prisoners, especially soldiers, in ships at all. Even sailors like to be on shore. I see that the admiral likes to live on shore, as well as

---

[*] I have some recollection (although I cannot find it in my journal) that Napoleon also told me that he had proposed to the English minister that both powers should simultaneously land their respective prisoners in such ports in England and France as might have been previously agreed upon, which proposal was not agreed to by his majesty's ministers.

[†] The height of barbarity.

every officer and seaman who can effect it. Man was born on shore, and it is natural for him to like it. Your ministers said that they had not any fortresses to put them in. Then, why not have exchanged or sent them to Scotland, instead of massacring them in *pontons?* I am very sorry that I did not carry my intentions into execution, as in the event of a war fifty or sixty years hence between the two countries, it will be said, but even Napoleon suffered the English to put the French prisoners in *pontons* without having retaliated. My intentions were to have put all the *milords* and the principal prisoners in *pontons*, and to have made them undergo precisely the same treatment as that practised upon my prisoners in the prison-ships in England. This would have had the desired effect, and would have been beneficial to both parties. For the complaints of '*my lords*,' to which I would have allowed every publicity to be given, would have produced such an outcry, such a sensation amongst you English, who are *egoïstes*, by making you feel yourselves that which you inflicted upon others, that your oligarchy would have been obliged to remove the French prisoners from the *pontons*, which would have been followed by a similar step on my part. I would have left the *canaille* in the fortresses, as they, poor devils, had nothing to do with the measures of your ministers, who, indeed, cared but little what they suffered. I would not," continued Napoleon, " desire a better testimonial in my favor than that of the prisoners of the different nations who have been in France. Many of your English sailors did not want to be exchanged. They did not wish to be sent again on board of their floating prisons. The Russians declared, that they were much better than in their own country, after they discovered that their heads were not to be cut off, which they at first had been persuaded to believe; and the Austrians would not have escaped, even if allowed."

"Another shocking act of your ministers," said Napoleon, " was the bundling (*jete*) of some hundred wounded and disabled soldiers who had been born in countries under me, and were wounded fighting your battles against me, on the coast of Holland, where they were liable by the laws of the country to be tried and shot within twenty-four hours, for having carried arms against it. When it was reported to me, and application made to try them, I said, 'Let them go on. Let them land as many as they like. They will tell what treatment they have received, and will prevent others of my troops from deserting and joining the English.' To say nothing of the inhumanity of the practice," said Napoleon, lifting up his hands with emotion, "it was very bad policy on the part of your ministers, as these poor mutilated wretches told it everywhere; and I also caused the names, countries, where wounded, &c., of many of them to be published in the Moniteur."

I endeavored to controvert the tenor of some of his assertions; but in consequence of not being sufficiently well acquainted with the circumstances, I could make but a feeble effort against a man who was master of the subject, to say nothing of the difficulty of contending against such an antagonist.

11*th*.—Told Sir Hudson Lowe what Napoleon had said relative to the restrictions, and the commissioners, &c. His Excellency asked why I had not told him this before? I replied, because it had only occurred yesterday, and that having often made him communications of a similar nature before, I had not thought it important. He observed that it was of *great* importance, as having taken place since he had sent his answer to their observations upon his restrictions. He then observed, that the principal cause of all the difficulties which he had to combat with the French people had arisen from Sir George Cockburn's having, upon his own authority, and beyond his instructions, taken upon himself to grant much more indulgence, and a much greater space for limits without being accompanied by a British officer, than he had any right to do; not only had he not the right, but it was contrary to his instructions, and that on his arrival, he had been astonished at Sir George Cockburn's conduct. He then spoke for some time about the letter which had been written by Madame Bertrand to Marquis Montchenu; which he seemed to consider as a very heinous offence. I observed that Count Bertrand had said that, at the time the letter was written, there had existed no prohibition against epistolary correspondence with persons domiciliated in the island as the marquis was, and that since that letter had been written by Madame Bertrand, six sealed letters had been received by her, amongst which was one from Sir George Bingham. His excellency did not appear to be well pleased with this observation of Count Bertrand's.

The quantity of wood and coals allowed not being near sufficient, Count Montholon desired me to represent to the governor, that in the admiral's time, when there were not near so many fires as at present, there was more than double the quantity of fuel allowed; that for some time they had been obliged to burn the wine-cases, and to request of him, if he did not think proper to increase the quantity furnished by government, that he would give directions that the purveyor might supply it, on their paying for it themselves. Went to Plantation House, and explained to the governor the above communication, particularizing the number of fires; who, after some discussion, replied, that he would give orders for an additional supply to be furnished.

12th.—Napoleon in his bath. Had some conversation about the governor. " If," said he, " the governor on his arrival here had told Bertrand that, in consequence of orders from his government, he was under the necessity of imposing fresh restrictions, and had described the nature of them, directing that in future we should conform ourselves to them, instead of acting in the underhand manner he has done, I would have said, this is a man who does his duty clearly and openly without tricks or shuffling. It is necessary that there should be in this world such men as jailers, scavengers, butchers, and hangmen; but still one does not like to accept of any of those employments. If I were in the Tower of London, I might possibly have a good opinion of the jailer for the manner in which he did his duty; but I would neither accept of his situation, nor make a companion of him. Captain H * * told Madame Bertrand, that in the whole British dominions, a worse man than this jailer could not be selected as governor; and that we should very shortly find such to be the case. In fact he described him to be just as we have found him.

But as we thought that he was desirous to induce Madame Bertrand to leave the island with her family, it was supposed that he had exaggerated the imperfections of this man, though we evidently saw that there was something in it."

After some conversation on the same subject, Napoleon said, "When I was at Elba, the Princess of Wales sent to inform me of her intention to visit me. I, however, on her own account, sent back an answer begging of her to defer it a little longer, that I might see how matters would turn out; adding, that in a few months I would have the pleasure of receiving her. I knew that at the time, it could not fail to injure the princess, and therefore I put it off. It is astonishing that she desired it, for she had no reason to be attached to me, as her father and brother were killed fighting against me. She went afterwards to see Marie Louise, at * *, and I believe that they are great friends."

"Prince Leopold," continued he, "was one of the handsomest and finest young men in Paris, at the time he was there. At a masquerade given by the queen of Naples, Leopold made a conspicuous and elegant figure. The Princess Charlotte must doubtless be very contented and very fond of him. He was near being one of my aid-de-camps, to obtain which he had made interest, and even applied; but by some means, very fortunately for himself, it did not succeed, as probably if he had, he would not have been chosen to be a future king of England. Most of the young princes in Germany," continued he, "solicited to be my aid-de-camps, and Leopold was then about eighteen or nineteen years of age."

Some conversation now took place relative to the infernal machine, and the different plots which had been formed to assassinate him. "Many of the plots of the Bourbons," said he, "and the * * * were betrayed to me by Frenchmen, employed and well paid by themselves, and in their confidence, but who in reality were agents of the French police. By means of them, I became acquainted with their plans, and the names of the contrivers of the plot, one of whom was the Comte d' * * *. Louis, the present king, always refused to give his consent. These agents had conferences with the Bourbon princes, and with some of your ministers, especially with Mr. H * * *, under-secretary of state, and rendered an account of every thing to the police. If I had acted right, I should have followed the example of Cromwell, who on the discovery of the first attempt made to assassinate him, the plot of which had been hatched in France, caused it to be signified to the French king, that if the like occurred again, he, by way of reprisal, would order assassins to be hired to murder him and a Stuart. Now I ought to have publicly signified, that on the next attempt at assassination, I would cause the same to be made upon king * * * and the Bourbon princes, to accomplish which last indeed, I had only to say that I would not punish the projectors."

13*th*.—Application made by me to Major Gorrequer (on the part of the maître d'hôtel) to request that the governor would give directions to Mr. Breame (the company's farmer) to let the establishment have two calves monthly, as Napoleon was partial to veal, and Mr. Breame had refused to dispose of them without leave from the governor.

Permission was accordingly granted by Sir Hudson Lowe to let the French have two calves monthly, for which the farmer was to be paid by the French themselves.

14*th*.—Napoleon in very good spirits. Asked me " why I had dined in camp yesterday?" I replied, " Because there was nothing to eat at Longwood." He laughed heartily at this, and observed, " *that* certainly was the best reason in the world."

Afterwards he conversed for some time about Moreau, and said that he was by no means a man of that superior talent which the English supposed; that he was a good general of division, but not adapted for the command of a great army. " Moreau was brave," said he, " indolent, and a *bon vivant*.* He did nothing at his *quartier général*,† but loll on a sofa, or walk about with a pipe in his mouth. He scarcely ever read a book. His disposition was naturally good, but he was influenced by his wife and mother-in-law, who were two intriguers. I recommended Moreau to marry her at the desire of Josephine, who loved her

* Good liver † Quarters.

because she was a creole. Moreau had fallen greatly in public estimation on account of his conduct towards Pichegru.* After Leoben, the Senate of Venice were foolish enough to stir up a rebellion against the French armies, without being either sufficiently strong themselves, or having adequate assistance from other powers to promise the slightest hope of success. In consequence of this, I caused Venice to be occupied by the French troops. An agent of the Bourbons, the Count d'Entraigues, whom I suppose you have heard of in England, was there at the time. Fearing the consequences, he escaped out of Venice, but on his way

---

* While Napoleon was at Moscow, Count Daru received a letter from Madame Moreau praying of him to ask the emperor to permit her to return to France for a few months on private and indispensable business. Daru knowing that the best mode of obtaining anything from Napoleon was by being candid and open, showed him the letter. "*Oui,*" replied the emperor, "*elle doit etre venue, et elle doit deja etre repartie.*"* Daru said that a woman could not be dangerous. "*Elle vient intriguer,*"† answered Napoleon. "Perhaps you are one of those who think that Moreau is a good citizen?" "*Sire,*" replied Daru, "*je crois que sous le rapport du civisme et du patriotisme, le caractere de Moreau est inattaquable.*"‡ "*Eh bien, vous vous trompez,*"§ said Napoleon, and the subject was dropped. At Dresden, in 1813, when Napoleon was at breakfast along with Maréchal Victor and Daru, a Russian flag of truce was announced. After the person who bore it had accomplished his mission, Napoleon asked him some questions relative to the disorder which he had observed in the advanced posts of the enemy's army on the preceding day, and if the Russians had not lost some officer of distinction. The officer replied, "No." "*Cependant,*" said Napoleon, "*il y a eu du desordre: a tel poste on a emporte quelqu'un blesse ou tue.*" "*Je ne sache pas,*" replied the officer, "*que nous ayons perdu personne, a moins que votre majeste, ne veuille parler du General Moreau, qui a ete blesse a mort aux avant postes.*"‖ "*Le General Moreau?*" repeated Napoleon, and afterwards making a sign with his head to Daru, "*eh bien!*"—Daru instantly recollected the conversation at Moscow, when Napoleon had made use of the same words, at which time he had supposed that the emperor's opinion had been influenced by personal motives, and allowed that he was now obliged to acknowledge that he had judged right, and that Moreau was far from being a good citizen.

* Yes, she ought to have come, and she ought also to have gone again.
† She comes to intrigue.
‡ Sire, I believe that in regard to his private character and patriotism Moreau is unassailable. § You are mistaken.
‖ Nevertheless (said Napoleon) there was much disorder, and in such a post there must have been some one wounded or killed. I do not know (replied the officer) that we have lost any person, unless your majesty would speak of General Moreau, who was mortally wounded at the out-posts.

to Vienna (I think he said) he was arrested on the Brenta by
Bernadotte, with all his papers. As soon as it was known who
he was, he was sent to me, being esteemed a man of some importance. Amongst his papers we found his plans, and the correspondence of Pichegru with the Bourbons. I had them immediately attested by Berthier and two others, sealed and sent to the
directory, as they were of the greatest consequence. I then
examined d'Entraigues myself, who, when he saw that the contents of his papers were known, thought there was no use in
attempting concealment any longer, and confessed everything.
He even told me more than I could possibly have expected; let
me into the secret plans of the Bourbons with the names of their
English partisans, and, in fact, the information I obtained from
him was so full and so important, that it determined me how to act
on the moment, and was the chief cause of the measures I then
pursued and of the proclamation which I issued to the army,
warning them, that if necessary, they would be called upon to
cross the mountains, and re-enter their native country to crush
the traitors who were plotting against the existence of the republic. At this time Pichegru was chief of the legislative body.
The Count d'Entraigues was so communicative, that I really felt
obliged to him, and I may say that he almost gained me. He
was a man of talent and acuteness, intelligent and pleasant to
converse with, though he proved afterwards to be a *mauvais sujet*.*
Instead of putting him in confinement, I allowed him to go where
he pleased in Milan, gave him every indulgence, and did not even
put him in *surveillance*.† A few days afterwards I received
orders from the directory to cause him to be shot, or what in
those times was equivalent to it, to try him by a military commission, and sentence to be immediately executed. I wrote to the
directory that he had given very useful information, and did not
deserve such a return; and finally, that I could not execute it;
that if they still insisted upon shooting him, they must do it
themselves. Shortly after this, d'Entraigues escaped into Switzerland, from whence the *coquin*‡ had the impudence to write a

* Bad subject.   † To have him watched.   ‡ Rascal.

libel, accusing me of having treated him in the most barbarous manner, and even with having put him in irons; when the fact was, that I had allowed him so much liberty, that it was not until after he had escaped for several days that his flight was discovered, and then only by having seen the arrival of the Cour· d'Entraigues notified in the Swiss papers, which at first was thought to be impossible, but on sending to examine his quarters it was found to be true. This conduct of d'Entraigues greatly displeased all who at Milan had been witnesses of the indulgent manner in which I treated him. Amongst others, some ambassadors and diplomatic characters were so much offended, that they drew up and signed a declaration contradictory of these accusations. In consequence of the information gained from d'Entraigues, Pichegru was banished to Cayenne."

"Immediately after the seizure of d'Entraigues, Desaix came to see me. Conversing with him about Pichegru, I remarked that we had been greatly deceived, and expressed my surprise that his treason had not been discovered sooner. 'Why,' said Desaix, 'we knew of it three months ago.' 'How can that be possible?' I replied. Desaix then recounted to me the manner in which Moreau, with whom he had been at that time, had found in the baggage of the Austrian general Klingspor a correspondence of Pichegru's, in which his plans in favor of the Bourbons were detailed, and those of the false manœuvres which he intended to put in practice. I asked Desaix if this had been communicated to the directory? He replied, 'no,' that Moreau did not wish to ruin Pichegru; and had desired him to say nothing about it. I told Desaix that he had acted very wrong; that he ought immediately to have sent all the papers to the directory, as I had done; that in fact it was tacitly conniving at the destruction of his native country. As soon as Moreau was informed that Pichegru was found out, he denounced him to the army as a traitor, and sent to the directory the papers containing the proofs of it, which he had kept concealed in his possession for some months, and allowed Pichegru to be chosen chief of the legislative body; though he knew that he was plotting the destruction of the republic. Moreau was accused this time, and with justice, of double treachery. 'Thou hast first,' it was said, 'betrayed thy country, by concealing the treason of Pichegru, and afterwards thou hast uselessly betrayed thy friend, by disclosing what thou oughtest to have made known before; but which, when concealed by thee until it was discovered by other means, ought to have ever remained a secret in thy breast.' Moreau never recovered the esteem of the public again."

I mentioned the retreat of Moreau, and asked if he had not displayed great military talents in it? "That retreat," replied the emperor, "instead of being what you say, was the greatest blunder that ever Moreau committed. If he had, instead of retreating, made a *détour*, and marched in the rear of Prince Charles," (I think he said,) "he would have destroyed or taken the Austrian army. The directory were jealous of me, and wanted to divide, if possible, the military reputation; and as they could not give credit to Moreau for a victory, they did for a retreat, which they caused to be extolled in the highest terms; though even the Austrian generals condemned Moreau for having done it. You may probably hereafter," continued Napoleon, "have an opportunity of hearing the opinion of French generals on the subject, who were present, and you will find it consonant to mine. Instead of credit, Moreau merited the greatest censure and disgrace for it. As a general, Pichegru had much more talents than Moreau."

"Moreau ridiculed the idea of the formation of the legion of honor. When he heard from some one that it was intended also to be given to those who had distinguished themselves in science, and not to be confined to feat of arms alone, he replied, 'Well, then, I shall apply for my cook to be made a commander of the order, as his talents are most superior in the science of cookery.'"

In reply to some arguments which I offered to convince him that * * * and the English * * * * * were ignorant of that part of Pichegru's plot which embraced assassination, Napoleon replied, "I do not suppose that * * * * or any other of the English * * * * * actually said to Georges or Pichegru, 'you must kill the first consul;' but they well knew that such formed the chief and indeed the only hope of success; and yet they, knowing this, furnished them with money, and provided ships, to land them in France, which, to all intents and purposes, rendered them accomplices; and if * * * had been tried by an English jury, he would have been condemned as such. Lord * * * * took great pains to persuade the foreign courts that they were ignorant of the project of assassination, and wrote several letters, in which he acknowledged that the English had landed men for the purpose of overturning the French government; but denied the other. However, he made a very lame business of it, and none of the continental governments gave any credit to his assertions. It was naturally condemned, as, on the ground of retaliation, none of the sovereigns or rulers were safe. It was at the time that I had it in contemplation to effect a descent in England. Your * * * did not want to get rid of 'Napoleon Bonaparte,' but of 'the first consul.' Fox had some conversations with me on the subject of the 3rd Nivose. He too, like you, denied that the * * * were privy to the scheme of assassination, but faintly, after hearing what I had to say, and condemned the whole transaction. Indeed his own measures were quite opposed to it. The conduct of the Emperor of Germany also formed a striking contrast. When I had possession of his capital, he, through religious motives, positively and with sincerity prohibited any attempt of the kind, which might have been executed daily, as I often walked about without suspicion."

During the conversation, I mentioned that Bernadotte had been strongly suspected of being lukewarm in the cause of the allies, if not of playing a double part; that he was called Charles Jean Charlatan, and supposed to be likely to join him if any reverse happened to the allies. Napoleon replied, " Probably they called him Charlatan, because he is a Gascon, a little inclined to boasting. As to joining me, if I had been successful, he would have done no more than all the rest. The Saxons, Wirtemburghers, Bavarians, and all those who abandoned me when I was unfortunate, would have joined me again if I had been successful. After Dresden, the Emperor of Austria went upon his knees to me,* called me *his dear son*, and begged me for the sake of his very *dear, dear daughter*, to whom I was married, not to ruin him altogether, but to be reconciled to him. Had it not been for the desertion of the Saxons with their artillery, I should have gained a victory at Leipsic, and the allies would have been far differently situated."

16*th*.—Napoleon, in his bed-room, complained of headache, and had his feet immersed in a pail of hot water. At first he was rather melancholy, but subsequently became tolerably lively and communicative. He spoke about Egypt, and asked me many questions ; amongst others, whether a three-decker could enter the harbor of Alexandria without having been lightened ? I replied that I thought it might, or if not, that it might be very easily lightened.† Napoleon observed, that he had sent an officer named Julien, from Cairo, with peremptory orders to Bruyes to enter the harbor of Alexandria, but that unfortunately he was killed by the Arabs on the way. " I called," continued he, " a fort which I built at Rosetta after him." He asked me if I knew that fort, to which I replied in the affirmative. " It was surprising," continued he, " how Bruyes could have thought of engaging at anchor without having first fortified the island with twenty or thirty pieces of cannon, and having brought out a Venetian sixty-four, and some frigates which he had in the fort of Alexandria. In a conversation which I had with Bruyes some weeks before, on board of the Orient, he himself demonstrated to me that a fleet ought never to engage at anchor, at least that a fleet which did so, must always be beaten, on account of the facility which the attacking ships would have of taking up their position ; and that an order (whether from Bruyes, or not, I did not understand) actually existed prohibiting it. Notwithstanding which, Bruyes

---

* This is a rigid translation of the words used by Napoleon, and were not intended to be understood, as must be evident, in their literal sense, but merely as a forcible manner of making me comprehend the earnestness with which the emperor of Austria made the application. Napoleon frequently used the same expression in similar instances.

† When at Alexandria, I saw the Tigre and Canopus enter the harbor. They were 80 gun ships of the largest class, and drew as much water as a three-decker

himself adopted it afterwards. Bruyes," continued he, "always believed, that if Nelson attacked him, it would be made on his right, thinking his left inexpugnable on account of the island, and had prepared matters accordingly. I endeavored to convince him that a ship or two of his left might be taken by a superior force, and an opening afforded thereby for the enemy's fleet to enter."

I observed, that if Bruyes had anchored head and stern, he might have gone in much closer to the shore, as he would not have been obliged to make an allowance for the ships to swing, and consequently no space would have been left for Nelson to pass between the French fleet and the land. Napoleon appeared to coincide in this opinion, and said that he would ask the opinion of the admiral on the subject. He added, that prior to the departure of Julien, orders had been sent to Bruyes, that he should not quit the coast of Egypt until after he had ascertained the physical impossibility of the fleet's being able to enter the harbor of Alexandria. If possible, he was ordered to carry it into execution; if not, to proceed to Corfu with his fleet. "Now, Bruyes," continued he, "not having ascertained the fact, as, on the contrary, Barré asserted that it was practicable, of which I was also myself convinced, did not think himself authorized to go away, and at the same time was afraid to enter the harbor even if possible, thinking it hazardous without having been first assured that we were in full possession of the country. He was ignorant of my success at Cairo until twenty-four hours before he was attacked by Nelson. In this manner he remained in balance, and neglected to secure himself. Moreover, he never expected that Nelson would have attacked him with an inferior force. If he had brought out his frigates, and well fortified the island, Nelson would either never have attacked him, or would have been beaten if he had. It was with great difficulty that I made Bruyes depart from Toulon. After sailing, he wanted to send four ships to attack Nelson, who was laying with three dismasted vessels at * * *, but I would not allow it, as the success of the enterprise was of too much importance to allow the capture of two or three ships to be put in competition with it. Bruyes afterwards wished to separate the fleet, which I would not permit. Bruyes was a man of unquestionable talent; but he wanted that decisive resolution that enables a man to seize an opportunity presented by the moment; which I conceive to be the most essential quality in a general or admiral. Probably from want of experience, he had not that confidence in his own ability and the propriety of his plans, which rarely anything else can impart. Unless nature forms a man of so peculiar a stamp as to be enabled to see and decide instantaneously, nothing but experience can give it. I, myself, commanded an army at twenty-two years of age, but nature made me different from most others. If Nelson had met Bruyes' fleet, in going to Egypt, I know not what might have happened, as I had placed three hundred and fifty, or four hundred veterans in each line-of-battle ship, who were trained to the guns twice a day, and had given orders that each ship should engage one of yours. Your vessels were small, and I believe not well manned, and I gave this order to prevent your obtaining any advantages by your superior skill in manœuvring."

Here some discussion took place upon the comparative merit of the English and French seamen. I urged that English sailors fought with more confidence; that if any accidents happened to the ships in action, they would remedy them much sooner, and would fight longer than the French seamen. Napoleon said, he agreed in every thing but the last. "*Signor Dottore*," said he, "*il marinero Francese è bravo quanto l'Inglese.*"*

" The French soldiers had a great contempt for the English troops, at the beginning of the war, caused, perhaps, by the failure of the expedition under the Duke of York, the great want of alertness, &c., in the English advanced posts, and the misfortunes which befell your armies. In this they were fools, as the English were well known to be a brave nation. It was probably by a similar error, that Regnier was beaten by General Stuart; as the French imagined that you would run away and be driven into the sea. Regnier was a man of talent, but more fit to give counsel

* Doctor, (said he,) the French sailors are as brave as the English.

to an army of twenty or thirty thousand men, than to command one of five or six. Your troops, on that day, were nearly all English, and Regnier's were chiefly Poles. It is difficult to conceive how little the French soldiers thought of yours, until they were taught the contrary. Of your seamen, they always spoke in terms of respect, although they would only allow that they were more expert and quick, but not more brave than their own."

"*When*" continued Napoleon, "*I was at Tilsit, with the Emperor Alexander and the king of Prussia, I was the most ignorant of the three in military affairs.* These two sovereigns, especially the King of Prussia, were completely *cu fait*,* as to the number of buttons there ought to be in front of a jacket, how many behind, and the manner in which the skirts ought to be cut. Not a tailor in the army knew better than King Frederick, how many measures of cloth it took to make a jacket. In fact," continued he, laughing, "I was nobody in comparison with them. They continually tormented me with questions about matters belonging to tailors, of which I was entirely ignorant, though, in order not to affront them, I answered just as gravely as if the fate of an army depended upon the cut of a jacket. When I went to see the King of Prussia, instead of a library, I found he had a large room, like an arsenal, furnished with shelves and pegs, in which were placed fifty or sixty jackets of various modes. Every day he changed his fashion, and put on a different one. He was a tall, dry-looking fellow, and would give a good idea of Don Quixote. He attached more importance to the cut of a dragoon or a hussar uniform, than was necessary for the salvation of a kingdom. At Jena, his army performed the finest and most showy manœuvres possible, but I soon put a stop to their *coglionerie*,† and taught them that, to fight, and to execute dazzling manœuvres, and wear splendid uniforms, were very different affairs. If," added he, "the French army had been commanded by a tailor, the King of Prussia would certainly have gained the day, from his superior knowledge in that art; but as victories depend more **upon the skill** of the general commanding the troops, than upon

* Certain. † Paradings.

that of the tailor who makes their jackets, he consequently failed."

The emperor then observed, that we are allowed too much baggage, and too many women to accompany our armies. "Women, when they are bad," said he, "are worse than men, and more ready to commit crimes. The soft sex, when degraded, falls lower than the other. Women are always much better, or much worse than men. Witness the *tricoteuses de Paris*,* during the revolution. When I commanded at the Col de Tende, a most mountainous and difficult country, to enter which the army was obliged to pass over a narrow bridge, I had given directions that no women should be allowed to accompany it, as the service was a most difficult one, and required the troops to be continually on the alert. To enforce this order, I placed two captains on the bridge, with instructions, on pain of death, not to permit a woman to pass. I went to the bridge myself, to see that my orders were complied with, where I found a crowd of women assembled. As soon as they perceived me, they began to revile me, bawling out, 'Oh, then, *petit caporal*, it is you who have given orders not to let us pass.' I was then called *petit caporal* by the army. Some miles further on, I was astonished to see a considerable number of women with the troops. I immediately ordered the two captains to be put in arrest, and brought before me, intending to have them tried immediately. They protested their innocence, and asserted that no woman had crossed the bridge. I caused some of those dames to be brought, when, to my astonishment, by their own confession, I found that they had thrown the provisions that had been provided for the support of the army out of some of the casks, concealed themselves in them, and passed over unperceived."

Napoleon observed, that he did not esteem the English cavalry to be by any means equal to the infantry. The men, by some fault, were not able to stop the horses, and were liable to be cut to pieces, if, in the act of charging, it became necessary to halt and retreat. That the horses were accustomed to be fed too lux-

* The knitters of Paris.

uriously, kept too warm, and from what he had learned, greatly neglected by the riders.

I offered some explanations about the quantity of baggage allowed by Lord Wellington; which I said did not exceed a small portmanteau for each officer; that only five women to a hundred men were allowed to embark for foreign service, and that new regulations had been adopted to prevent the horses of the cavalry from being kept too warm, or too highly pampered. Napoleon replied, that he had been informed by French officers, that the baggage of one English officer in France, or in Belgium, was greater than that of ten French.

18th.—Major Fehrzen came to Longwood. Being asked, why he did not call upon the Bertrands occasionally; he replied, that the governor had signified his desire that no communication, beyond that of a common salutation, should take place between the officers of the 53d regiment and the persons detained in St. Helena. He admitted that the dark and mysterious conduct pursued towards the French was of a nature likely to excite suspicion, but assured them, that in the 53d regiment there were no assassins to be found.

22nd.—Napoleon in his bath, and suffering from headache. Had some conversation about Montchenu, who, he said, would perfectly agree with the idea which the English had formerly held of the French, viz., that they were a nation of dancing-masters; in which opinion they must have been strengthened during the revolution, by seeing arrive amongst them a set of vain triflers, who had been expelled their own country for their arrogance and tyranny. "This idea," added Napoleon, "was impressed so strongly upon the minds of the English, that when I sent Duroc as ambassador to Petersburg, Lord St. Helens, the English envoy there, being curious to see what he was like, took an opportunity of observing him closely on his entrance into that capital; and on being afterwards asked his opinion of him, replied, '*Ma foi, au moins il n'a pas l'air danseur;*'* expressing thereby that Duroc was the only Frenchman he had seen who had not the appear-

* Upon my word, *he* at least has not *the air* of **a dancer.**

ance of a dancing-master; which I can hardly believe, as probably until that time he had seen no other Frenchmen than *imbéciles** like Montchenu, with whom England was overrun. *Vraiment c'est trop fort, l'envoyer une telle bête ici,*† to a settlement of a rival nation, in order to render his own an object of contempt, and confirm the English in their old prejudices. Does not Montchenu," said he, " answer the idea you formerly entertained of the French nation?"

After leaving the bath, Napoleon spoke about Russia, and said, that the European nations would yet find that *he* had adopted the best possible policy at the time he had intended to re-establish the kingdom of Poland, which would be the only effectual means of stopping the increasing power of Russia. It was putting a barrier, a dyke to that formidable empire, which it was likely would yet overwhelm Europe "I do not think," said he, "that I shall live to see it, but you may. You are in the flower of your age, and may expect to live thirty-five years longer. I think that you will see that the Russians will either invade and take India, or enter Europe with four hundred thousand Cossacs and other inhabitants of the deserts, and two hundred thousand real Russians. When Paul was so violent against you he sent to me for a plan to invade India. I sent him one, with instructions in detail." (Here Napoleon showed me on a map the routes, and the different points from whence the army was to have proceeded.) "From a port in the Caspian Sea he was to have marched on to India. Russia," continued he, " must either fall or aggrandize herself, and it is natural to suppose that the latter will take place. By invading other countries, Russia has two points to gain,—an increase of civilization and polish, by rubbing against other powers,‡ the acquisition of money, and the rendering friends to herself the inhabitants of the deserts, with whom some years back she was at war. The Cossacs, Calmucks, and other barbarians, who have accompanied the Russians into France, and other parts of Europe, having once

---

* Simpletons.
† Really it is too bad to send such a numscull here.
‡ The literal English of his words.

acquired a taste for the luxuries of the south, will carry back to their deserts the remembrance of places where they had such fine women, fine living, and not only will not themselves be able to endure their own barbarous and sterile regions, but will communicate to their neighbors a desire to conquer these delicious countries. In all human probability, Alexander will be obliged either to take India from you, in order to gain riches and provide employment for them, and thereby prevent a revolution in Russia; or he will make an irruption into Europe, at the head of some hundred thousand of those barbarians on horseback, and two hundred thousand infantry, and carry everything before him. What I say to you is confirmed by the history of all ages, during which it has been invariably observed, that whenever those barbarians once got a taste of the south of Europe, they always returned to attempt new conquests and ravages, and have finally succeeded in making themselves masters of the country. It is natural to man to desire to better his condition; and those *canaille*, when they contrast their own deserts with the fine provinces they have left, will always have an itching after the latter, well knowing also, that no nation will retaliate, or attempt to take their deserts from them. Those *canaille*," continued he, " possess all the requisites for conquest. They are brave, active, patient of fatigue and bad living, poor, and desirous of enriching themselves. I think, however, that all depends upon Poland. If Alexander succeeds in incorporating Poland with Russia, that is to say, in perfectly reconciling the Poles to the Russian government, and not merely subduing the country, he has gained the greatest step towards subduing India. My opinion is, that he will attempt either the one or the other of the projects I have mentioned, and I think the last to be most probable."

I observed that the distance was great, and that the Russians had not the money necessary for such a grand undertaking. "The distance is nothing," replied the emperor; "supplies can be easily carried upon camels, and the Cossacs will always ensure a sufficiency of them. Money they will find when they arrive there. The hope of conquest would immediately unite armies of Cossacs and Calmucks without expense. Hold out to them the plunder of some rich cities as a lure, and thousands would flock to their banners. Europe," continued he, "and England in particular, ought to have prevented the union of Poland with Russia."

"A great object for England," added Napoleon, "ought to be to keep Belgium always separate from France; as France having Belgium, might be said in case of war with England, to have possession of Hamburgh, &c. It would, however, have been better for England that Austria had it, than that it should be possessed by Holland, because Austria is stronger; and when France arises from her present state of nothingness, Holland being too weak to stand alone, will always be at her feet."

"If I had succeeded, in my expedition to Russia," added he, "I would have obliged Alexander to accede to the continental system against England, and thereby have compelled the latter to make peace. I would also have formed Poland into a separate and independent kingdom." I asked what kind of a peace he would have given to us. "A very good one," replied Napoleon. "I would only have insisted upon your discontinuing your vexations at sea." I asked if he would have left us Malta; to which he replied in the affirmative, adding, that he was tired of war, and was as well adapted for the former as the latter; that he would have employed himself in the improving and adorning France, in the education of his son, and in writing his history. "At least," said he, "the allied powers cannot take from me hereafter the great public works which I have executed, the roads which I made over the Alps, and the seas which I have united. They cannot place their feet to improve where mine have not been before. They cannot take from me the code of laws which I formed, and which will go down to the latest posterity. Thank God, of these they cannot deprive me."

I said that I had been seeking for the number of ships which had been seized by the English, prior to the proclamation issued by him for the detention of the English in France, and could only discover that two chasse marées had been taken in Quiberon Bay. "Two chasse marées?" said Napoleon, "why there was property to the amount of seventy millions, and I suppose above two hundred ships detained, before I issued the proclamation. But it is what England has always done. In the year of 1773, you did the same, and you gave as a reason, that you had always done so. The great cause of dispute between you and us was, that I would not allow you to do what you liked at sea; or at least, if so, that I would act as it pleased me by land. In short, I did not wish to receive laws from you, but rather to give them. Perhaps in this I pushed matters too far. Man is liable to err. When you blockaded France, I blockaded England; and it was not a paper blockade, as I obliged you to send your merchandise round by the Baltic, and occupy a little island in the North Sea, in order to smuggle. You said that you would shut me out from the seas, and I said that I would shut you out from the land. You succeeded; but had it not been for accidents, you would not. Your country is nothing the better for it, through the imbecility of your ministers, who have aggrandized Russia instead of their native country."

I asked Napoleon again, as I was anxious to put the matter beyond a doubt, whether, if Talleyrand had delivered the Duc d'Enghien's letter in time to him, he would have pardoned the writer? He replied, "It is probable that I might; for in it he made an offer of his services; besides, he was the best of the family. He behaved very bravely and with much dignity before the court-martial, and denied nothing. It is true that I, as well as the nation, was very desirous of making an example of one of the family; that was against him; but still I think that I would have pardoned him."

I asked if he would have pardoned Pichegru? "Pichegru," said he, "had fallen into great contempt, and was not likely to do me much mischief. In remembrance of the conquest of Holland, it is possible that I might, on condition of banishment to America."

"If," said he, "Lord Castlereagh were to offer to place me again upon the throne of France on the same conditions that Louis fills it, I would prefer remaining where I am. There is no man more to be pitied than Louis. He is forced upon the nation as king, and instead of being allowed to ingratiate himself with the people, the allies oblige him to have recourse to measures which must increase their hatred instead of conciliating their affections. Royalty is degraded by the steps they have made him adopt. *On le rend si salle et méprisable,** that it reflects upon the throne of England itself. In place of making him respectable, *on l'a couvert d'ordure."†*

"The French nation," continued he, "would never willingly consent to receive the Bourbons as kings, because the allies wish it. They would desire me, because the allies do not; but putting me out of the question, the French are desirous to see the throne filled by one chosen by themselves, and for whom no enemies or foreign powers had interfered. Ask yourselves, you Englishmen, what your sentiments would be in a similar case? The wish of your ministers to re-establish despotic power and superstition in France, cannot be agreeable to the English. A free people, unless indeed a desire to humble and to injure prevails, cannot wish to see another nation enslaved. Ill-treated as I have been, and deprived of everything dear to me," added he, " I prefer my sojourn on this execrable rock, to be seated on the throne of France like Louis, as I know that posterity will do me justice. Another year or two will probably finish my career in this world, but what I have done will never perish. Twelve hundred years hence, my name will be mentioned with respect, while those of my oppressors will be unknown, or only known by being loaded with infamy and opprobrium."

" I am inclined," continued Napoleon, " to doubt very much what has been said of Cromwell. It has been asserted that he always wore armor, and continually changed his abode, through fear of assassination. Now both these assertions have been made of me, and both I know to be false, as were most likely those imputing the same to him."

" The conduct of your government in attempting to put down liberty, and enslave the English, surprises me," continued Napo-

---

* They render him so despicable.

† They have covered him with filth

leon; "for Russia, Prussia, and Austria to do so, I wonder not, as they do not merit the name of liberal, or of free nations. In them, the will of the sovereign was always law, the slaves must obey; but that England should do so, surprises me; unless, as I said to you on a former occasion, political motives, jealousy, and a wish to humble and lessen those who have enriched themselves by trade, prevail with your prince, and amongst your oligarchy."

23d.*—A message sent for me to attend the governor at Plantation House. Found him in the library with Sir Thomas Reade. His excellency said, "that the day before yesterday some newspapers of a later date than any of his own, had been received by Mr. Cole the postmaster, some of which were lent to me in direct violation of the act of parliament, which positively prohibited communication, verbal or written, with General Bonaparte, or any of his family, or those about him, without his (the governor's) knowledge. That he therefore wished to know from myself, whether I had lent those papers, or any others to General Bonaparte?" I replied that I had lent those and many others at various times to Napoleon, as I had been constantly in the habit of lending papers to him, since I had been on the island. That Sir George Cockburn had in more instances than one, given me newspapers to take to Longwood before having perused them himself. Sir Hudson Lowe replied, that it was a violation of the act of parliament. I replied, that I was not included in the act of parliament, as I had made an express stipulation that I should not be considered or treated as one of the French, and would immediately resign my situation, if I were required to hold it upon such terms. His excellency said, that "he desired me to understand, that for the future I was not to lend General Bonaparte any newspaper, or be the bearer of any information—news or newspapers—to him, without having previously obtained his sanction." I observed, that I felt it difficult how to act, for if, after the arrival of a ship, Napoleon asked me if there were any news? I could not possibly pretend ignorance. His excellency

---

* I am not positive that this conversation did not occur on the 22d, as in some pages of my journal it is so dated.

said, " as soon as a ship arrived, both Captain Poppleton and myself ought to be shut up in Longwood, until the whole of the information or news brought was made known to him, and *then* I could obtain from him whatever news was proper to be communicated to General Bonaparte." I replied, that I would not remain an hour in my situation subject to such a restriction.

His excellency observed, that " some months ago, information of the greatest importance had been communicated by me to General Bonaparte, before he (the governor) had himself known it, viz. that of the dissolution of the chamber of deputies in France ; that I had myself told him, that I had informed General Bonaparte of it, and concluded by asking, if I had communicated this intelligence verbally, or by means of a newspaper, and if the paper had not been lent to me by Sir Pultney Malcolm ?"

I replied, that at such a distance of time I could not recollect whether the communication made by me had been verbal or by means of a newspaper ; that most probably it had been both, and that I did not recollect from whom I had received the newspaper. His excellency said, that " a person possessed as I was of a memory so extraordinarily good, could not pretend want of recollection," and repeated the question. I answered, that trifles did not long remain impressed upon my memory. The governor observed it was singular I could not recollect that it had been lent by the admiral, and in a sneering way asked " if it was not a *Scotch* paper ?" I answered that I never had seen a Scotch paper at Longwood. That Sir Pultney Malcolm often had selected two or three papers of the oldest dates for me, and sent the recent ones to him (Sir Hudson.) His excellency then demanded, " if the papers lent by the admiral had been for myself, or if Sir Pultney knew that they would be submitted to General Bonaparte for perusal." I replied, " For myself, and I do not know whether he is aware of the use I put them to or not." Sir Hudson said, that " it was very extraordinary I could not tell if the admiral knew of it. That by the signature of his majesty's ministers, nobody but himself had any right to communicate in any manner whatever with General Bonaparte." I observed that Sir George

Cockburn had never considered it necessary to keep back newspapers from Napoleon; that the only instructions he had given me on the subject were, that it would be better not to show him any thing personally very offensive. Much more conversation took place, during which the governor often recurred to the *Scotcn* paper.

24tn.—Found Napoleon in his bed-room, afflicted with headache. Recommended him to use cold applications to his forehead and temples, which he immediately put in practice with considerable benefit.

In the course of conversation afterwards, he observed, that a great discordancy existed among the libels which had been published at his expense. Some asserting that his lust had carried him to the length of having an incestuous correspondence with his sisters, &c., while others maintained *impuissance** equally forcible. "This last report," continued he, "was so prevalent, that when a marriage between me and a sister of the Emperor Alexander was in agitation, the empress, her mother, said to Alexander, that she would not consent to sacrifice her daughter, and throw her into the arms of one who *ne peut rien faire;*† that if her daughter were married to me they would be obliged to act as Gustavus had done with his queen, which she could not reconcile with religion. Do you know," added he, " that history about Gustavus?" I replied in the negative. "Why, *Gustave était impuissant,*‡ and not having an heir to the throne, *il fit coucher un de ses chambellans avec la reine,*§ from which sprang that madman who resigned the crown a few years ago. In one of his fits of madness, that *imbécile* since confessed that the Swedes had acted with justice in deposing him, as he had no right to the crown. 'My dear mother,' said Alexander, 'is it possible that you can believe these stories? I assure you that I should not wish you better fortune than to be sufficiently young to be married to him, and you would not long want an heir.' Kourakin,"

* Impotence. † Could do nothing.
‡ Gustavus was impotent.
§ He sent one of his chamberlains to bed with the queen.

said he, "told me this anecdote afterwards, which created great mirth at Paris."

Napoleon then spoke about Madame de Staël. "Madame de Staël," said he, "was a woman of considerable talent and great ambition; but so extremely intriguing and restless, as to give rise to the observation, that she would throw her friends into the sea that at the moment of drowning she might have an opportunity of saving them. I was obliged to banish her from court. At Geneva, she became very intimate with my brother Joseph, whom she gained by her conversation and writings. When I returned from Elba, she sent her son to be presented to me on purpose to ask payment of two millions, which her father Neckar had lent out of his private property to Louis XVI., and to offer her services, provided I complied with this request. As I knew what he wanted, and thought that I could not grant it without ill-treating others who were in a similar predicament, I did not wish to see him, and gave directions that he should not be introduced. However, Joseph would not be denied, and brought him in, in spite of this order, the attendants at the door not liking to refuse my brother, especially as he said that he would be answerable for the consequences. I received him very politely, heard his business, and replied that I was very sorry it was not in my power to comply with his request, as it was contrary to the laws, and would do an injustice to many others. Madame de Staël was not, however, contented with this. She wrote a long letter to Fouché, in which she stated her claims, and that she wanted the money in order to portion her daughter in marriage to the Duc de Broglie, promising that if I complied with her request, I might command her and hers; *that she would be black and white for me.* Fouché communicated this, and advised me strongly to comply, urging that in so critical a time she might be of considerable service. I answered that I would make no bargains."

"Shortly after my return from the conquest of Italy," continued he, "I was accosted by Madame de Staël in a large company, though at that time I avoided going out much in public. She followed me every where, and stuck so close that I could not shake her off. At last she asked me, 'who at this moment is *la première femme du monde?*'* intending to pay a compliment to me, and expecting that I would return it. I looked at her, and coldly replied, 'she who has borne the greatest number of children,' turned round, and left her greatly confused and abashed. He concluded by observing, that he could not call her a *wicked* woman, but that she was a restless *intrigante*,† possessed of considerable talent and influence."

He then conversed upon the bad state of England, and said that he had made a calculation, and found that it would require fifty years of an uninterrupted peace to enable England to pay off the national debt, a circumstance which had never occurred, and never would

Saw Sir Hudson Lowe at Plantation House, with whom I had a conversation, chiefly upon subjects connected with the admiral. Informed him that maccheroni formed an item of magnitude in the expenditure of Longwood; as for the two pounds of that article, which they consumed daily, they were obliged to pay twenty-four shillings to Mr. Solomon. His excellency observed that there was plenty of it in the government store.‡

Cipriani in town making the customary purchases of provisions.

26*th*.—Napoleon indisposed with catarrh, inflammation and tumefaction of the right cheek and gums, with head-ache, caused probably by exposure yesterday to the cold wind in the garden.

27*th*.—Napoleon better. Right cheek, however, is still tumefied. Had some conversation with him about the ambassador. "If," said he, "a million of francs had been given to the first mandarin, everything would have been settled, and it would not have been a reproach to the nation; as that embassy was not one which regarded the honor of the country. It was, and ought to be considered more as an affair of merchandise than as one immediately affecting the nation. It was in fact an embassy

---

* The greatest woman in the world.
† Intriguer.
‡ When some were sent up a few days after, it was found to have been rendered unfit for use from long keeping.

to China from the tea-merchants in England, and therefore advantages might with great honor be purchased. Besides, when you send ambassadors to those barbarians, you must humor them and comply with their customs. They do not seek you. They never have sent ambassadors in return for yours, nor asked you to send any. Now great commercial advantages may be lost to England, and perhaps a war with China be the consequence. If I were an Englishman, I should esteem the man who advised a war with China to be the greatest enemy to my country in existence. You would in the end be beaten, and perhaps a revolution in India would follow."

" In the course of a few years," added he, " Russia will have Constantinople, the greatest part of Turkey, and all Greece. This I hold to be as certain as if it had already taken place. Almost all the cajoling and flattering which Alexander practised towards me was to gain my consent to effect this object. I would not consent, foreseeing that the equilibrium of Europe would be destroyed. In the natural course of things, in a few years Turkey must fall to Russia. The greatest part of her population are Greeks, who you may say are Russians. The powers it would injure, and who could oppose it, are England, France, Prussia, and Austria. Now as to Austria, it will be very easy for Russia to engage her assistance by giving her Servia, and other provinces bordering upon the Austrian dominions, reaching near to Constantinople. The only hypothesis that France and England may ever be allied with sincerity will be in order to prevent this. But even this alliance would not avail. France, England and Prussia united cannot prevent it. Russia and Austria can at any time effect it. Once mistress of Constantinople, Russia gets all the commerce of the Mediterranean, becomes a great naval power, and God knows what may happen. She quarrels with you, marches off to India an army of seventy thousand good soldiers, which to Russia is nothing, and a hundred thousand *canaille*, Cossacs and others, and England loses India. Above all the other powers, Russia is the most to be feared, especially by **you**. Her soldiers are braver than the Austrians, and she has the **means** of raising as many as she pleases. In bravery, the French and English soldiers are the only ones to be compared to them. All this I foresaw. I see into futurity farther than others, and I wanted to establish a barrier against those barbarians by re-establishing the kingdom of Poland, and putting Poniatowski at the head of it as king; but your *imbeciles* of ministers would not consent. A hundred years hence, I shall be praised, (*encense*,) and Europe, especially England, will lament that I did not succeed. When they see the finest countries in Europe overrun, and a prey to those northern barbarians, they will say, 'Napoleon was right:' the Russians are beginning already with you; I see that they have prohibited the introduction of your merchandise. England is falling. Even Prussia prohibits your goods. What a change for England! Under the great Chatham, you forbade the most powerful sovereign in Europe, the Emperor of Germany, to navigate the Escaut, or to establish an extensive commerce at Ostend. This was barbarous and unjust, but still you had the power to prevent it, because it was against the interests of England. *Now* Prussia shuts her ports against you. What a falling off! In my opinion the only thing which can save England will be abstaining from meddling in continental affairs, and by withdrawing her army from the continent. Then you may insist upon whatever is necessary to your interests, without fear of reprisals being made upon your army. You are superior in maritime force to all the world united; and while you confine yourself to that arm, you will always be powerful and be dreaded. You have the great advantage of declaring war when you like, and of carrying it on at a distance from your home. By means of your fleets you can menace an attack upon the coasts of those powers who disagree with you, without their being able materially to retaliate. By your present mode of proceeding, you forfeit all those advantages. Your most powerful arm is given up, and you send an army to the continent where you are inferior to Bavaria in that species of force. You put me in mind of Francis the First, who had a formidable and beautiful artillery at the battle of Pavia. But he placed his cavalry before it, and thus masked the battery, which, could it have fired, would have ensured him the victory. He was beaten, lost everything, and was made prisoner. So it is with you. You forsake your ships, which may be compared to Francis's batteries, and throw forty thousand men on the continent, which Prussia, or any other power who chooses to probibit your manufactures, will fall upon and cut to pieces, if you menace or make reprisals."

"So silly a treaty as that made by your ministers for their own country," continued the emperor, "was never known before. You give up everything, and gain nothing. All the other powers gained acquisitions of country and millions of souls, but you give up colonies. For example, you give up the isle of Bourbon to the French. A more impolitic act you could not have committed. You ought to endeavor to make the French forget the way to India, and all Indian policy, instead of placing them half way there. Why did you give up Java? Why Surinam, or Martinique, or the other French colonies? To avoid doing so you had nothing more to say than that you would retain them for the five years the allied powers were to remain in France. Why not demand Hamburgh for Hanover? Then you would have an *entrepôt** for your manufactures. In treaties, an ambassador ought to take advantage of everything for the benefit of his own country."

Napoleon then said, that if I were asked any questions by the ambassador about a reception at Longwood, I should say, that he (Napoleon) was not on good terms with the governor, and could not think of receiving him with that person. That if he were desirous of being introduced, he would receive him presented by Count Bertrand or by the admiral. "I have no doubt," added he, "that this governor will tell him that I am very much dissatisfied with him for doing his duty, and that I am sulky. That having been so long used to command myself, I have not philosophy enough to bear restraint. That I have been treated very well, and have made a very bad return for it. If the ambassador asks you, you may say that I have my own way of receiving persons who wish

---

* A mart.

to be introduced to me. That I do not wish to affront him, far from it, but that I cannot see the governor."

28*th.*—A servant, named William Hall, dismissed from Longwood. After leaving it, he underwent a long interrogation at Plantation House by the governor, relative to what he had seen and heard during his residence at Longwood.

The Ocean, Experiment, and another ship, arrived from England yesterday.

Saw Sir Hudson Lowe, who told me, with some embarrassment, that "his conduct had undergone a parliamentary investigation, and that I should see in the newspapers an account of a motion relative to General Bonaparte, that had been made by Lord Holland in the House of Lords, but that *he* had not as yet received any official account of it from Lord Bathurst. That the reports of his lordship's reply, as given in the newspapers, might be incorrect or unfaithful, which I had better say, if General Bonaparte asked me any questions."

30*th.*—Napoleon sent for me to his bed-room to explain several passages in the Times newspaper, particularly in the speech imputed to Lord Bathurst in reply to Lord Holland's motion for the production of papers relative to him. Having read those parts, which stated that every change which had taken place in the situation of the complainant had been for his own benefit; that the reason for lessening his limits had been his tampering with soldiers or inhabitants; that he had only received one letter; that the communication with officers and inhabitants was unrestricted and free; that people had gone to Longwood in disguise, &c. &c. "*Je suis bien aise,*" said Napoleon, "*de voir que le ministre Anglaise a justifie sa conduite atroce envers moi au parlement, à sa nation, et à l'Europe avec des mensonges ; triste ressource, qui ne dure pas long temps.* Il regno di bugie non durerà per sempre,"* continued he, "I felt greatly ashamed, and

---

* I am happy (said Napoleon) to see that the English minister has justified his conduct towards me, to parliament, to the nation, and to Europe, with lies; a miserable resource which cannot last long.—The reign of lies will not last for ever.

ready to sink into the earth, and stammered out the excuse that had been suggested to me by Sir Hudson Lowe." "It is even worse," said he, "in the Morning Chronicle. In the Times, it appeared as if *prepared* for publication in a ministerial office but in the Chronicle, it looks as if coming from his own mouth. I have ordered Bertrand," added he, "to make a faithful translation of it, and to consult you about any phrase or delicacy of language, of the sense of which he may be doubtful. Lord Bathurst," continued he, "has shown great indelicacy in having shown or told to Montchenu in London, the contents of a letter written by Gourgaud to his mother, which the old blockhead repeated to all the world here. He asserts that I only received one letter, that from my brother Joseph, which is false. He ought to act like a confessor, to hear everything, and divulge nothing; but it is of a piece with the rest of his outrageous conduct. He wants to debase and to lower me. There are some of his pleasantries that I do not well comprehend. I shall, however, soon be able to give him a proper answer. If the governor questions you, tell him what I have said."

Napoleon then observed it was strange that a sovereign, who by the grace of God, was born lord and master of so many millions, could not receive a sealed letter. "How," said he, "can complaints be made to the sovereign of a corrupt or vile minister if such be the rule? In time of war, if a minister betrays and sells his country, how can it be known to the king, if the complaint must go through the hands of the persons complained of? At whose option it will be either to varnish and color it over as best suits his views, or suppress it altogether."

"Santini," continued he, "has published a *brochure** full of trash. There are some truths in it, but every thing is exaggerated. There was always enough to exist upon, but not enough for a good table."

31st.—Gave Napoleon a translation I had made by his desire, of a letter, which appeared in the Courier newspaper. After reading it, he expressed his opinion that it had been written by

* Pamphlet.

the governor himself, and that the seeming incorrectness of one part, was only to mask the real author.

He then spoke at length about the state of England: observed, that it was necessary not to yield too much to the people, or to allow them to think that it were conceded through fear. That perhaps the suspension of the habeas corpus act might, for a short time, be a proper step, as well as an army kept up to intimidate the *canaille*. " But," said he, " I consider these to be only topical applications, which if used without general remedies, that should act upon the constitutional disease, might prove repellent and dangerous, by driving the complaint to nobler parts. England may be likened unto a patient requiring to have his system changed by a course of mercury. The only radical remedy is that which will affect the constitution, that is to say, relieve the misery which exists. This can only be effected by procuring a vent for your manufactures, and by reduction of expenditure, ministers setting the example themselves, by giving up the sinecures, &c. This would contribute essentially to calm the public agitation. Had the ministers come forward like men, at the opening of the session of parliament, and thrown up their sinecures, this, with the example set by the Prince Regent, would have quieted all tumults and complaints.

" The people, in expectation of experiencing something radically beneficial from so good a beginning, would have united, and time would have been gained to adopt measures to relieve the general distress. An exclusive commercial treaty for twenty years with the Brazils and Spanish South America might still be demanded with success. Or assist the colonies in rendering themselves independent, and you will have all their commerce. A war with Spain, if she refused to agree to your demands, would divert the attention of the public, employ soldiers and sailors, and a great portion of manufacturers.—All your miseries, I maintain to be owing to the imbecility and ignorance of Lord Castlereagh, and his inattention to the real prosperity of his own country. Had Lords Grenville or Wellesley been ambassadors, I am convinced that the interests of England would have been consulted. What would those Englishmen, who lived one hundred years ago, say, if they could rise from their graves, be informed of your glorious successes, cast their eyes upon England, witness her distress, and be informed that, in the treaty of peace not a single article for the benefit of England had been stipulated! that, on the contrary, you had given up conquests and commercial rights necessary to your existence. When Austria gained ten millions of inhabitants, Russia eight, Prussia ten, Holland, Bavaria, Sardinia, and every other power, obtained an increase of territory, why not England? who was the main organ of all the success? Instead of establishing a number of independent maritime states, such as Hamburgh, Stralsund, Dantzic, Genoa, to serve as *entrepôts*, for your manufactures, with conditions, either secret or otherwise, favorable to your commerce, you have basely given up Genoa to the King of Sardinia, and united Belgium to Holland. You have rendered yourselves hated by the Italians and Belgians, and have done irreparable injury to your trade. For, although it is a great point for you, that Belgium should be separated from France, it is a serious disadvantage to you that she should be united to Holland. Holland has no manufactories, and consequently would have become a dépôt for yours, from whence a prodigious influx would be kept up on the continent. Now, however, that Belgium has been made a part of Holland, this last will naturally prefer taking the manufactures of her subjects to those of a stranger, and all Belgium may be called a manufacturing town Independent of this, in case of any future war with France, Holland must join the latter through fear of losing the provinces of Belgium. People always consider the danger that is most imminent. They will reason thus: 'If we declare against France, we lose, directly, Belgium and our manufactures; if against England, what can she do? Blockade our ports, and effect disembarkations. We shall still have the commerce of the continent, and shall have time enough to prepare ourselves. We must, therefore, declare for France.' It would have been much better that you should have given it to Austria, or why not have made it an independent country, and placed an English prince as sovereign? Now let us see the state you are actually in. You are nearly as effectually shut out from the continent, as when I reigned and promulgated the continental system. I ask you what peace dictated by me, supposing that I had been victorious, could have been worse in its effects for England, than the one made by Lord Castlereagh, when she was triumphant. The hatred which your ministers bear to me, has precipitated them into an abyss. You recollect I told you some time ago, that I thought it bad policy to leave the English troops in France, and make Lord Wellington commander-in-chief. You now see the effect of it. Prussia denies entrance to your merchandise. What can you do? You can neither attempt to intimidate, nor proceed to extremities, as Prussia could fall upon Lord Wellington and his forty thousand men. While you retain your troops on the continent, you will never be independent. Had you, after the grand blow was given, when I was disposed of, withdrawn your troops from the continent, you would have been independent; you would not have drawn down the hatred and jealousy of the continental powers, especially at seeing Lord Wellington commander-in-chief, and they never would have dared to shut their ports against you. You could then have sent your ships, blockaded their ports, and have declared, 'if you do not permit my merchandise to enter, no other shall either go in or come out.' They would soon have listened to reason.—*Now*, your hands are tied; your meddling in continental affairs, and trying to make yourselves a great military power, instead of attending to the sea and commerce, will yet be your ruin as a nation. You were greatly offended with me for having called you a *nation of shopkeepers*. Had I meant by this, that you were a nation of cowards, you would have had reason to be displeased; even though it were ridiculous and contrary to historical facts; but no such thing was ever intended. I meant that you were a nation of merchants, and that all your great riches and your grand resources arose from commerce, which is true. What else constitutes the riches of England? It is not extent of territory, or a numerous population. It is not mines of gold, silver, or diamonds. Moreover, no man of sense ought to be ashamed of being called a shopkeeper. But your prince and your ministers appear to wish to change altogether *l'esprit** of the English, and to render you another nation; to make you ashamed of your shops and your trade, which have made you what you are, and to sigh after nobility, titles, and crosses; in fact, to assimilate you with the French. What other objects can there be in all those cordons, crosses and honors, which are so profusely showered? You are all nobility now, instead of the plain old Englishmen. You are ashamed of yourselves, and want to be a nation of nobility and *gentlemen*.† Nothing is to be seen or heard of now in England, but 'Sir John,' and 'My lady.' All those things did very well with me in France, because they were conformable to the spirit of the nation, but believe me, it is contrary both to the spirit and the interest of England. Stick to your ships, your commerce, and countinghouses, and leave cordons, crosses and cavalry uniforms to the continent, and you will prosper. Lord Castlereagh himself was ashamed of your being called a nation of merchants, and frequently said to France, that it was a mistaken idea to suppose that England depended upon commerce, or was indebted to it for her riches; and added that it was not by any means necessary to her. How I laughed when I heard of this false pride. He betrayed his country at the peace. I do not mean to say," continued he, laying his hand over his heart, "that he did it from here, but he betrayed it by neglecting its interests. He was in fact the *commis*‡ of the allied sovereigns. Perhaps he wanted to convince them that you were not a nation of merchants, by showing clearly that you would not make any advantageous bargain for yourselves; by magnanimously giving up everything that nations might cry, 'Oh! how nobly England has behaved.' Had he attended to the interest of his own country, had he stipulated for commercial treaties, for the independence of some maritime

* The Spirit.
† This he said in English, as well as the words marked with commas, which follow.
‡ Clerk, deputy.

states and towns, for certain advantages to be secured to England, to indemnify her for the waste of blood, and the enormous sacrifices she had made, why then they might have said, 'What a mercenary people! they are truly a nation of merchants; see what bargains they want to make:' and Lord Castlereagh would not have been so well received in the *drawing-rooms!*"

"Talent he may have displayed in some instances," continued the emperor, "and great pertinacity in accomplishing my downfall: but as to knowledge of, or attention to, the interest of his own country, he has manifested neither the one nor the other. Probably for a thousand years, such another opportunity of aggrandizing England will not occur. In the position of affairs, nothing could have been refused to you. But now after such romantic and unparalleled successes; after having been favored by God and by accidents, in the manner you have been; after effecting impossibilities—I may say, effecting what the most sanguine mind could never have entertained the most distant idea of, what has England gained?—the cordons of the allied sovereigns for Lord Castlereagh!"

"When," continued Napoleon,* "a nation has been favored so much as yours has been, and that misery exists in that nation, it must be owing to the imbecility of the ministers. The transition from war to peace cannot explain it. It is of too long a continuance. Had I been the English minister, or had the minister been possessed of common sense, and not blinded by vanity, or one who would not have allowed himself to be duped by the attentions of kings and emperors, you would have been rich, the seas covered with your ships, and your manufactures would have been wealthy and flourishing. Lord Castlereagh will be an object of reprehension for the nation and for posterity."

I told Napoleon that in one of the Couriers sent him by the governor, I had observed a speech attributed to Sir Francis Burdett, accusing him of having established eight *bastiles* in France. Napoleon replied, "In some respects it is true. I established a few prisons, but they were for certain persons who

* This conversation was communicated by me in 1817, to official persons.

were under sentence of death; as I did not like to have the capital punishment executed, and could not send them to a Botany Bay; as you were masters of the sea and would have released them, I was obliged to keep them in prisons."

"There were," continued he, "some Vendean chiefs, Chouans, and others, who had been arrested for rebellion and other crimes, to whom the choice was given, either to be tried, or to remain in prison as long as the government might think it necessary for the safety of the state. Those jails were inspected twice a year by a committee composed of a counsellor of state, and two judges; who each time offered the prisoners the choice of continuing in prison as they were, or of being brought to trial; but they always preferred the former. They were allowed three francs a day for their subsistence. No abuses," continued he, "were known to be committed in the prisons; in fact, instead of being a crime as imputed to me in that paper, it was a mercy. But," added he, "where is the country without jails? Are there not some in England?"

June 2d.—An orderly dragoon brought a letter directing me to proceed immediately to Plantation House. Found his excellency in the library, who asked what were General Bonaparte's remarks upon the discussions in parliament. I repeated Napoleon's expressions, (as I had been desired to do.) When I mentioned the remarks he had made upon the assertion imputed to Lord Bathurst, that every change which had taken place had been for the benefit of the complainant, also his observations on the indelicacy of disclosing the contents of letters, Sir Hudson Lowe took up a number of the Times newspaper, and with a countenance in which embarrassment was visible, observed, "that Lord Bathurst was right in having asserted, that whatever alterations had been made, had been for the better, because his lordship must have alluded to the different manner in which letters were now sent to Longwood; for *instead of passing through the hands of inferior officers* as before, they were now only seen and read by himself" (the governor.)

Some conversation then took place relative to the quantity of provisions allowed to Longwood. Sir Hudson Lowe maintained that the quantities had been fixed by Count Montholon, and that he (Sir Hudson) had never heard any complaints made of a deficiency. I explained to his excellency, that Count Montholon had not fixed the quantities, and also called to his recollection that the scantiness of the allowance had been frequently reported to him by the orderly officer, by the purveyor, by myself, and also by the maître d'hôtel. Sir Hudson Lowe persisted that the quantities had been specified by Count Montholon, and sent for Major Gorrequer, to prove the correctness of his assertion. Major Gorrequer, however, did not support his excellency; as he declared that the quantity of the wine only had been fixed by the Count, and that of the remaining articles by a scale framed by orders of his excellency himself. Notwithstanding a little confusion produced by this, Sir Hudson Lowe persisted in asserting that he was ignorant of the insufficiency of the allowance of provisions; upon which I thought it necessary to enumerate the days on which representations to that effect had been made to him by me, by Mr. Balcombe, and by the maître d'hôtel; and also observed, that the assistance rendered by Sir Thomas Reade twice a week in procuring divers articles of eatables for Longwood, for which payment had been frequently made in his presence by Cipriani, could not have left Sir Thomas in ignorance respecting the wants of the French. The governor sneeringly observed, "It appeared that I should be the best witness *those* people could call.'

4*th.*—An increase of twenty-eight pounds daily in the meat furnished by government to Longwood, ordered by Sir Hudson Lowe.

Independent of the usual guard, an officer has been stationed at Hut's Gate since the arrival of the ships from England, with orders to inspect minutely every one approaching Longwood, and to allow "*no suspicious persons*" to pass.

5*th.*—Count and Countess Montholon went to town shopping, and to pay a visit to Admiral and Lady Malclom. The officer who accompanied them was ordered by the governor to "follow them into the Admiral's, and to pay attention to their conversation."

6th.—Saw Napoleon, who was in very good spirits. Told me that Count Montholon had been informed yesterday that a person who had seen the Grand Lama had just arrived in the island; he therefore desired, that as soon as I went to town, I should endeavor to get acquainted with him, and inquire what ceremonies had been made use of; whether adoration was practised, and inform myself of every possible particular. "I am," said he, "very curious to get some information about this Grand Lama. I have never read any accounts about him that I could rely upon, and sometimes have doubted of his existence."

Saw Sir Hudson Lowe in town, with whom I had some conversation relative to Napoleon's observations on Lord Bathurst's speech. His excellency gave me a message to be delivered to him in reply. Mentioned to him that Napoleon had also remarked, when speaking of Lord B., "*Quasi tutti li ministri son bugiardi. Talleyrand, ni' il caporale, poi viene Castlereagh, poi Metternich, Hardenberg,*"* &c. Informed him also that Napoleon had desired me to endeavor to make myself acquainted with a gentleman lately arrived, who, it was reported, had seen the Grand Lama. Sir Hudson *appeared* not to know that such a person was in the island.

Shortly afterwards I met Capt. Balston, of the Hon. Company's sea-service, who reminded me of our former acquaintance. By him I was informed that a gentleman had arrived from China, with a letter of introduction to me from Mr. Urmston, of Macao, with whom I had been on terms of intimacy. On seeing the gentleman afterwards, I found that his name was Manning, and that he was the person of whom I was in search. He wore a long black beard, and had travelled through the kingdom of Thibet as far as the frontiers of China. I told him that the emperor had expressed great curiosity about the Grand Lama, and that if he came up to Longwood, there was every probability that he would

* Almost all ministers are liars. Talleyrand is their corporal; next come Castlereagh, Metternich, Hardenberg.

see him. Mr. Manning related that he had been a prisoner in France, and had been released by Napoleon, and furnished with a passport, as soon as the emperor had learned that he was a person travelling for information, which might ultimately benefit society; that as a mark of his gratitude for this favor, he had sent some little presents to the governor for him, with a request that they might be forwarded, and that he would ask a pass for the purpose of endeavoring to see him.

A report current in town, that a marble bust of young Napoleon was brought out in the Baring, and that Sir Thomas Reade had recommended the captain of the vessel to throw it overboard and say nothing about it. This was asserted as a positive fact to Cipriani and to me by Captain * *, who said that the captain of the Baring had confessed that insinuations to that effect had been made to him.

7th.—Mr. Manning, accompanied by Captain Balston, came up to Count Bertrand's. The former told me that he had been directed by the governor, for what reason he could not divine, not to communicate to the Count that he had sent a few presents to him for Napoleon. After they had been about an hour at Count Bertrand's, Napoleon came in, accompanied by General Montholon. He accosted Captain Balston first, and observed, "Oh, I have seen you here before." He then asked Mr. Manning some questions. Manning related that he had been in France in 1805, (I think,) and was one of the persons who had been detained; that he had written a letter to him (Napoleon,) stating that he was travelling for the benefit of the world at large, which had procured his release. "What protection had you?" asked Napoleon "Had you a letter from Sir Joseph Banks to me?" Manning replied that he had no protection whatever, nor letter from Sir Joseph Banks, nor had he any friends to interest themselves in his behalf; that he had merely written a letter to him stating his situation. "Was it your simple letter which obtained your liberty?" asked Napoleon. "It was my simple letter," replied Manning, "that induced you to grant it to me, for which I am very grateful, and beg to thank you." Napoleon asked him where he had

1817.—JUNE.

lived, &c., and looked at the map of the countries in the atlas of Las Cases, asking a variety of questions about the route he had taken; whether he had seen the Grand Lama; the manners, customs, &c., of the countries he had passed through.

Manning gave him a clear and concise reply to every question, said that he had seen the Lama, whom he described to be an intelligent boy of seven years old, and had performed the same ceremonies in his presence as were done by others who were admitted to it. Napoleon said, "How did you escape being taken up as a spy?" "I hope," replied Manning, "that there is nothing in my countenance which would indicate my being a spy;" at which Napoleon laughed, and said, "How came it to pass, that you being *profane* according to their ideas, could gain admission to the presence of the Lama?" Mr Manning answered that he honored and paid respect to all religions, and thereby gained admission. Napoleon desired to know if he had passed for an Englishman, and observed that the shape of his nose would indicate his being a European? The other replied that he had passed for a native of Calcutta, but he believed it was known that he was an Englishman; that there were some races of men there who had a similar formation of nose. Napoleon then observed with a smile, that "*Messieurs les voyageurs** frequently told *contes*,† and that the exsitence of the Grand Lama had been denied by several." Manning answered, "*Je ne suis pas du nombre de ces voyageurs là ;*‡ that truth was not falsehood," at which Napoleon laughed, and asked many other questions. Manning related, that the chief part of the revenues of the Grand Lama arose from presents made to him by the princes and others who believed in him; that temporarily, however, he was subject to the Chinese; that he never married, neither did his priests; that the body into which, according to their belief, the spirit passed, was discovered by signs known only to the priests. Napoleon then asked several questions about the Chinese language, the late embassy, if the Russians had ever penetrated in that direction, and whether he intended to publish an account of his travels; after which he asked Balston some ques-

* Travellers.   † Fibs,   ‡ I am not one of that sort of travellers.

tions about his ship, wished them a good morning, and departed!

Gave Napoleon a copy of Santani's pamphlet in French, which he read, observing as he went through it, according as the passages seemed to deserve it, " true," " partly true," " false," " stuff," &c

He observed that they had spelled his name with a *u* (*Buonaparte*), and told me that when he first commanded the army of Italy, he had used the *u* in order to please the Italians; that, however, either the one or the other was equally proper; that after his return from Egypt he had dropped it; that in fact the chiefs of the family and those who had been highest, had spelled their names with the *u*, adding, " that a mighty affair had been made of so trifling a matter." He concluded by remarking, that " Santani would have done better to have confined himself strictly to the truth, which would have had a much stronger effect on the public mind than the exaggerations he had promulgated, which indeed appeared to have been framed by some person in England, as Santani was incapable of writing a pamphlet himself."

8th.—Mr. Cole (of the firm of Balcombe and Co., the purveyors,) came up to Longwood by order of Major Gorrequer, to acquaint General Montholon that the liveries of the servants must be changed from green to blue, and the quantity of gold lace upon the coats diminished.

For some time back complaints have been made by the maître d'hôtel of the badness of the mutton, of the fowls, the indifferent quality and want of variety of the vegetables, &c. Mr. Cole informed me that it was not their fault, as by order of Sir Hudson Lowe, the purveyor was obliged to take the sheep from the company's stock-yard. That this day permission had been received to purchase from the farmers, restricting them however to a certain price; that the vegetables furnished were received from the garden of the governor.

9th.—An official complaint made in writing by Captain Poppleton to Major Gorrequer of the badness of the above-mentioned articles; also that Mr. Cole said that the vegetables were furnished from Plantation House garden.

10th.—Napoleon in his bed-room. Told him that I had received a Portsmouth paper, in which were contained extracts from a work published in London under his name. He looked over it, and observed that he had not written a line of it, though some parts resembled his manner. He added that there was a Scotchman, whose name he did not recollect, who had written several articles so much in his style, that when in France he had caused some of his works to be translated into French.

I informed him that Colonel Macirone, aid-de-camp to Murat, had published some anecdotes of his late master. "What does he say of me?" said Napoleon. I replied, that I had not seen the book, but had been informed by Sir Thomas Reade that he spoke ill of him. "Oh," said he laughing, "that is nothing; I am well accustomed to it. But what does he say?" I answered, it was asserted that Murat had imputed the loss of Waterloo to the cavalry not having been properly employed, and had said that if he (Murat) had commanded them, the French would have gained the victory. "It is very probable," replied Napoleon, "I could not be every where; and Murat was the best cavalry officer in the world. He would have given more impetuosity to the charge. There wanted but very little, I assure you, to gain the day for me. *Enforcer deux ou trois bataillons,** and in all probability Murat would have effected that. There were not I believe two such officers in the world as Murat for the cavalry, and Drouot for the artillery. Murat was a most singular character. Four and twenty years ago, when he was a captain, I made him my aid-de-camp, and subsequently raised him to be what he was. He loved, I may rather say, adored me. In my presence he was as it were struck with awe, and ready to fall at my feet. I acted wrong in having separated him from me, as without me, he was nothing. With me, he was my right arm. Order Murat to attack and destroy four or five thousand men in such a direction, it was done in a moment; but leave him to himself he was an *imbécile*† without judgment. I cannot conceive how so brave a man could be so *lache*.‡ He was no where

* To drive two or three battalions. † Weak. ‡ Sluggish.

brave unless before the enemy. *There* he was probably the bravest man in the world. His boiling courage carried him into the midst of the enemy, *couvert de pennes jusqu'au clocher*,* and glittering with gold How he escaped is a miracle, being, as he was, always a distinguished mark, and fired at by every body Even the Cossacs admired him on account of his extraordinary bravery. Every day Murat was engaged in single combat with some of them, and never returned without his sabre dripping with the blood of those whom he had slain. He was a paladin, in fact a Don Quixote in the field ; but take him into the cabinet, he was a poltroon without judgment or decision. Murat and Ney were the bravest men I ever witnessed. Murat, however, was a much nobler character than Ney. Murat was generous and open ; Ney partook of the *canaille*. Strange to say, however, Murat, though he loved me, did me more mischief than any other person in the world When I left Elba, I sent a messenger to acquaint him with what I had done. Immediately he must attack the Austrians. The messenger went upon his knees to prevent him; but in vain. He thought me already master of France, Belgium, and Holland, and that he must make his peace, and not adhere to *demi-mesures*.† Like a madman he attacked the Austrians with his *canaille*, and ruined me. For at that time there was a negotiation going on between Austria and me, stipulating that the former should remain neutral, which would have been finally concluded, and I should have reigned undisturbed. But as soon as Murat attacked the Austrians, the emperor immediately conceived that he was acting by my directions and indeed it will be difficult to make posterity believe to the contrary. Metternich said, ' Oh, the Emperor Napoleon is the same as ever. A man of iron. The trip to Elba has not changed him. Nothing will ever alter him ; all or nothing for him.' Austria joined the coalition, and I was lost. Murat was unconscious that my conduct was regulated by circumstances and adapted to them. He was like a man gazing at the scenes shifting at the opera, without ever thinking of the machinery behind,

* Covered with badges of honor even to crippling. † **Half measures.**

by which the whole is moved. He never, however, thought that his secession in the first instance would have been so injurious to me, or he would not have joined the allies. He concluded that I should be obliged to give up Italy and some other countries, but never contemplated my total ruin."

Sir Hudson Lowe at Longwood. Went to Count Bertrand's, where he remained for some time. In the evening Napoleon sent for me, and said, that Sir Hudson Lowe had been to Bertrand, to inform him, that Lady Holland had sent out some presents for Madame Bertrand's children, two books for himself, and some other articles, with a letter; that although it was contrary to the regulations, which prescribed that every thing should come through the secretary of state's office, he would take it upon himself to send them. That Mr. Manning had also left some trifling presents for him (Napoleon,) which he wished to know if he would accept. That there was also another circumstance still more embarrassing, viz. that a sculptor at Leghorn had made a bad bust of young Napoleon, and which he had forwarded to St. Helena by the Baring, in charge of a man now very ill with a fever, with a letter, stating that the artist had been already satisfied, but that if he (Napoleon) wished to pay any more, one hundred guineas was the price, which he conceived to be a large sum of money for a badly executed bust. That he wished to be informed if Napoleon would desire to have it. " Bertrand," continued Napoleon, " replied, that doubtless the emperor would wish to see the statue of his son. He regretted it had not been forwarded at an earlier period. That it would be better to send it that very evening than detain it until to-morrow, and that the emperor would be happy to receive Mr. Manning's presents." Bertrand says, that he looked disturbed, and appeared to attribute great merit to himself for having offered to send up those things, because they had not passed through the hands of the secretary of state, and surprised that Bertrand was not abounding in thanks to him for his great goodness. I do not know what he meant by saying that a hundred guineas was too much for the statue, or if he intended it as an insult, or as a reflection upon us. Surely no sum could be too much for a *father* to pay under similar circumstances. But this man has no feeling."

Napoleon then asked me if I knew anything about the statue? I replied, that I had heard of it some days before. "Why did you not tell me?" asked the emperor. I felt a little confused, and answered, that I expected the governor would have sent it up. Napoleon said, "I have known of it for several days. I intended, if it had not been given, to have made such a complaint as would have caused every Englishman's hair to stand on end with horror (*alzare i capelli*.) I would have told a tale which would have made the mothers of England execrate him as a monster in human shape. I have been informed that he has been deliberating about it, and also that his prime minister Reade ordered it to be broken. I suppose that he has been consulting with that little major, who has pointed out to him that it would brand his name with ignominy for ever, or that his wife had read him a lecture at night about the atrocity of such a proceeding. He has done enough, however, to dishonor his name by retaining it so long,* and by even allowing a doubt to exist of its being sent up."

The emperor afterwards spoke of his own family. "My excellent mother," said he, " is a woman of courage and of great talent, more of a masculine than a feminine nature, proud and high-minded.† She is capable of selling everything even to her *chemise* for me. I allowed her a million a year, besides a palace, and giving her many presents. To the manner in which she formed me at an early age, I principally owe my subsequent elevation. My opinion is, that the future good or bad conduct of a child entirely depends upon the mother. She is very rich. Most of my family considered that I might die, that accidents might happen,

---

* The bust had been in the island for fourteen days, during several of which it was at Plantation House.

† Madame Mère, when I had the honor of seeing her at Rome in 1819, was still the remains of a fine woman. Her manners were dignified and commanding, and her deportment such as one would expect to find in a queen, or in the mother of Napoleon. Her thoughts were divided between her God and her son. She saw but little company, and I believe that the Duke of Hamilton and myself were the only Britons who had dined at her table. Her establishment was splendid, though private and unostentatious.

and consequently took care to secure something. They have preserved a great part of their property.

"Josephine died worth about eighteen millions of francs. She was the greatest patroness of the fine arts that had been known in France for a series of years. She had frequently little disputes with Denon, and even with myself, as she wanted to procure fine statues and pictures for her own gallery, instead of the museum Now, I always acted to please the people; and whenever I obtained a fine statue, or a valuable picture, I sent it there for the benefit of the nation. Josephine was grace personified (*la grazia in persona.*) Everything she did was with a peculiar grace and delicacy. I never saw her act inelegantly during the whole time we lived together. She had grace even *en se couchant.** Her toilet was a perfect arsenal, and she effectually defended herself against the assaults of time."

"When the Pope was in France," added Napoleon, "I allotted him a most superb palace, elegantly furnished at Fontainebleau, and one hundred thousand crowns a month for his expenses. Fifteen carriages were kept for himself and the cardinals, though he never went out. He was a good man, but a fanatic. He was greatly annoyed by the libels which had been published, containing assertions of my having ill treated him, and contradicted them publicly, stating, that except politically, he had been very well treated. At one time," continued the emperor, "I had it in contemplation to take away all his temporal power, to make him my almoner, and Paris the capital of the Christian world."

11*th.*—This day was sent up a beautiful white marble bust of young Napoleon, about the natural size, and very well executed, with an inscription, Napoléon François Charles Joseph, &c., and decorated with the grand cross of the legion of honor. The presents from Lady Holland and Mr. Manning accompanied it. Napoleon did not eat anything until eight o'clock in the evening.

Some time after the bust arrived, Napoleon sent for me. It was placed on the mantel-piece in the drawing-room. "Look at that," said Napoleon, "look at that image. Barbarous and atro-

---

* In getting into bed.

cious must the man be who would break such an image as that. I esteem the man capable of executing, or of ordering it, to be worse than him who administers poison to another. For the latter has some object to gain, but the former is instigated by nothing but the blackest attrocity, (*l'atrocità la più nera*) and is capable of committing any crime. That countenance would melt the heart of the most ferocious wild beast. The man who gave orders to break that image, would plunge a knife into the heart of the original, if it were in his power."* He gazed on the statue for several minutes with great satisfaction and delight; his face covered with smiles, and strongly expressive of paternal love, and of the pride which he felt in being the father of so lovely a boy. I watched his countenance narrowly, which I had an excellent opportunity of doing while he was contemplating attentively the beautiful, though inanimate features sculptured on the marble. No person who had witnessed this scene, could deny that Napoleon was animated by the tender affections of a father.

Napoleon afterwards vented his feelings about the alleged order for the destruction of the bust. When I endeavored to reason upon the uncertainty of the fact, and that it assuredly had not been given by the governor, he interrupted me by saying, " that it was in vain to attempt to deny a known fact. The statue to me," continued he, " was worth a million, though this governor contemptuously said that a hundred pounds was a great price for it."

Mr. Balcombe came up to Count Bertrand's about some money concerns, and had an interview afterwards with Napoleon, who walked with Count Bertrand and him to the end of the wood.

12*th*.—Saw Napoleon in his bath, in which he remained for four hours and a half. Gave him M. Macirone's interesting facts respecting Joachim Murat. With very little assistance from me, he read it through, making observations occasionally. " He will not be pitied," said he, " because he was a traitor. He never mentioned to me that he was determined to defend his kingdom;

---

* This conversation was communicated by me to official persons shortly after it occurred.

neither had I ever told him that my intentions were to unite the kingdoms of Italy and Naples, take them from him, and make him constable of the empire. I certainly made an instrument of him, to answer grand projects that I had in view for Italy, and intended, as I told you before, to have dispossessed Murat of the crown of Naples; but the time was not come; and besides, I would have given him a suitable indemnification. His letter to Macirone was ridiculous, and his enterprise that of a madman. What reason had he to complain of the Emperor of Austria, who had behaved generously, and offered him an asylum, wherever he pleased, in his dominions, subject to no other restriction than that of not quitting it without permission; which was very necessary. In the actual state of things, what more, in God's name, could he desire? I, myself, never should have expected more in England. It was a generous act on the part of the Emperor of Austria, and a return of good for evil, as Murat had endeavored to deprive him of Italy; had published proclamations exciting insurrection amongst the Italians; attacked the emperor's troops like a blockhead without reason; and like a madman engaged without judgment in an expedition without a plan, and so badly arranged that he never had been able to unite even his own guard. In his proclamations to the Italians, he never even mentioned my name, though he knew that they adored me."

"*Ma bisogna dire la verita*,"* continued he, "Murat had not acted in that double manner in his correspondence with me of which he has been accused. The papers shown to prove it, were falsified. At that time, Murat had no understanding with me. Lord Exmouth appears to have acted fairly and honorably, by candidly informing him that he would receive him on no other terms than as a prisoner of war. I do not believe that he offered a thousand louis for the arrestation of Murat. * * *, who is described to be so good and honorable a character, is neither the one nor the other. He certainly is a person greatly attached to me, but he is a man of the police; you know," added he, laughing, "what kind of honor those gentry have." *Belle armee*† in-

---

* But I am obliged to tell the truth. † A fine army.

deed, repeated he, using an expression of contempt, alluding to Murat's expression about the Neapolitan army. " You know what the Neapolitans are.—Murat undertook an expedition *da coglione al fondo*,* to invade Naples with two hundred Corsicans at the time that it was occupied by twenty thousand Austrians, and terminated his life like a madman. He will be lamented by none, though at the same time he was far from being guilty of that double treachery imputed to him."

He then repeated the opinion he had formerly given, had the cavalry been commanded by Murat at Waterloo; but added, that the army considered him as a traitor.

13th.—Saw Napoleon in the billiard-room. He was in very good spirits. Spoke about the possibility of his having remained in France after the battle of Waterloo, in spite of the efforts of the allied powers. " My own opinion was," said he, "that I could not have done so, without having shed the blood of hundreds by the guillotine. I must have plunged my hands up to this in blood"—stretching out one arm, and applying the finger of the other to his arm-pits. " Had the legislative body displayed courage, I might have succeeded, but they were frightened and divided amongst each other; La Fayette was one of the chief causes of the success of the enemies of France. To have given me a chance, I must have had recourse to the most sanguinary measures. The conduct of the allies, in declaring that they waged war against me alone, had a great effect. Had it been possible to have rendered me inseparable from the nation, no efforts of the allied powers would have succeeded; but as it was, by isolating me, and declaring that if I were once removed, all obstacles to a peace would cease, people became divided in their sentiments, and I determined to abdicate, and remove, as far as I was concerned, every difficulty. Had the French nation guessed at the intentions of the allies, or that they would have acted as they have done since, they would have rallied round me. But they were overreached like the lambs of the fable, when the

* To the extent of their force.

wolves declared they only waged war against the dogs; **but the dogs once removed, they fell upon and devoured the lambs."**

"There is a great difference of opinion," continued the emperor, "as to what I ought to have done." Many were of opinion that I ought to have fought to the last. Others said that fortune had abandoned me, that Waterloo had closed my career of arms for ever. My own opinion is, that I ought to have died at Waterloo; perhaps a little earlier. Had I died at Moscow, I should probably have had the reputation of the greatest conqueror ever known. But the smiles of fortune were at an end. I experienced little but reverses afterwards; hitherto I had been unconquered. I ought to have died at Waterloo, (*j'aurais du mourir à Waterloo.*) But the misfortune is, that when a man seeks the most for death, he cannot find it. Men were killed around me, before, behind, everywhere, but no bullet for me."

A letter written to Sir Hudson Lowe by Count Bertrand, stating that he had not yet seen the captain of the vessel who had brought the bust, and expressing a wish that he might be permitted to come to Longwood.

Napoleon walked in the evening for some time with Count Montholon.

18*th*.—A reply was returned by the governor to Count Bertrand's note, stating that the bust had not been brought out by the captain of the Baring. A request was however again made by the Count, that he should be permitted to visit Longwood, and on this day Captain Lamb (a half-pay lieutenant of the navy) came to see Count Bertrand. On his return I asked him to favor me with some information about the bust. He stated, that it had been passed and sent on board from the customhouse, in charge of the gunner of his ship, an Italian, who formerly had been for many years in the British navy. That the day after his arrival at St. Helena, he had mentioned the circumstance at a gentleman's house, and had demanded to be informed of the best mode of transmitting it to Bonaparte, when he was directed to apply to Sir Thomas Reade, who had made numerous inquiries on the subject; amongst others, whether he had mentioned the circumstance to any person in the island, to which he answered that he had related it; he had spoken of it at a dinner party. He was then asked how he could think of bringing out such an article, it being contrary to the instructions; and was finally desired by Sir Thomas Reade to say nothing about the matter, and also to request of those to whom he had mentioned it, to be equally silent. I observed that he must be aware of the report which was current in the island, relative to a recommendation said to have been made to him to throw it overboard, or break it into pieces, a contradiction of which I was anxious to hear from his own mouth. Captain Lamb replied that he had heard the report, which was very general, but not true, and professed that he did not know what it could have arisen from.

On this gentleman's return to town he alighted at Sir Thomas Reade's, and after a stay of a few minutes, proceeded to Plantation House on one of the governor's horses.

19th.—The Podargus brought the intelligence that the Conqueror, with the new admiral (Plampin), had arrived at the Cape. Letters received for Count Bertrand, General Gourgaud, and Marchand.

The admiral and Lady Malcolm, with Major Boys of the marines, and Captain Jones, royal navy, paid a visit to Napoleon. Colonel Fagan, formerly judge advocate in India, had also an interview with him afterwards. The colonel, who spoke French like a native, said that Napoleon asked him many questions in his profession which puzzled him, and that he was extremely shrewd in his remarks.

Saw Napoleon in the evening. He informed me that he had seen Sir Pultney and Lady Malcolm, also Colonel Fagan. "The admiral," said he, "endeavored to support the governor, and said that I might depend upon it he had sent my observations on the restrictions to England. Indeed he advocated his conduct so much, that I told him he was like the rest of the English, *trop égoïste*,* that not being myself an Englishman, their laws did not protect me, and I had no justice to expect from them. *E troppo*

---
* Too much of an egotist.

Inglese.* I told him that in Lord ———'s speech there were three calumnies and ten lies, and that I intended to answer it. He tried to excuse him in the same manner the governor did, by stating that the report of the speech in the newspapers might not be correct, or faithful, and was not to be depended upon. He is mistaken, however. In France, even during the time of the revolutionary fury, the speeches were faithfully reported. I gave *Milédi*† one of my fine porcelain cups with a figure of Cleopatra's needle upon it, as a mark of the esteem which I entertain for her, and the sense I have of her attentions. She insisted upon taking it down herself. I cannot," added he, " conceive how the admiral can think of attempting to excuse a man so unlike himself, and whose conduct I know he cannot approve of in his heart."

Napoleon then said that he had asked Colonel Fagan several questions about the military penal code. " Of this subject," added he, " I am master, as I framed many of the laws myself. I am a doctor of laws, and while the code Napoleon was forming I had repeated disputations and discussions with the compilers of it, who were astonished at the knowledge which I possessed on the subject. I also originated many of the best of its laws."

20*th.*—An order received by Captain Poppleton from Sir Hudson Lowe, to reply by signal, *yes* or *no*, whether Lady Malcolm, Major Boys, and Captain Jones had been in with General Bonaparte at the same time with the admiral.

Learned that the governor appeared to be very uneasy that some observations made by Napoleon on Lord Bathurst's speech should have been repeated by a captain in the navy at Solomon's shop; which circumstance had been reported to him by Sir Thomas Reade immediately after it occurred.

An official report again made to his excellency by the orderly officer, of the quality of the bread supplied to Longwood, which was so bad, that for a considerable time Napoleon had been obliged to make use of biscuit.

24*th.*—Napoleon's cheek swelled and inflamed, chiefly caused by a carious tooth.

* He is too much of an Englishman.   † My Lady.

Some uneasiness manifested at Plantation House at the declaration made by two captains in the navy of their intentions towards Sir Thomas Reade, whom they accuse of some practices of espionage towards them, which had not been warranted either by their situation or conduct.

27*th*.—Lord Amherst arrived.

28*th*.—Lord Amherst and suite, accompanied by the governor, paid a visit to Count and Countess Bertrand.

Napoleon observed, that the civilities of the governor were those of a jailer. "When he came to Bertrand's with the ambassador," said he, " he merely introduced him as Lord Amherst, and then, without sitting down or conversing for a moment like a gentleman, turned about and took his leave, like a jailer or turnkey who points out his prisoners to visitors, then turns the key, and leaves them together. Having come up with Lord Amherst, he ought to have remained for a quarter of an hour and then left them."

July 3rd.—Admiral Plampin, who arrived two or three days ago in the Conqueror, came to Longwood with Captain Davie (his flag captain,) and his secretary, Mr. Elliott. They were introduced to Napoleon by Sir Pultney Malcolm.

Saw Napoleon afterwards, who remarked the singular difference of appearance between Sir Pultney Malcolm and his successor. " Few men," said he, " have so prepossessing an exterior and manner as Malcolm ; but the other reminds me of one of those drunken little Dutch *schippers* that I have seen in Holland, sitting at a table with a pipe in his mouth, a cheese, and bottle of Geneva before him."

On my return from town, dined with the emperor *tête-à-tête* in his writing-room. He was in very good humor. Spoke about Sir Pultney and Lady Malcolm ; asked if I had seen the new admiral ; made some remarks on the late attacks made on the validity of his title to the crown. " By the doctrines put forth by your government writers," said he, " upon the subject of legitimacy, every throne in Europe would be shaken from its foundation. If I was not a legitimate sovereign, William the Third was a usurper of the throne of England, as he was brought in chiefly by the aid of foreign bayonets. George the First was placed on the throne by a faction, composed of a few nobles; I was called to that of France by the votes of nearly four millions of Frenchmen. In fact, the calling of me a usurper is an absurdity which your ministers will in the end be obliged to abandon. If my title to the crown of France was not legitimate, what is that of George the Third?"

The dinner was served on a little round table. The emperor sat on the sofa, and I on a chair opposite. I was very hungry, and did great justice to what was presented to me. Napoleon said that he should like to see me drunk, and ordered Marchand to bring a bottle of champagne, of which he took one glass himself, and made me finish the rest, calling out in English several times, " *Doctor, drink, drink.*"

4th.—Sir Pultney and Lady Malcolm sailed for England in the Newcastle frigate.

Having mislaid some sheets of my journal, I have been under the necessity of chiefly trusting to my recollection for the following details. The manner in which Captain Lamb had related the history of the bust, had, instead of dissipating the suspicions at Longwood, rather convinced them that some such proposal or insinuation had been made. This was confirmed by the visit at Longwood of two of the captains of the lately arrived store-ships, both of whom saw Napoleon in the garden. One, whose name it is not *now* necessary to mention, assured Napoleon himself, and other residents at Longwood, that he had heard Captain Lamb say, that some insinuations had been made to him purporting that the bust should be thrown overboard, the gunner who brought it confined to his ship, and nothing more said of the matter. Previous to this, I succeeded in persuading Napoleon that the charge against Sir Thomas Reade was unfounded, and even obtained his permission to communicate his sentiments on the subject to that officer. The affair was buzzed about the island, and gained considerable credit.

It was reported that the bust in question had been executed at Leghorn by orders of the Empress Marie Louise, and that she had sent it to her husband by the gunner, as a silent though convincing proof that her affections were unchanged. Napoleon, who was extremely partial to the empress, was inclined to believe this supposition, which in itself was very probable, and made him very anxious to ascertain the truth. To accomplish this object, he directed Count Bertrand to apply for permission to be granted to the gunner to come to Longwood. After some delays and assertions that the man was sick, during which time he was examined on oath at Plantation House and minutely searched, it was signified to Bertrand that leave was granted to him to go to Longwood. A few minutes after his arrival at Count Bertrand's, and while speaking to the Countess, Captain Poppleton was sent into the room by the governor, with orders not to allow him to speak to any of the French, unless in his presence. This proceeding, combined with the disingenuous manner in which it was executed, was considered as an insult, and the gunner was immediately directed to withdraw.

Two or three days after Lord Amherst's arrival, I had the honor of dining in company with him at Plantation House. As I have lost the notes which I made on that occasion, I shall merely state, to the best of my recollection, the purport of what I had the honor of explaining to his lordship, viz. "that I conceived myself bound to inform him, that if he went to Longwood with a view of seeing Napoleon, accompanied by the governor or by any of his staff, he would certainly meet with a refusal; which, though far from the intention of Napoleon, might by others be construed into an insult. That considered in any way, it was a circumstance desirable to be avoided. That if his lordship came up with only his own staff, I had little doubt but that he would be received, provided Napoleon should be sufficiently recovered from a swelling in his cheek, with which he was then afflicted."

His lordship was pleased to thank me for the suggestion.

At the end of June, or beginning of July, Count Bertrand waited upon Lord Amherst, and informed him that Napoleon had been unwell for several days, and was at that moment suffering under a tooth-ache. He added, however, that if the emperor should be in a state to see visitors before his lordship's departure, he would receive him. Accordingly, on the 2d or 3d his lordship proceeded to Longwood, accompanied by his suite, and by Captain Murray Maxwell, of his majesty's late ship the Alceste. About half past three, the ambassador was introduced to Napoleon, with whom he remained alone for nearly two hours. Previous to leaving him, his lordship presented the members of his suite and Captain Maxwell, to each of whom Napoleon addressed some observations. Mr. Ellis, the secretary, conversed with him about a quarter of an hour. He observed to Captain Maxwell, that he had taken a frigate of his off the island of Lissa, in the Adriatic, in 1811, which would amply compensate for the loss of the Alceste. To Mr. Griffiths, the chaplain, he also addressed several questions, and in a smiling way recommended him to his lordship's patronage.

9th.—Some packages and cases containing a superb set of chessmen and table, two magnificent carved ivory work-baskets, and a set of ivory counters and box, all of Chinese manufacture, sent to Count Bertrand for Napoleon. They were accompanied by a letter, stating that they had been made by order of the Hon. Mr. Elphinstone, for the purpose of being presented to the distinguished personage whose initials they bore, as a mark of the gratitude entertained by the donor for the extraordinary humanity displayed by him, which was the means of saving the life of a beloved brother.* A letter from Sir Hudson Lowe also came with them, stating, that when he had promised Count Bertrand a day or two before that they should be sent, he was little aware, that on opening them, he should have discovered something so objectionable, and which, according to the letter of his instructions, ought to prevent their being sent.

It appeared that on the presents was engraved the letter *N*,

* The day before the battle of Waterloo, Captain Elphinstone had been severely wounded, and made prisoner. His situation attracted the attention of Napoleon, who immediately ordered his surgeon to dress his wounds; and perceiving that he was faint from loss of blood, sent him a silver goblet full of wine from his own canteen. On the arrival of the Bellerophon in England, Lord Keith sent his grateful thanks to Napoleon for having saved his nephew's life.

surmounted by a crown, which his excellency esteemed to be highly objectionable and dangerous. Captain Heaviside, who had brought them from China, on having obtained permission to visit Longwood soon after his arrival, was ordered by the governor to maintain a strict silence on the subject to all the French

In the evening, Napoleon looked at those articles, which he greatly admired, and signified his intention to send the workbaskets to the Empress Marie Louise, the box of counters to his mother, the chessmen and superb table to his son.

11th.—Saw Napoleon in his writing room. Had some conversation touching Ferdinand of Spain and the Baron Kolli. "Kolli," said he, "was discovered by the police, by his always drinking a bottle of the best wine, which so ill corresponded with his dress and apparent poverty, that it excited a suspicion amongst some of the spies, and he was arrested, searched, and his papers taken from him. Amongst them was a letter from * * *, inviting him to escape, and promising every support. A police agent was then dressed up, instructed to represent Kolli, and sent with the papers taken from him to Ferdinand; who, however, would not attempt to effect his escape, although he had no suspicion of the deceit practised upon him. While at Bayonne, I offered him permission to return to Spain, informing him however at the same time, that immediately on his arrival in his own country, I should declare war against him. Ferdinand refused to return, unless under my protection. No force or compulsion was employed to induce him to sign his abdication; neither was he confined at the time, but had his friends, and as many of the nobles as he thought proper, about him. Had he been treated like me in this island," continued he, "the case would have been different; although if your Prince Regent were now to offer me a reception in England, provided I would resign the throne of France, acknowledge myself a prisoner of war, and sign a treaty as such, I would refuse it, and prefer remaining here, although I have already abdicated: and therefore the first would be of no consequence. To sign a treaty, acknowledging that the injustice of the English parliament in detaining me as a prisoner of war in time of peace was lawful,

I would never do. A treaty not to quit such part of England as might be allotted to me, nor to meddle with politics, and be subject to certain restrictions, I would gladly consent to; and moreover would desire to be naturalized as a British subject. The two grand objects of my policy were, first to re-establish the kingdom of Poland as a barrier against the Russians, in order to save Europe from those barbarians of the north; and next, to expel the Bourbons from Spain, and establish a constitution which would have rendered the nation free, have driven away the inquisition, superstition, the friars, feudal rights, and immunities; a constitution which would have rendered the first offices in the kingdom attainable to any person entitled to hold them by his abilities, without any distinction of birth being necessary. With the *imbéciles* who reigned, Spain was nearly useless to me. Besides, I discovered that they had made a secret treaty to betray France. With an active government, the great resources which Spain possesses would have been made use of against England with such vigor, that you would have been forced to make a peace according to liberal maritime rights. Also I did not like to have a family of enemies so near to me, especially after I had discovered this secret treaty. I was anxious to dispossess the Bourbons; they were so with me. It mattered little whether my brother or another family were placed on the throne, provided the Bourbons were removed; in thirty or forty years the ties of relationship would signify nothing, when the interests of a kingdom were under discussion."

"Fox," said he, " was sincere and honest in his intentions; had he lived, there would have been a peace, and England would now be contented and happy. Fox knew the true interests of your country. He was received with a sort of triumph in every city in France through which he passed. Fêtes and every honor the inhabitants could confer, were spontaneously offered, wherever he was known. It must have been a most gratifying sensation to him to be received in such a manner by a country which had been so long hostile to his own, particularly when he saw that they were the genuine sentiments of the people. Pitt, probably, would have been murdered. I liked Fox, and loved to converse with him. There was a circumstance occurred, which, though accidental, must have been very flattering to him. As I paid him every attention, I gave orders that he should have free admission every where. One day he went with his family to see St. Cloud, in which there was a private cabinet of mine, which had not been opened for some time, and was never shown to strangers. By some accident Fox and his wife opened the door, and entered. There he saw the statues of a number of great men, chiefly patriots, such as Sidney, Hampden, Washington, Cicero, Lord Chatham, &c., and amongst the rest, his own, which was first recognized by his wife, who said, ' my dear, this is yours.' This little incident, though trifling and accidental, gained him great honor, and spread directly through Paris. The fact was, that a considerable time before, I had determined upon forming a collection of statues of the greatest men, and the most distinguished for their virtues, of all nations. I did not admire them the less because they were enemies, and had actually procured busts of some of the greatest enemies of France, amongst others, that of Nelson. I was afterwards diverted from this intention by occurrences which did not allow me time to attend to the collecting of statues."

"It would," continued Napoleon, " have been a very easy matter to have made the French and English good friends and love one another. The French always esteemed the English for their national qualities, and where esteem exists, love will soon follow, if proper measures be pursued. They are very nearly akin. I myself have done much mischief to England, and had it in contemplation to do much more, if you continued the war; but I never ceased to esteem you. I had then a much better opinion of you than I now have. I thought that there was much more liberty, much more independence of spirit, and much more generosity in England than there is, or I never would have ventured upon the step I have taken."

I asked him his opinion of Lord Whitworth. "*Un homme ho-*

oile, un intrigant,"* said he, "as far as I could observe him. A man of address, *uu bel homme.*† Your ministers had no reason to complain of him, for he answered their purposes well. The account which was published by your ministers of his interview with me was *plein de faussetés.*‡ No violence of manner or impropriety of language was used by me. The ambassadors could not conceal their surprise when they read such a mass of misrepresentation, and publicly pronounced it to be false. His wife, the Duchess of Dorset, was greatly disliked by the English at Paris. They said publicly that she was *sotte*§ with pride. There was much disagreement between her and many English ladies about presentation at court. She refused to introduce any who had not previously been presented at St. James's. Now there were many of your countrywomen who either could not or would not be presented there, but were anxious to be presented to me, which was refused by her and her husband. This excited great ill-will towards them. Your chargé d'affaires also, Mr. Merry, was disliked by the English for the same reason. Some of them threatened to horsewhip him publicly, and he made application to me to protect him against his own countrymen."

Napoleon then recounted the noble manner in which Fox had made known to him the proposal that had been made to assassinate him, which generous act he did not fail to compare with the treatment he now received, and with the attempts made upon his life by wretches paid by * * * * in 1803, and landed in France by British men of war. He also mentioned that his assassination had been recommended in the English ministerial papers of the time as a meritorious action. He subsequently related some anecdotes of General Wurmser. "When I commanded at the siege of Mantua," said he, "a short time before the surrender of that fortress, a German was taken endeavoring to effect an entrance into the town. The soldiers, suspecting him to be a spy, searched, but found nothing upon him. They then threatened him in French, which he did not understand. At last a Frenchman, who spoke a little German, was brought, who

* An ingenious man.   † A fine man.   ‡ Full of falsehoods.   § Foolish

threatened him with death in bad German if he did not immediately tell all he knew. He accompanied his menaces with violent gestures, drew out his sword, pointed it at his belly, and said that he would rip him up. The poor German, frightened, and not understanding perfectly the broken jargon spoken by the French soldier, concluded, when he saw him point at his belly, that his secret was discovered, and cried out that there was no occasion to rip him up, for if they waited a few hours, they would have it by the course of nature. This led to further inquiries, when he confessed that he was the bearer of despatches to Wurmser, which he had swallowed when he perceived himself to be in danger of being taken. He was immediately brought to my head-quarters and some physicians sent for. It was proposed to give him some purgative, but they said it would be better to wait the operation of nature. Accordingly he was locked up in a room, and two officers of the staff appointed to take charge of him, one of whom constantly remained with him. In a few hours the wished for article was found. It was rolled up in wax, and was not much bigger than a hazel-nut. When unrolled, it proved to be a despatch from the Emperor Francis to Wurmser, written with his own hand, enjoining him to be of good heart, to hold out a few days longer, and that he would be relieved by a large force which was coming in such a direction under the command of Alvinzi. Upon this I immediately broke up with the greatest part of my troops, marched in the route indicated, met Alvinzi at the passage of the Po, totally defeated him, and returned again to the siege. Wurmser then sent out General * * * with proposals to treat for the evacuation of the fortress. He stated that though the army had provisions for four months, he was willing to surrender upon honorable terms. I signified to him that I was so well pleased with the noble manner in which Wurmser had defended the fortress, and entertained so high an opinion of him, that, although I knew he had not provisions for three days more, I was willing to grant him an honorable capitulation; in fact, that I would concede to Wurmser every thing he desired. He was greatly astonished at the good information I possessed of the deplorable state of the troops, and still more with the good terms I offered, acquainted as I was with his distress. Wurmser was won by it, and ever afterwards entertained a great esteem and regard for me. After we had agreed upon the principal conditions, I sent an officer into the town, who found that there was only one day's provisions remaining for the garrison. Previous to this, Wurmser used to call me *un garcon.** He was very old, brave as a lion, but so extremely deaf, that he could not hear the balls whistling around him. He wanted me to enter Mantua after we had agreed upon the capitulation; but I considered that I was better where I was. Besides, I was obliged to march against the Pope's troops, who had made a treaty with me, and afterwards broke it. Wurmser saved my life afterwards. When I got to Rimini, a messenger overtook me with a letter from him, containing an account of a plan to poison me, and where it was to be put in execution. It was to have been attempted at Rimini, and was framed by some of the *canaglie*† of priests. It would in all probability have succeeded, had it not been for this information. Wurmser, like Fox, acted a noble part."

Napoleon then informed me of the precautions which he made his army take when before Mantua, in order to preserve their health in that sickly country. One of which was, burning large fires all night, and obliging the troops to keep by them. He spoke about the measures which he had caused to be taken at Jaffa. "After the assault," said he, "it was impossible to restore any kind of discipline until night. The infuriated soldiers rushed into the streets in search of women. You know what kind of people the Turks are. A few of them kept up a fire in the streets. The soldiers who desired nothing more, whenever a shot was discharged, cried out they were fired upon from certain houses, which they immediately broke open, and violated all the women they found. This, together with their having plundered pelisses and other articles of Turkish dress, many of which were infected, produced the plague amongst them. The following day I gave orders that every soldier should bring his plunder into the

* A boy. † Rabble.

square, where all articles of apparel were burnt. But the disease had been already disseminated. I caused the sick to be immediately sent to the hospitals, where those infected with the plague were separated from the rest. For a short time, I succeeded in persuading the troops that it was only a fever with buboes, and not the plague; and in order to convince them of it, I went publicly to the bed-side of a soldier who was infected, and handled him. This had a great effect in encouraging them, and even some of the surgeons who had abandoned them became ashamed, and returned to their duties. In consequence of the advice of the medical officers, I ordered that all the buboes which did not appear likely to suppurate should be opened. Previous to giving this order I had the experiment made upon a certain number, and allowed an equal number of others to be treated in the usual manner, by which it was found that a much greater proportion of the former recovered."

17th.—Saw Sir Hudson Lowe in town, who was in a very surly humor, and with whom I had a long conversation, part of it not of a very agreeable nature. He said, that it did not appear "that I had made use of arguments of a nature sufficiently forcible to undeceive General Bonaparte; and that he would write to Lord Bathurst, that all the time General Bonaparte was so much in the *dark* respecting *his* character, no Englishman excepting Admiral Malcolm and myself had access to him."

I informed his excellency, that Sir Pultney Malcolm had done every thing in his power to conciliate and to reconcile matters, and had endeavored by all means to justify his (Sir Hudson's) conduct; so much so, indeed, that Napoleon had expressed his discontent at it; as to myself, I had often exerted myself to the utmost of my ability to effect the same. I also suggested to his excellency, that if Captain Lamb were to make an affidavit of the falsity of the charge relative to the supposed proposal to break the bust, it would effectually silence all calumniators. Sir Hudson Lowe replied, " I judge from effects, sir. You do not appear to have testified sufficient indignation at what General Bonaparte said and did. *You ought to have told him that he was guilty of a dirty action!*"

His excellency then said that Napoleon had caused Bertrand to write him the most impertinent letter* which he had ever received, in reply to one written by him relative to the chess-men, and another equally so for the purpose of being given to the gunner of the Baring. That he was authorized to turn General Bertrand off the island for his impertinence. He then desired me to "express to General Bonaparte, that he had sent for me in order to inquire who was the author of a report so false as that the gunner who had brought out the bust, had been prevented from going on shore and disposing of his goods, and had in consequence sustained losses, and suffered bad treatment. Also, that he was greatly astonished at the tenor of the last letter he had received, more so indeed than at that of any that had been sent to him since he arrived on the island."

18th.—Saw Napoleon, to whom I communicated the message I had been ordered to deliver by Sir Hudson Lowe. He replied, that the gunner had declared before Madame Bertrand, that he had been prevented from going on shore for several days, and consequently had been obliged to sell his little venture to Solomon, or some other shop-keeper for half price,† and had thereby sustained a great loss. "I have been informed, and I believe it," continued the emperor, "that this bad treatment was caused by his having brought out the bust of my son. The governor has expressed astonishment at the tenor of the letters sent to him. I want nothing from his caprice. He says, that according to the *règlemens établis en vigueur*,‡ he was not authorized to send up those presents. Where are those regulations? I have never seen them. If they are new restrictions, let them be made known. But I never have heard that because there was a crown upon toys, they were to be prohibited. I protest against all restrictions which are not made known to me previous to their

---

* Appendix, No. IX. and that to the gunner, No. X.
† This was an unquestionable fact, and notorious on the island.
‡ Rules established in vigor.

being put into execution. By Lord Bathurst's speech, he has no right to make any new restriction. Could he not have said that he protested against the crown, and we should have laughed at it. But, no. He must give a *coup d'épingle*, refer to unknown restrictions, and throw in insinuations that it is to his goodness I am indebted for them. To a dungeon, to chains upon his legs and arms, *l'uomo s'accostuma, ma al capriccio d'altrui, è impossible*, (a man may accustom himself, but to another's caprice, it is impossible,) I do not desire any favor from him. Perhaps he requires that I should write him a letter of thanks daily for the air which I breathe. *Un uomo che m'ammazza ogni giorno ;** and then desires that I should thank him for it. He reminds me of a German *bourreau*, who, while bastinadoing with all his might an unfortunate sufferer, cried after each blow, ' *Pardon, Monsieur pour grande liberte que je prends.*' " (Pardon, Sir, for the great liberty which I take.)

I asked what answer I should return. " 'Tell him," said Napoleon, " *che io non son obbligato di render nessun conto al mio boja.*"†

After walking about for a moment, he said, with energy, " *Vous me faites des insinuations, c'etoit la manière d'agir de tous les petits tyrans d'Italie. Cet homme paroit n'avoir d'autre but que de me tuer à coup d'épingles, soit au morale, soit au physique. Un bourreau me tueroit d'un seul coup. Sa conduite est tortueuse et environnée de mystere. Le crime seul marche dans les ténèbres. Un jour son prince et sa nation seront instruits et sa méchante conduite sera connue, et s'il échappe à la justice de la loi qu'il viole, il n'echappera pas à la justice de l'opinion de tous les hommes éclairés et sensibles. Il est un mandataire infidèle, il trompe son gouvernement, comme le montrent les vingt mensonges et les calomnies qui sont dans le discours de Lord* * * *. *Se conduite pour le buste de mon fils, qui est prouvée, est horrible et digne de tout ce qu'il a fait depuis un an.*"‡

* Who kills me with vexation.
† That I am not obliged to answer to my executioner.
‡ You deal in insinuations: it is the way all the little tyrants of Italy act This man appears to have no other object in view than to kill me by little and

This answer he desired me to deliver, which, he observed, would convince him of the real opinion he entertained of his character.

After this, he said, that he had informed Lord Amherst of the conduct pursued towards him. "The ambassador," said he, "declared that such were not the intentions of the bill; that the object of it was not to render worse, but to ameliorate my situation as a prisoner, and that he would not fail to make known the representations I had made to him to the Prince Regent, to Lord Liverpool, and to Lord Bathurst. He asked permission to report what I said to the governor; I replied, certainly. I told him that I had observed the governor taking him round the new road he had made, but that I supposed he had not communicated to him, that I could neither quit it, nor go into any houses; and that a prohibition had formerly existed, which debarred me from speaking to such persons as I might meet. At this he was *beaucoup frappé* (greatly struck.) He proposed that I should see the governor; I replied, ' Neither your prince, nor both of your Houses of Parliament, can oblige me to see *mon geolier et mon bourreau. Ce n'est pas l'habit qui fait le geolier, c'est la manière et la mœurs.'*
I told him that he had pushed matters to such an extremity, that in order to leave nothing in his power, I had confined myself to my room, expecting that he would surround the house with sentinels. I left nothing for him to effect, except violating my privacy, which he could not have done without walking over my corpse.† That I would not commit suicide, but would exult in

---

little; either morally or physically. An executioner would kill me by a single blow. His conduct is disingenuous, and encircled with mystery. Crime alone walks in darkness. One day his prince and his nation will be instructed, and his wicked conduct will be known; and if he escapes from the justice of the law which he violates, he will not escape the justice of the opinion of all enlightened and sensible men. He is an unfaithful steward; he deceives his government; as is shown by the twenty lies and calumnies which are in the speech of Lord * * *. His conduct relative to the bust of my son, which is proved, is horrible, and worthy of every thing he has done the year past.

* My jailer and executioner. It is not the dress which makes the jailer, it is the conduct and manners.

† The emperor was so firmly impressed with the idea that an attempt would

being assassinated by an Englishman. Instead of drawing back, (*réculer*,) it would be a consolation to me in my last moments."

The emperor concluded by telling me that he had no objection that the governor should be acquainted with every sentiment which he had expressed to me.

18*th*.*—Went to town in pursuance to Sir Hudson Lowe's directions, to whom I repeated the message which I had been ordered to deliver. His excellency commenced his reply by denying that he had ordered me to say, " that he, the governor, was surprised at the tenor of the two last notes he had received, and that he had called out to me, on leaving the room, to repeat the former only ; he then said, darting a furious look at me, " General Bonaparte's expressions convince me, sir, more and more, that no means have been taken to justifiy my character to him. Tell him," continued he, not in the most moderate tone of voice, " that to show I am not afraid to send any thing home, I shall send what he has stated to ministers."

He then demanded me to communicate any thing else I was charged with. When I came to that part in which Napoleon (describing what he had related to Lord Amherst) had said, " but I suppose he did not tell you that I was not permitted to leave the road ;" his excellency, whose appearance I shall not attempt to describe, started up, and with a degree of violence which considerably impeded his utterance, exclaimed, " 'Tis false! 'Tis false ! I did tell him." When he had recovered a little his powers of speech, he reproached me, in a violent manner, with not having contradicted the assertion, also with having manifested little warmth in his defence. After he had expended some portion of his wrath, I observed that I had attempted his defence to the best of my abilities, but that I did not think he ought to be much surprised at Napoleon's not being upon good terms with him, when he considered what material alterations had taken place in

be made to forcibly intrude on his privacy, that from a short time after the departure of Sir George Cockburn, he always kept four or five pair of loaded pistols, and some swords in his apartments, with which he was determined to dispatch the first who entered against his will.

* In some of the pages of my journal, this conversation is dated on the 19th.

his situation since his arrival, all of which tended to render it more unpleasant. A long discussion now followed, during which I recounted to his excellency some of his own restrictions; amongst others, that one in which he prohibited Napoleon from speaking; at which he again became very angry, and insisted that it was not a prohibition, *it was only a request;* that it was not his fault, if General Bonaparte did not choose to ride out. I took the liberty, then, of asking the following question: 'Place yourself, sir, in Napoleon's situation, would you have availed yourself of the permission to ride out, coupled with the restrictions imposed upon him?" His excellency refused to reply to this question, which he pronounced to be an insult to him, as governor and representative of his majesty. He then desired me to give my opinion respecting Lord Bathurst's speech. I pointed out, that many of his lordship's positions were at variance with the truth. After hearing my opinion, his excellency expressed much anger at "my presuming to speak so freely of a speech made by one of his majesty's secretaries of state; that I appeared to be an advocate for the French, and that nobody else in the island held similar opinions, or would dare to express them," &c. He concluded by telling me, that "I was not permitted for the future to hold any conversation with General Bonaparte, unless upon professional subjects, and ordering me to come to town every Monday and Thursday, in order to report to him General Bonaparte's health and his habits."

21st.—Had another conversation with Sir Hudson Lowe, of a nature nearly similar to that of yesterday. A long and very disagreeable discussion took place, with which I shall not fatigue the reader, further than by stating, that I requested of him to remove me from my situation.

24th.—Went to town, according to Sir Hudson Lowe's orders. His excellency made me undergo an interrogation before Sir Thomas Reade and Major Gorrequer, during which he again expressed much anger, because my sentiments did not accord with his own.

Finding that Sir Hudson Lowe made me in a manner responsible for all Napoleon's actions and expressions, and took every opportunity of venting upon me all the ill-humor he could not personally discharge upon his prisoner, and perceiving that all hopes of accommodation between the parties had vanished when Admiral Malcolm departed, and that all my efforts to ameliorate the situation of the captive were fruitless, I determined to confine myself, as much as possible, to my medical duties, and to avoid all unnecessary communication with a man, who could avail himself of his irresponsible situation, as a means of insulting an inferior officer.

August 2nd.—Went to report Napoleon's health as usual.

Saw Napoleon on my return, who observed that he had seen in the papers some extracts from a work written by the Duke of Rovigo, detailing several circumstances relative to Pichegru, Wright, &c. He lamented the death of Réal,* and remarked that Savary and Réal were the persons, especially Réal, (at that time the Duke of Rovigo, was not in a situation to enable him to know personally the circumstances relative to those two,) who from their employments knew the names of the jailers, turnkeys, gendarmes, and others, and could say, 'such a man was present, let him be examined. Perhaps he is now in the service of the king.' In the exalted situation which I occupied, I could know nothing of these minute details. Savary," added he, " relates a circumstance which is perfectly true, and appears to have preserved some order that I wrote on the occasion, as well as recollected some of my expressions. I did not like to have it publicly mentioned, as it deeply implicated so near a relation to my son. I did not wish to have it known, that one so nearly allied by blood to him, could be capable of proposing so atrocious an act as that made by Caroline to me. It was to make a second Sicilian Vespers; to massacre all the English army, and the English in Sicily, which she offered to effect, provided I would support and afford her assistance after the deed was done. I threw the agent who was the

---

* Réal was grand judge at the time alluded to, and his death had been reported in the last papers that arrived at St. Helena; which was afterwards contradicted.

bearer of the proposal into prison, where he remained until the revolution which sent me to Elba. He must have been found amongst others in the prisons that were allotted for state criminals.* It was my intention, whenever, I made a peace with England, to have sent him over to your ministers for examination."

10*th*.—Had some conversation with Napoleon upon a report contained in one of the papers relating to his removal to Malta, to which he did not give any credit, observing that he should create less alarm in England than in Malta. He remarked upon the impolicy of the governor, in having by his treatment rendered him (Napoleon) an object of sympathy to Europe. "The greatest indignation," continued he, "will be excited by it. Nothing could have happened to lessen the English so much in the estimation of other nations. It will confirm them in the opinions of your government which the emigrants who returned from England have disseminated. They returned filled with hatred against your ministers, whom they accused of having acted in the most parsimonious manner, and descending to the most minute and unworthy details. That they certainly furnished them with money, but so barely as merely to keep them from starvation. That they should have been truly wretched, had it not been for the generosity which they experienced from some private individuals, many of whom they allowed to possess great liberality."

"The emperors of Austria and Russia, and the king of Prussia," added he, "have all three told me that I was much mistaken in believing that they had received such large subsidies from England. They alleged that they had never actually obtained more than one-half of the sums which they were nominally supposed to have received, through the deductions made for freightage, poundage, and numbers of other charges, and that frequently a large portion was paid in merchandise. Those sove-

---

* It is a singular circumstance that the wretch who was thrown into prison for having been the bearer of a confidential letter and message from Queen Caroline, containing a proposal to massacre the whole of the English army in Sicily, should have been subsequently released by the successes of that very army whose destruction he had contemplated and proposed.

reigns complained greatly of the conduct of your ministers, and I am inclined to believe with some reason. Here, through a mistaken and scandalous parsimony, they have counteracted their own views, which were, that as little as possible should be said of me, that I should be forgotten. But their ill-treatment, and that of this man, has made all Europe speak of me. He formerly thought that nothing which passed here would be known in Europe. He might as well have attempted to obscure the light of the sun with his hat. There are still millions in the world who are interested for me. Had your ministers acted wisely, they would have given a *carte blanche* for this house. This would have been making the best of a bad business, silenced all complaints and attempts made for me, and in the end, with such men as Cockburn or Malcolm, would not have cost more than 15 or 16,000*l* a year. But this * * * * *c'est un homme qui a les manières ignobles, l'esprit astucieux et le cœur méchant. Cockburn au moins avait la marche droite et sincere. C'était un homme, un Anglaise, mais, mon Dieu! cet homme ci, la nature l'a fait pour un mauvais bourreau.** That under-secretary doubtless said to Lord B., '*J'ai trouvé votre homme.*'† I have little doubt but * * *'s intentions at first were by a series of ill-treatment to force away every Frenchman from about me, and to induce me to commit suicide, or to have me altogether at his disposal. The force of public opinion has made them change a little afterwards."

"If the Emperors of Austria and Russia," continued Napoleon, "were to make me offers of whatever money I pleased, I would not accept of it. *J'ai eu la sottise*,‡ to put myself in John Bull's hands, and I must swallow whatever pill may be prepared for me."

In reply to an observation of incredulity expressed by me as to the correctness of his supposition of the probable intentions of

---

* He is a man of ignoble manners, of a crafty mind, and a wicked heart. Cockburn was, at least, candid and sincere. He was a man, an Englishman, but, my God, as for this man, nature made him for a bad hangma

† I have found your man.

‡ I have had the foolishness.

those who sent him to St. Helena, he observed, "Doctor, a man must be worse than a blockhead who does not perceive that I was sent here to be * * * * * * * *, either by the natural effects of ill treatment, combined with the badness of the climate, or by the probability of my being induced to commit suicide, as I have said, or by * * *.

"Were I in England," added Napoleon, "I would receive but few visitors, and never speak upon political subjects: here I do, because I am *here* and am ill-treated. To live quietly, to enjoy occasionally the company of some *savans*, take a ride now and then, reading and finishing my history, and educating my son, would form my occupations. Here the want of books greatly retards the advance of my works."

He informed me that the governor had sent answers to the letter which had been written about the Chinese articles and to the gunner; but that he had ordered Bertrand not to bring them to him until he asked for them.

Saw his reply to Lord Bathurst's speech, commencing in the following manner: "*Le bill du parlement anglaise, n'est ni une loi, ni un judgment:*"* and proceeding to compare it with the proscriptions of Sylla and Marius, "*aussi juste, aussi nécessaire, mais plus barbare ;*†" that Sylla and Marius issued their decrees '*avec la pointe encore sanglante de leurs épées ;*"‡ but that of the English parliament was issued in time of peace, and sanctioned by the sceptre of a great nation.

11th.—Told Sir Hudson Lowe again (having mentioned it to him before, about a fortnight ago,) that Napoleon wished to have the garden freed from an alkalescent and fetid weed, (spurge,) with which it was overrun at present, and desired that it should be converted into grass, or sown with oats or barley, as it was useless at present. That he wished to have something green to look at out of his window, and to see something growing about him. That if it were not done within a fortnight, the season

---
* The bill of the English parliament is neither a law nor a judgment.
† As just, as necessary, but more barbarous.
‡ With the points of their swords yet bloody

would be over. His excellency replied, that he would go to Longwood in a day or two.

14th.—Went yesterday to Plantation House, in consequence of an order from the governor that I should go there on Tuesdays and Saturdays, instead of Mondays and Thursdays in town. The governor, after having asked some questions, said, that I had on a former occasion mentioned that General Bonaparte told me he had made use of observations concerning him to Lord Amherst, which he desired I would repeat. Although I foresaw the consequences, I did not think myself authorized to refuse, as I had been permitted to communicate them to him; and having previously warned him that what he insisted upon might cause an access of irritation, I therefore repeated what Napoleon had observed, viz.: "Neither your prince nor both your houses of parliament can oblige me to see *mon geolier et mon bourreau. Ce n'est pas l'habit qui fait le geolier, c'est la maniere et les mœurs.*"*

Sir Hudson Lowe walked about for a few moments, looking very angrily, and asked me to give him General Bonaparte's reasons for making use of such expressions. I replied that this was out of my power. He then began, as I had foreseen, to vent upon me all the ill-humor which he entertained towards the author of the epithets; brought up the old affair of the Scotch newspaper, and concluded by saying, "You are not authorized, sir, by me, to communicate with General Bonaparte on any other than medical subjects; and if you hold any others with him it is at your own peril, unless you make such communications known to me, and thereby free yourself from the responsibility. Your business is not to act from your own judgment or discretion, but to ask what you may be permitted to do."

Napoleon has been up at four o'clock for several mornings writing, without calling any of his generals to assist him. He took a walk of two hours, and appeared to be in good spirits. Saw him on his return in the billiard-room. Had some conversa-

---

* My jailer and my executioner. It is not the dress which makes the jailer, it is the conduct and manners.

tion about Egypt, and some of the characters who had accompanied him there. He mentioned one Poussilguere (or Poussière,) who had served under him during the campaigns of Italy. "Poussilguere," said he, "had been employed by me upon diplomatic and other services from Milan to Genoa, during which time he acquired my confidence. He was then sent to Malta to feel the way before I attacked it. The information he obtained was very useful, and rendered great service. He accompanied me to Egypt, where I appointed him to an office high in the commissariat and loaded him with favors. When I quitted Egypt, Poussilguere, who was left behind for some unaccountable reasons, conceived a great hatred for me, and wrote letters *pleines d'horreurs** of me to the directory. I was then appointed first consul, which was unknown to Poussilguere, and was the person who opened his letters. Though astonished and indignant at his conduct, I took no notice of them. When I was made Emperor, Poussilguere's brother, who was a distinguished surgeon, and well known to me, came to supplicate employment for him, and begged of me to grant his prayer, although he admitted that his brother had behaved to me badly and most ungratefully. "Who is your brother?" I replied. "I know him not. Poussilguere betrayed General Bonaparte, but the emperor knows him not. I will grant him no favor myself, but if the minister of finance chooses to name him, I will sign the nomination. His brother went to the minister, told him what I had said, a recommendation for a very lucrative situation was made out, which I signed, and he enjoyed it for several years."

He afterwards spoke about the Mamelukes, and said, that in the combats between the French cavalry and them, whenever the numbers of the parties engaged exceeded a hundred men, the superiority of discipline procured the victory to the French, but under that number, or individually, the Mamelukes prevailed.

15*th*.—Napoleon's birth-day. He was dressed in a brown coat. All the generals and ladies dined with him at two o'clock; also all the children, excepting the two infants of Counts Bertrand and Montholon, who were brought in and shown for a short time.

* Full of horrors.

To each of the children he gave a present, and amused himself, for some time, playing with them.

17th.—Saw Napoleon at two o'clock. He was in extremely good humor, and very facetious, cracking jokes upon various subjects, and rallying me about a young lady in the island.

Told me, that when he was at Boulogne, two English sailors arrived there, who made their escape from Verdun, and had passed through the country undiscovered. "They had remained there for some time. Having no money, they were at a loss how to effect their escape, and there was such a vigilant watch kept upon the boats, that they despaired of being able to seize upon one. They made a sort of vessel of little ribs of wood, which they formed with their knives, living as well as they could upon roots and fruits. This bark of theirs they covered with calico, which they stretched over the ribs. When finished, it was not more than about three feet and half in length, and of a proportionate breadth, and so light, that one of them carried it on his shoulders. In this machine they determined to attempt their passage to England. Seeing an English frigate approach very near the shore, they launched their bark, and attempted to join her; but before they had proceeded very far they were discovered by the *douaniers*, seized and brought back. The story got wind in consequence of the astonishment excited at seeing two men venture out to sea in such a fragile conveyance. I heard of it, and ordered them with their little ship to be brought before me. I was, myself, struck with astonishment at the idea of men trusting their lives to such an article; and asked them if it was possible they could have intended to have gone to sea in that? They replied, that to convince me of it, they were ready that moment to attempt it again in the same vessel. Admiring the boldness of the attempt, and the bluntness of the reply, I ordered that they should be set at liberty, some Napoleons given to them, and a conveyance to the English squadron provided for them. Previous to this, they were going to be tried as spies, for several persons had seen them lurking about the camp for some days."

"When I made my triumphal entry into Berlin," said Napoleon, "the mother of the Prince of Orange, the sister of the king, was left behind sick in the upper apartments of the palace, and very badly off, having been abandoned without money, and neglected by almost every body. A day or two after my arrival there, some of her attendants came to ask for assistance, as they had not wherewithal to procure even fuel for her use. The king, indeed, had neglected her most shamefully. The moment it was made known to me, I ordered a hundred thousand francs to be instantly sent, and went to see her myself afterwards. I caused her to be furnished with every thing befitting her rank, and we had frequent interviews together. She was much obliged to me, and a kind of friendship commenced between us. I liked her conversation. When her son, the Prince of Orange, was aid-de-camp to Wellington, he went over from Spain or Portugal to London, at the time that the intended marriage between the Princess Charlotte and him was in contemplation. From London he wrote several letters to his mother, giving a description of the whole of the royal family, beginning with the queen, and going through every branch nominatively, filled with *horreurs* and *sottises*,* particularly of the * * * *, against whom he appeared to be particularly indignant. He did not even spare * * * whom he painted as ambitious, and desirous of command, and that he should be a mere cipher and a stallion if * * * * to which he declared he never would submit. There were many fine and heroic sentiments expressed in them, which, though in a romantic style, did the writer honor, but he tore the whole * * * * to pieces. Those letters he sent by an agent to Hamburgh, for the purpose of being forwarded to his mother. This agent was arrested, his papers seized and despatched to Paris, where they were examined and laid before me. I read them in a cursory manner, and laughed very heartily at their contents. Afterwards, in order to retaliate a little for all the abuse heaped upon me, I ordered them to be sent to the Moniteur and published. Meanwhile, however, the agent acquainted the prince's mother with his arrest and the seizure of his papers, with the contents of

* Horrors and foolishness.

which he was partly acquainted. Before the publication was completed, I received a letter from her, conjuring me not to make them public, stating to me what injury it would do to her son and her family, and calling to my recollection the time I had been at Berlin. I was touched with her letter, and countermanded the publishing of the letters, which would have made a great noise in Europe, and have been extremely disagreeable to the persons described in them."

Napoleon then spoke of the late Queen of Prussia in very high terms, said that he had an esteem for her, and that if the king had brought her at first to Tilsit, it would in all probability have procured him better terms. "She was elegant, ingenuous, and extremely well informed," continued Napoleon. "She bitterly lamented the war. 'Ah,' said she to me, '*la mémoire du grand Frédéric nous a fait égarer. Nous nous crumes pareils à lui, et nous ne le sommes pas.*'"*

I observed to the emperor that his enemies had accused him of having treated her very barbarously. "What," said he, "do they say that I poisoned her too?" I replied, no; but that they asserted that he had been the means of her death in consequence of the misfortunes which he had caused to befall her country. "Why," replied Napoleon, "that grief for the fallen situation of her husband and her country, and for the losses they had sustained, and the humiliated state they were reduced to, may have accelerated her death, is very probable. But that was not my fault. Why did her husband declare war against me? However, instead of treating her barbarously, nobody could have paid her more attention or respect, or have esteemed her more, for which I received her thanks. The Princess of Salms was extremely beautiful and witty; but in point of virtue and other good qualities, she was far below her sister. She would make a charming mistress, but not a * * * *. She had * * * *."

Napoleon then made some observations about Malta, an abode with which he declared he would be satisfied for some years, pro

---

* The memory of the great Frederick has made us err—we believed ourselves equal to him, but we are not.

fessing at the same time his disbelief of such being the intentions of government. He added that the best thing our government could do, would be to make a kind of treaty with him, by which he would bind himself not to quit Malta for a certain number of years without the permission of the Prince Regent, with a condition that at the expiration of the time he should be received in England. This would save the nation six or eight millions of francs yearly. ' It would," added he, " have been much more honorable for England (and indeed for the coalesced powers) and more humane, to have caused me to be shot on board of the Bellerophon, in the rage of the moment, than to have condemned me to be exiled to such a rock as this. They might have excused themselves by saying, ' It is necessary for the tranquillity of Europe to put this man out of the way.' This would have at once freed them from all alarm, and saved millions to their treasury, besides being much more humane. When the discussions about the sentence on Louis the Sixteenth took place, Condorcet declared that his conscience would not allow him to vote for death, but in place of that he voted that the unfortunate Louis should be condemned to the galleys for life. This proposal met with universal disapprobation, even from the most violent of the Jacobins, and great odium was thrown upon Condorcet for having voted for that, which in the opinion of all, was worse than death. Now exile here, particularly under the man they have chosen, is infinitely worse than condemnation to the galleys. For there you have the sun of Europe, and if you have money, can enjoy comparatively a tolerable existence. I recollect at Toulon," (I think he said) " a colonel who had been condemned to the galleys for life. He was certainly confined, but he never was obliged to work, and had everything allowed him, at his own expense, which could render his situation supportable. The keeper, unless he was like this governor, would never degrade a man who had held such a situation by obliging him to labor. Besides, for money a man can always get somebody to work for him. I therefore maintain, that it would have been more honorable, more consistent with policy, and, above all, more humane, to have caused me to be quietly *fusille** on board of the Bellerophon. It would have been preferred by myself. I really think that Lord * * * imagined that by a series of ill-treatment and humiliation, they would induce me to commit suicide, and for that purpose found *son homme*.† The very idea of this, if I ever had any thoughts of doing so, would effectually prevent my putting it into execution."

22nd.—Saw Napoleon at twelve o'clock. He has continued to rise at four o'clock in the morning, and to employ his time in reading and writing. Pointed out to me that he had been obliged to cause his coat to be turned, as there was no green cloth on the island, except of what the French call *couleur de merde d'oie*.‡ Spoke about his detention in so horrible an abode, " *Il y avait quelque chose de sauvage*.§ The * * * did not know how to separate the man from the situation. As first consul, as emperor, being at war with England, I did her as much harm as I could; but as Napoleon Bonaparte now, when all the world is at peace, what right have they to detain me as a prisoner? It is a great nation going to war with one man."

" I have," continued he, " reflected upon my conduct towards the English, and have nothing to reproach myself with, except not having done enough against them as an enemy. I ought to have put their prisoners in *pontons*, not to punish the poor prisoners, as it was not their fault, but to force your oligarchy to remove the French from those in which they had immured them."

He then observed that the eyes of the English would soon be opened with respect to his character. " They will see," said he, " the folly and injustice of keeping me in this island; an island so bad, that I can compare it to nothing else than the face of the wretch they have sent out as governor. This and the enormous expense will cause my removal."

I observed, that I was afraid the present disturbed state of England would operate most powerfully against his being permitted to go to England. " Bah," replied he, " your ministers are not silly enough to believe that I would lose my character

* Shot. † His man.
‡ Goslin green. § There was something savage.

so far as to put myself at the head of a *canaille*, even if the latter were willing to place a foreigner at their head, which is very unlikely. Even in France I refused to do it. I have too great a regard for the reputation I shall leave to posterity to act the adventurer. No, no, it is hatred, and the fear they have of the information I could give. They are afraid I should say *it was not true*,* in reply to the histories of many political events which they have explained in their own way."

"What do you think," said he, "of all things in the world would give me the greatest pleasure?" I was on the point of replying, removal from St. Helena, when he said, "To be able to go about *incognito* in London and other parts of England, to the *restaurateurs*, with a friend, to dine in public at the expense of half a guinea or a guinea, and listen to the conversation of the company; to go through them all, changing almost daily, and in this manner, with my own ears, to hear the people express their sentiments, in their unguarded moments, freely and without restraint; to hear their real opinion of myself, and of the surprising occurrences of the last twenty years." I observed, that he would hear much evil and much good of himself. "Oh, as to the evil," replied he, "I care not about that. I am well used to it. Besides, I know that the public opinion will be changed. The nation will be just as much disgusted at the libels published against me, as they formerly were greedy in reading and believing them. This," added he, "and the education of my son, would form my greatest pleasure. It was my intention to have done this, had I reached America. The happiest days of my life were from sixteen to twenty, during the *semestres*, when I used to go about, as I have told you I should wish to do, from one *restaurateur* to another, living moderately, and having a lodging for which I paid three louis a month. They were the happiest days of my life. I was always so much occupied, that I may say I never was truly happy upon the throne. Not that I have to reproach myself with doing evil whilst seated there; on the contrary, I restored fifty thousand families to their country, and the improvements I

---

* These words were spoken in English.

made in France will speak for themselves. I made war, certainly; of this there is no doubt; but in almost every instance I was either forced to it, or I had some great political object in view."

"Had I died at Moscow," continued he, "I should have left behind me a reputation as a conqueror, without a parallel in history. A bullet ought to have put an end to me there: whereas, when a man like me dies in misfortune, his reputation is lessened. *Then* I had never received a check. No doubt afterwards at Lutzen and Bautzen, with an army of recruits and without cavalry, I re-established my reputation, and the campaign of 1814, with such an inferior force, did not lessen it."

I observed that the generality of the world was surprised that he had not made a peace at Chatillon, when circumstances were apparently desperate for him. Napoleon replied, "I could not consent to render the empire less than what it was when I mounted the throne; I had sworn to preserve it. Moreover, the allied powers each day brought forth some condition more inadmissible than on the preceding one. You may think it strange, but I assure you that I would not sign it now. Had I remained on the throne after the return from Elba, I would have kept it, because I found it made, but I would not have made it myself originally. My great fault was in not having made peace at Dresden. My error was in having made that armistice. Had I pushed on at that time, my father-in-law would not have been against me."

Napoleon then said, that notwithstanding the occupation of Paris by the allies, he should still have succeeded had it not been for the treachery of Marmont, and have driven them out of France. His plan was arranged. He was to have entered Paris in the dead of the night. The whole of the *canaille** of the city were at the same time to attack the allies from the houses, who, fighting against troops acquainted with the localities, would have been cut to pieces, and obliged to abandon the city with immense loss. The *canaille* were all ready. (I think he also said that he would have cut off the allies from their park of artillery.) Once driven

* Populace.

from Paris, the mass of the nation would have risen against them. "I mentioned this plan," added he, "to Baron Koller, who admitted the danger of it. Marmont will be an object of horror to posterity. As long as France exists, the name of Marmont will not be mentioned without shuddering. He feels it," added Napoleon, "and is at this moment probably the most miserable man in existence. He cannot forgive himself, and he will terminate his life like Judas."

I took the liberty of asking what he considered to be the happiest time of his life, since his elevation to the throne. "The march from Cannes to Paris," was his reply.

"When Castlereagh was at Chatillon with the ambassadors of the allied powers, after some successes of mine, and when I had in a manner invested the town, he was greatly alarmed lest I might seize and make him a prisoner; not being accredited as an ambassador, nor invested with any diplomatic character to France, I might have taken him as an enemy. He went to Caulaincourt, to whom he mentioned that he 'labored under considerable apprehensions, that I should cause violent hands to be laid upon him,' as he acknowledged I had a right to do. It was impossible for him to get away without falling in with my troops. Caulaincourt replied that, as far as his own opinion went, he would say that I would not meddle with him, but that he could not answer for what I might do. Immediately after, Caulaincourt wrote to me what Castlereagh had said and his own answer. I signified to him in reply, that he was to tell Lord Castlereagh to make his mind easy, and to stay where he was; that I would consider him as an ambassador. At Chatillon," continued he, "when speaking about the liberty enjoyed in England, Castlereagh observed, in a contemptuous manner, that it was not the thing most to be esteemed in your country, that it was a *usage* which they were obliged to put up with; but had become an abuse, and would not answer for other countries."

I ventured to express my surprise to Napoleon that the Empress Marie Louise had not made some exertion in his behalf. "I believe," replied the emperor, "that Marie Louise is just as much a state prisoner as I am myself, except that more attention is paid to decorum in the restraints imposed upon her. I have always had occasion to praise the conduct of my good Louise, and I believe that it is totally out of her power to assist me; moreover, she is young and timorous. It was, perhaps, a misfortune to me that I had not married a sister of the Emperor Alexander, as proposed to me by Alexander himself at Erfurth. But there were inconveniences in that union, arising from her religion. I did not like to allow a Russian priest to be the confessor of my wife, as I considered that he would have been a spy in the Tuileries for Alexander. It has been said that my union with Marie Louise was made a stipulation in the treaty of peace with Austria, which is not true. I should have spurned the idea. It was first proposed by the Emperor Francis himself, and by Metternich, to Narbonne."

"Of all the ambassadors I ever employed," added Napoleon, "Narbonne* was the ablest. He had *beaucoup d'esprit*,† and his moral character was unexceptionable. While he was at Vienna, France was never duped by Metternich as she had been before. He penetrated Metternich's projects in a few days. Had such a man as Narbonne been sent to Alexander in 1812, it is probable that peace would have been made. Russia demanded Dantzic, and an indemnification for the Duke of Oldenberg. Romanzoff persuaded Alexander that I would make any sacrifices to avoid war, and that the favorable moment for him to make demands had arrived. After the first success I had gained, Alexander sent a message to me, that if I would quit his territory, and retreat to the Niemen, he would treat with me. However, I did not believe that he was of good faith, and judged it to be a *ruse*,‡

---

* I was informed by Cipriani, that Narbonne was the natural son of Louis the Fifteenth, and the fruit of an incestuous intercourse which that *legitimate* maintained with his own daughter Adelaide; and that documents were in existence, and even persons living, who could incontestably prove it. In justice, however, I must say, that Napoleon, to whom I communicated the assertion, told me that he disbelieved the fact of the incest, but not the rest.
† Great genius.
‡ Artifice.

otherwise we might have treated in person at Wilna, and settled everything."

23rd.—Yesterday, Mr. Smithers, midshipman of the Conqueror, came up to Longwood with a pass from Sir Hudson Lowe to go to Count Bertrand's. After having passed the guard-room at the entrance, he was called back by the officer, and told that his pass was found to be for the 21st, and consequently he could not be permitted to enter, as the date of the passport had expired the day before.*

At no greater distance of time than last Tuesday, Sir Hudson Lowe manifested great ill-humor towards me for having presumed to assert that he sometimes had given passes in which the day was specified, and related to him a very strong instance in that of Mr. Urmston. His excellency also officially denied the fact to Count Bertrand.

Previous to Mr. Smithers being permitted to come up, he was subjected to a long interrogation upon the nature of his business there; how he knew the Bertrands; that he *surely* must have some letters to them from Captain Hamilton of the navy, and many other indications of suspicion and distrust of an officer high in rank.

General Gourgaud informed me this day, that at the close of the battle of Waterloo, when the charge made by the French had failed, and the English charged in their turn, a part of the cavalry of the latter, with some *tirailleurs* intermingled with them, approached within a hundred or a hundred and fifty toises of the spot where the emperor was standing, with only Soult, Drouot, Bertrand, and himself. Close to them was a small French battalion drawn up in a square. Napoleon ordered Gourgaud to fire some shots from two or three field-pieces which belonged to the battalion, to drive away the cavalry, which were approaching nearer. This was put into execution, and one of those shots carried away the Marquis of Anglesea's leg. Napoleon then placed himself with the column, and wanted to charge,

---

* The orderly officer, when this was reported to him, took it upon himself to order the officer of the guard to allow Mr. Smithers to enter.

exclaiming, "*Il faut mourir ici, il faut mourir sur le champ de bataille.*"* At this time the English *tirailleurs* were firing at them, and they expected every moment to be charged. Labedoyère was galloping about like a madman, with his arms extended before him, seeking to be killed. Napoleon was prevented from throwing himself amongst the enemy by Soult, who laid hold of the bridle, exclaiming, that he would not be killed but taken prisoner, and with the aid of the others, finally succeeded in compelling him to leave the field at the time there was none other than the above-mentioned small column to oppose the Prussians, who were advancing. Napoleon was so fatigued, that on the road to Jamappe and Philipville, he would have frequently fallen from his horse, had he not been supported by Gourgaud and two others, who were the only persons with him for some time. He was silent for a long time. When on the road to Paris, it was decided at one moment, that the emperor should instantly on his arrival go booted and spurred to the senate, which would have had a great effect, but this resolution unfortunately was not acted upon.

24*th.*—Went to Plantation House, where, as customary, I had to suffer a long interrogation and much ill-humor. Amongst other matters, his excellency, after asking how I came to know that Cipriani had a conversation with him relative to the deficiencies at Longwood, said, "that I had no business to have any conversation with the maître de hôtel of Longwood concerning the provisions allowed; that in everything not strictly medical, I was to ask *him* what I was to be permitted to do; that I was not to use my own discretion or judgment with respect to any conversation with General Bonaparte, not medical, or reply to his questions, unless I made such communications known to him, as he (the governor) was the only judge of their propriety."

I replied, that if he expected me to communicate to him the conversations I held with Napoleon, he was mistaken. That, with the exception of what I had frequently stated to him before, I should be silent. That according to the doctrine he laid down, I

* We ought to die here, we ought to die on the field of battle.

must communicate to him all that passed ; by his own words I had no right to employ my own judgment or discretion, and consequently must tell him everything, as retaining any part of a conversation would be an exercise of my judgment.

He shuffled for a while in reply to this, and brought the old threadbare subject of the Scotch newspaper again on the carpet.

Had some conversation with Napoleon about Lord Castlereagh. "Never yet," said he, "has there been so much political imbecility displayed by man as there has been by Lord Castlereagh. A king is forced upon the throne contrary to the wishes and to the opinion of the people, and then, as a mode of ingratiating himself with that people, and of conciliating them, he is compelled to make them pay contributions ruinous to the country. They have made the Bourbons *les bourreaux de leur peuple*,* of the Vendeans and others who have bled for them, and by whose means they gained the battle of Waterloo; for had it not been for that business in La Vendée, I should have had thirty thousand men more at Waterloo. Then again those Bourbons have made a concordat with the pope, which would not have answered in the tenth or fifteenth century. They have agreed to establish by degrees all the laws of the church. What does this mean but the suppression of Protestantism and of all other religions except the Roman Catholic? You know that the Roman doctrine is, that out of the pale of the church, no one can be saved. It is in fact re-establishing all the old bigotry and superstition, and even the inquisition, as that was one of the laws of the church. The Protestants must see that the intention of this concordat is to deprive them of the liberty of worship, and to tolerate no religion but the Roman Catholic. The proprietors of national domains that once belonged to the church must tremble, as it leads to the restitution of them. The Protestants will be worse than before the revolution, at which time if one of them wanted to marry, he was obliged to say that he was a Catholic. Though their churches were then in a manner tolerated, yet if they frequently opened them, they were visited and tormented by the police. That *pa-*

* The executioners of their people.

paccio, that *pretaccio** has been imbecile enough to give his consent to a measure that will ultimately cause the assassination of the priests. At one time I had myself the greatest difficulty in preventing the people from accomplishing it. Oh, those Bourbons! Well may the French say, *ils n'ont rien appris, ils n'ont rien oblié.*† They rest upon a sleeping lion. I see France in a flame. I see rivers of blood flowing. You will behold a general massacre of the Bourbons take place, the old noblesse, the priests, and many an innocent Englishman and friend to liberty will pay the forfeit of his life to expiate the wicked policy of Lord Castlereagh. The imagination always exceeds the reality, and the great latitude given in the concordat to the king and to the priests to revive all the ancient superstition and intolerance, will set France in a flame, and produce another revolution of '*bonets rouges*,' and '*à bas les calottes*.'‡

25*th*.—Napoleon in high spirits Saw him in the drawing-room, dressed in a gray double-breasted coat. He was very facetious in his remarks about the governors of Benguilla, the Cape de Verde Islands, &c.

Had some conversation with him relative to Spain. I asked if it were true that the Queen had said to Ferdinand in his presence, that he was *her* son, but not the son of the king, thus proclaiming her own infamy? Napoleon assured me, that she had never made use of such expressions before him. That she had told him he was not worthy of being the son of the king I observed that it had been asserted that he had offered to give Ferdinand one of his relations in marriage, and make him king of Naples; to marry another of his relations to Don Carlos, and to grant him a sovereignty. Napoleon replied, " All those assertions are false. Ferdinand himself repeatedly asked me to give him one of my relations in marriage, but I never asked him." I said, that in a publication of great circulation it was broadly asserted, that he had given Ferdinand the choice between abdication and death :

---

* Shadow of a pope, (that) shadow of a priest.
† They have learned nothing ; they have forgotten nothing.
‡ Red caps and down with the priests.

that in consequence of this, and the threats of King Charles against himself and his followers, he had abdicated. "That is also false," replied Napoleon. "There was no threat made use of, or compulsion. If, indeed, Ferdinand had been treated as I am here, or put to the torture, or deprived of food, it might be said that he was forced to it. Your * * * would willingly have put me to death, but finding that the nation would not consent, they sent me here, in order that I might die a death slow enough to appear natural, or in the hope that I might commit suicide. The fact is, that had it not been for their broils and quarrels amongst themselves, I should never have thought of dispossessing them." I said that some of the publications against him asserted that he had been the contriver of the whole himself, in order to take advantage of it afterwards. "A man like me," replied the emperor, "is always either *un dio* or *un diavolo* (a god or a devil). It is as true as is the assertion that I brought over Pichegru and Georges to Paris purposely to ruin Moreau. When I saw those *imbéciles* quarrelling and trying to dethrone each other, I thought that I might as well take advantage of it, and dispossess an inimical family; but I was not the contriver of their disputes. Had I known at first that the transaction would have given me so much trouble, or that it would even have cost the lives of two hundred men, I never would have attempted it: but being once embarked, it was necessary to go forward."

He spoke about the battle of Esling (or Eylau), and observed, that it admitted a great deal to be said on both sides. He had remained on the field of battle, but had retired in the night, and it might be thought, that he had sustained a reverse. Lutzen* and Bautzen, he observed, he had most decidedly gained. "When only seventeen," said Napoleon, "I composed a little history of Corsica, which I submitted to the Abbé Raynal, who praised, and wished that I would publish it; adding, that it would do me much credit, and render great service to the cause then in agitation. I am," continued Napoleon, "very glad that I did not, as it was

* General Gourgaud informed me, that at Lutzen, the emperor had only two regiments of cavalry.

written in the spirit of the day, at a time when the rage for republicanism existed, and contained the strongest doctrines that could be promulgated in support of it. It was full of republicanism, and breathed freedom in every line, too much so indeed: I have since lost it. When at Lyons, in 1786, I gained a gold medal from the college on the following theme: 'What are the sentiments most advisable to be recommended, in order to render men happy.' When I was seated on the throne, a number of years afterwards, I mentioned this to Talleyrand, who sent off a courier to Lyons to procure the treatise, which he easily obtained, by knowing the theme, as the author's name was unknown. One day afterwards, when we were alone, Talleyrand took it out of his pocket, and thinking to please and pay his court to me, put it into my hands, and asked if I knew it. I immediately recognized the writing, and threw it into the fire, where it was consumed, in spite of Talleyrand's endeavors to save it. He was greatly mortified, as he had not taken the precaution of causing a copy to be made previous to showing it to me. I was very much pleased, as the style of the work was similar to that on Corsica, abounding in republican ideas, and exalted sentiments of liberty, suggested by the warmth of a fervid imagination, at a moment when youth and the rage of the times had inflamed my mind. The sentiments in it were too exalted ever to be put into practice."

I asked his opinion about Robespierre. "Robespierre," replied Napoleon, "was by no means the worst character who figured in the revolution. He opposed trying the queen. He was not an atheist; on the contrary, he had publicly maintained the existence of a Supreme Being, in opposition to many of his colleagues. Neither was he of opinion that it was necessary to exterminate all priests and nobles, like many others. Marat, for example, maintained that, to ensure the liberties of France, it was necessary that six hundred thousand heads should fall. Robespierre wanted to proclaim the king *hors de la loi*,[*] and not to go through the ridiculous mockery of trying him. Robespierre was a fanatic, a monster, but he was incorruptible, and

---

[*] Outlawed.

incapable of robbing, or of causing the deaths of others, either from personal enmity, or a desire of enriching himself. He was an enthusiast, but one who really believed that he was acting right, and died not worth a sou. In some respects, Robespierre may be said to have been an honest man. All the crimes committed by Hebert, Chaumette, Collot d'Herbois, and others, were imputed to him. Marat," continued he, "Billaud de Varennes, Fouché, Hebert, and several others, were infinitely worse than Robespierre. It was truly astonishing," added Napoleon, "to see those fanatics, who, bathed up to the elbows in blood, would not for the world have taken a piece of money, or a watch, belonging to the victims they were butchering. There was not an instance, in which they had not brought the property of their victims to the comité of public safety. Wading in blood at every step, they believed they were doing right, and scrupled to commit the smallest act bordering upon dishonesty. Such was the power of fanaticism, that they conceived they were acting uprightly, at a time when a man's life was no more regarded by them than that of a fly. At the very time that Marat and Robespierre were committing those massacres, if Pitt had offered them two hundred millions, they would have refused it with indignation. They even tried and guillotined some of their own number (such as Fabre d'Eglantine,) who were guilty of plundering. Not so Talleyrand, Danton, Barras, Fouché : they were *figurants*,* and would have espoused any side for money. Talleyrand, *c'est le plus vil des agioteurs, homme corrompu, sans opinion, mais homme d'esprit.*† A *figurant* ready to sell himself, and everything, to the best bidder. Barras was such another. When I commanded the army of Italy, Barras made the Venetian ambassador pay him two hundred thousand dollars (I think he said) for writing a letter, begging of me to be favorable to the Republic of Venice, with which I," (here he made use of a most significant gesture,) " I never paid any attention to

---
* Hirelings.
† He was the vilest of the jobbers ; a corrupt man without opinion, but a man of genius.

such letters. From my first career, I always commanded myself. Talleyrand, in like manner, sold everything. Fouché in a less degree; his traffic was in an inferior line."

I asked how it had been possible that Barrére had escaped during the different ebullitions of the revolution? " Barrére ?— *parceque c'est un homme sans caractère.** A man who changed and adapted himself to every side. He has the reputation of being a man of talent, but I did not find him so. I employed him to write, but he did not display ability. He used many flowers of rhetoric, but no solid argument. Nothing but *coglionerie*† wrapped up in high-sounding language."

"Of all the sanguinary monsters," added the emperor, " who reigned in the revolution, Billaud de Varennes was the worst. Carnot, *c'est le plus honnête des hommes*.‡ He left France without a sou."

"Madame Campan," continued Napoleon, " had a very indifferent opinion of Marie Antoinette. She told me that a person, well known for his attachment to the queen, came to see her at Versailles, on the 5th or 6th of October, where he remained all night. The palace was stormed by the populace. Marie Antoinette fled, undressed, from her own chamber to that of the king for shelter, and the lover descended from the window. On going to seek the queen in her bed-room, Madame Campan found that she was absent, but discovered a pair of breeches, which the favorite had left behind in his haste, and which were immediately recognized."

"After the events in Brumaire," said he, " I had a long conversation with Sieyes, during which I entered considerably into the state of France, and divers political matters. Sieyes went immediately after to sup with some stern republicans, his most intimate friends. After the servants had left the room, he took off his cap, and throwing it upon the ground, "*Messieurs*," said he, " *il n'y a plus de republique, elle est déjà morte*.§ I have con-

---

* Because he was a man without any character
† Boastings.
‡ He is the most honest of men.
§ Gentlemen (said he), there is no longer a republic, it is already dead.

versed to-day with a man who is not only a great general, but of himself capable of every thing, and who knows every thing. He wants no counsellors, no assistance; politics, laws, the art of governing are as familiar to him as the manner of commanding an army. He is young and determined. The republic is finished. " But," cried the republicans, "if he becomes a tyrant, *il faut le poignard de Brutus, &c."* " *Helas, mes amis, alors nous tomberons dans les mains des Bourbons ce qui est pire.*"*

" Fouché," added he, " never was my confidant. Never did he approach me without bending to the ground. For *him*, I never had esteem. As a man who had been a terrorist, and a chief of Jacobins, I employed him as an instrument to discover, and get rid of the Jacobins, Septembrizers, and others of his old friends. By means of him I was enabled to send into banishment to the Isle of France two hundred of his old associate Septembrizers, who disturbed the tranquillity of France. He betrayed and sacrificed his old *camarades*† and participators in crime. He never was in a situation to demand my confidence, or even to speak to me without being questioned, nor had he the talents requisite for it. Not so Talleyrand. Talleyrand really possessed my confidence for a long time, and was frequently acquainted with my projects a year or two before I put them into execution. Talleyrand is a man of great talents, although wicked, unprincipled, and so covetous of money, as not to care by what means he obtains it. His rapacity was so great, that I was obliged, after having in vain warned him several times, to dismiss him from his employments. Sieyes also possessed my confidence, and was a man of great talent, but, unlike Talleyrand, Sieyes was an upright man. He loves money, but he will not try to obtain it otherwise than by legitimate means; unlike the other, who will grasp at it in any form."

26*th*.—The following observations upon our embassy to China were delivered by Napoleon.

"It appears, that your ambassador, Lord Macartney, was

---

* The dagger of Brutus is necessary—alas my friends, then we shall fall into the hands of the Bourbons, which is worse.

† Comrades.

obliged, in 1793, to submit to the *ko-tou*, without doing which he would not have been received. Your ministers, who must have foreseen this, and in fact, who did foresee difficulty in etiquette, had, in sending out Lord Amherst, authorized him to comply with it; and it appears, that his private opinion was, that he ought to perform it, and that in refusing to do so, he suffered himself to be guided by bad advisers."

" It is an error, but still one which is very generally believed, that an ambassador represents the sovereign. An ambassador, however, does not represent his sovereign, as in fact none of the stipulations of affairs which he signs are valid until after a ratification; and as to his rank in etiquette, there never has been an example of sovereigns having treated them as equals, never having returned their visits; never having given way for them, nor treated them as they would have treated a foreign sovereign. The false idea that ambassadors represented the sovereign is a tradition of the feodal customs. According to which, at the rendering of homage, when a great vassal was prevented from tendering it in person, he caused himself to be represented by an ambassador. In this case the ambassador really received the honors due to his master. The character of an ambassador is of the same nature as that of a minister plenipotentiary, or an envoy, with this difference, that an ambassador is in the first degree; a minister, the second; and an envoy, the third; and in negotiations, these three have the same rights; whatever they stipulate or sign, must be submitted for the ratification of their prince; but in etiquette there is a great difference; the ambassador in precedency ought to be treated like the first lord in the country, like princes or dukes, and ministers of state. The minister plenipotentiary like nobles of the second rank in precedency at court, and envoys like those of the third. As to chargé d'affaires, they are not accredited with the sovereign, but with the minister.

" The English and Russian ambassadors had a right to the same distinctions, and ought to have followed the same etiquette as was practised by the princes and the chief mandarins. Now, these last performed the *ko-tou*, and therefore the ambassadors ought to have done the same; and the Emperor of China had a right to require it. It has been said, that a French captain, named Rock, who had been in China during the reign of Louis XIV., had refused to perform the *ko-tou*. But it must be considered that this officer was *not* an ambassador, nor a minister plenipotentiary, nor an envoy, and he was at liberty to act as he pleased, equally as the Chinese government was at liberty to consider him as being of more or less importance. But a man charged with a diplomatic mission ought to have performed the *ko-tou*; and could not refuse it without being wanting in respect to the emperor, in the same manner as this last could not refuse to receive him, without showing disrespect to his character of ambassador.

"Lord Macartney, and it appears Lord Amherst, thought of divers expedients, which had been also tried by the Russian minister. They proposed that a mandarin of equal rank to the ambassador should perform the *ko-tou* before the picture of the king of England, or that by a public declaration the Chinese monarch should promise, that if he sent an ambassador to England, he should perform the *ko-tou*. The Chinese rejected these proposals, and with good reason. If a Chinese ambassador were received in London, he would have no right to perform the *ko-tou*; but he ought to follow the same etiquette in the presence of the king of England as that observed by the princes, the ministers of state, and the knights of the garter, when they are admitted before the throne, which would be the English *ko-tou*. These proposals were therefore unreasonable, as the principle we have advanced naturally evinces. A third suggestion was made, which was not to perform the *ko-tou*, but to follow exactly the etiquette of England, which is, to place one knee upon the ground close to the throne, in presenting the credentials. It certainly is an extraordinary presumption for you to attempt to regulate the etiquette of the palace of Pekin by that of St. James's; the simple principle which has been laid down, that in negotiations as well as in etiquette, the ambassador does not represent the sovereign, and has only a right to experience the same treatment as the highest grandee of the place, clears up the whole of the question, and removes every difficulty."

"Only one reasonable objection presents itself to the mind, to wit, that the *ko-tou* is a religious act, that such religious act has something idolatrous in it, and is consequently contrary to the principles of Christianity. The mandarins perfectly comprehended the force of this objection, and repelled the idea, by declaring in an official manner, that the *ko-tou* was not a religious act, but simply a law of etiquette, which ought to have removed every scruple. Russia and England should instruct their ambassadors to submit to the *ko-tou*, upon the sole condition that the Chinese ambassador should submit in London and Petersburgh to such forms of etiquette as are practised by the princes and grandees."

"Your embassy cost you some hundred thousand pounds, which have been thrown away, and in place of being the means of approximation, will be a foundation for separation and of ill-blood between the Chinese and you, and all this by a ridiculous misunderstanding. In paying respect to the customs of a country, you make those of your own more sacred; and every homage which is rendered to a great foreign sovereign in the forms which are in use in his own country, is becoming and honorable. Besides, had not your ministers an example of it in what has always taken place with the Porte, which has constantly obliged *all* ambassadors to submit to the etiquette in use there? The ambassador is not admitted to the feet of the sublime sultan, unless he is clothed in a caftan, and is obliged to perform such ceremonies as the civilization of the Porte, and its greater or lesser degree of power, have prescribed and changed; but which still preserve traces of their original character. Is there any great difference between prostrating one's self, in order to perform the *ko-tou*, and kissing the dust at the feet of the sultan? You say that you might awe them by means of a maritime armament, and thus force the mandarins to submit to the European etiquette. This idea is madness. You would be very badly advised indeed, if you were to call to arms a nation of two hundred millions of inhabitants, and to compel them in their own defence to build ships against yours. Every sensible man in your country therefore can consider the refusal to perform the *ko-tou* no otherwise than as unjustifiable and unfortunate in its consequences."

September 1st.—Yesterday the Maria transport arrived from the Cape, with mails. A letter from young Las Cases was sent to Madame Bertrand, stating that they had at length obtained permission to quit the Cape, and were on the point of embarking on board of a brig for England, but were ignorant if permission to land would be granted them; that his father was very unwell, and expressed his fears that he would fall a victim to his complaints before he arrived, as there was no medical person in the brig. He added, that no letter had been received from Longwood since his father and himself had arrived at the Cape. A letter also arrived to Count Bertrand, from Messrs. Baring, Brothers, and Co., of London, informing him that two years ago the sum of £12,000 had been deposited in their hands for his use.

Napoleon has been in good spirits for several days, and has taken rather more exercise than formerly. On the 30th, he went to the sentry-box on the left of the house, where he remained for some time looking at the progress which had been made in a new road, greatly to the surprise of the sentinel, who stood gazing at him at the distance of a few yards.

In one of the Cape newspapers which I received, there was an article, stating that his sister Caroline had married a certain General Macdonald. Upon this Napoleon remarked, that after the recent assassination of her husband, he did not think it possible that his sister would marry; especially in so public a manner, unless she were mad, or had been forced to it with a pistol at her throat; "especially," said he, "when I consider that my sister is a woman arrived at an age when her passions are no longer *brulantes ;** that she has four children, and is possessed of a strong, masculine understanding, and talents superior to the generality of her sex. However," continued Napoleon, " there is no accounting for the actions of a woman."

He then made some remarks upon a diatribe, which had been

* Ardent.

published about him in the Courier, and observed, that now scurrility and obloquy would rather serve than hurt him. That those attempts to *flétrir son caractéré** would now be unavailing, in consequence of the free communication of the English with France. "The vast number of English," said he, "who have had access to the continent, will long ago have discovered and published that I am not that monster I have been described in the English and French libels. They have found out their mistake, and will blush at the idea of having been so grossly deceived. I would desire no better vindication of my character than their opinion. The time for libels against me is past. A moderate criticism upon my actions, well managed, well written, and not too highly exaggerated, would be infinitely more injurious to me than all the furious diatribes in the Quarterly Review style."

Some extracts of a pamphlet said to have been published by the Duke of Rovigo upon the death of Captain Wright, now attracted his observation. "If," said he, "Wright was put to death, it must have been by my authority. The Duke de Rovigo mistakes in throwing out insinuations against Fouché. If he was put to death in prison, I ordered it. Fouché, if even so inclined, never would have dared to do it. He knew me too well. But the fact is, Wright killed himself, and I do not believe that he was even personally ill-treated in prison. That Fouché may have threatened him with a view of extracting discoveries, is possible. Sidney Smith has acted in a manner unworthy of himself, and unworthy of a man of honor, in the epitaph which he wrote upon Wright. For in it he throws out insinuations, or at least leaves room to suppose, that he was secretly despatched, though he does not dare to say it openly. After having made every search and inquiry in his power, after having exhausted all his means in endeavoring to prove that he was murdered, after having had an opportunity of examining the jailers and turnkeys, and finding that nothing of the kind had happened, he ought, like a man of honor, to have openly declared, ' that there was no proof to admit of such an accusation,' instead of making insinuations, espe-

* To tarnish his character.

cially when his old enemy, against whom he had so often fought, was in the hand of his countrymen. Sidney Smith, above all men, knew, from having been so long in the Temple, that it was impossible to have assassinated a prisoner, without the knowledge of such a number of persons as would have rendered concealment impossible; and also must have been aware that nobody could have entered the prison, unless by an order from the minister of police."

"Nevertheless," added he, "Sidney Smith displayed great honor in informing Kleber of the refusal of Lord Keith to consent to the convention of El-Arish. Had he delayed it for twenty-four hours longer, Kleber would have evacuated the forts to the Turks, and would have been obliged to surrender to the English. He treated the French prisoners of war very well. *Un intrigant.** He, however, committed gross faults, in not having confined himself to operations purely naval: except in the instance of Acre, where he acted perfectly right, in sending men and officers to assist the Turks. He neglected cutting off communications by sea, which he might have done, had he attended more closely to his squadron. By this oversight, he allowed me to escape. At Acre, he caused his ships to fire broadsides at my troops at such a distance as to be harmless; indeed, on the contrary, it rendered us essential service, as there was a scarcity of shot, and every soldier who picked up one of the English balls, received five sous. However, notwithstanding," continued Napoleon, "that Sidney Smith has ill-treated me, I should still have a pleasure in seeing him. I should like to receive *ce gaillard là* † He has certain good qualities, and as an old enemy, I should like to see him."

"Have you ever heard," said he, "that Lord Wellington was the person who first proposed to send me to St. Helena?"‡

---

* An intriguer. † This gallant.

‡ It is said, that the Duke of Wellington returned to England from India in a frigate commanded by Captain (now Sir George) Cockburn, and remained at St. Helena for some days, during which time he narrowly escaped death by drowning, having been upset in a boat in one of the squalls so prevalent in that anchor

I replied, that I had heard so, but did not give the report any credit. "If it be true," said he, "it will reflect but little honor upon him in the eyes of posterity."

2nd.—Went to Plantation House, according to Sir Hudson Lowe's direction. After acquainting him with Napoleon's state of health, I proceeded to ask him, by General Bertrand's desire, information respecting the measures necessary to be taken towards obtaining a certificate of life for Countess Bertrand, and a power of attorney for the Count, and begged to know whether Mr. Brooke (the secretary to the council) was not the person who performed the duties of notary public. Sir Hudson Lowe replied roughly, "Let Count Bertrand ask Captain Blakeney." Soon afterwards, however, he said that he would not let me return without an answer, and desired me to say that there was no public notary on the island; that Mr. Brooke was not vested with powers sufficient to allow him to take such a deposition; that to legalize acts they must be signed by him as chief magistrate of the island. He then asked, "What motives could Count Bertrand have, in wishing to perform it before Mr. Brooke? Why not have asked me, as chief magistrate?" I replied, that one of Count Bertrand's motives was to spare Madame Bertrand the inconvenience and trouble of going five miles distance from Longwood, in the bad weather which prevailed, especially as she was suckling an infant, and in an extremely delicate state of health. That Count Bertrand, in the supposition that Mr. Brooke performed the duties of notary public, had desired me to inquire, and if so, to ask permission for him to come to Longwood. "Those are not his motives, sir," said Sir Hudson Lowe; "he wants to get the Marquis Montchenu to Longwood, in order to have an opportunity of conversing with

age; also, that when Napoleon was at Elba, his grace suggested to the congress, that he should be removed from thence to St. Helena, urging the latter place to be the best adapted for his perpetual imprisonment, from his own local knowledge. I merely give this report as an *on dit*, though I know that it is believed by many. If true, however, perhaps the duke may esteem it to be one of his most brilliant achievements, and only surpassed by the manifestation of generosity and humanity he displayed in the fate of his old antagonist, **Ney.**

him, before Mr. Brooke, who does not understand French. Do you not think, sir, that that is their motive?" I replied, that it had never occurred to me, that such was their intention or motive. "Then it does you but little credit, sir. You are very sharp at finding out and observing everything to their advantage;" and added, that I was an instrument in their hands. I observed to his excellency, that if asking for information from himself constituted me an instrument, I must plead guilty. That I was at a loss to conceive why they should have recourse to so much trouble to have a conversation with Marquis Montchenu in Longwood, when they had frequently met and conversed for a long time, with all the commissioners outside of it, as he must well know, without any British officers being present. His excellency said, very gruffly, that the less communication I had with them, (the French,) unless on professional subjects, the better. After repeating his insinuations, and sarcastically expressing his surprise that I should not have discovered their real motive, (which I could have told him, was solely the invincible repugnance every body at Longwood had to his presence), he asked if I had anything to communicate from General Bonaparte. I replied in the negative. He then asked how many conversations with him I had had, and for how long. I replied, that I did not recollect how many, or how long. They might have lasted for an hour, perhaps longer; and took my departure.

3rd.—Found the emperor in the drawing-room, reading aloud the Old Testament. In very good spirits. Told me that he had seen Mr. Cole at Madame Montholon's a few days since, and had taken him for a Jew. "I asked Madame Montholon," said he, "What Jew is that? *Vraiement il a l'air d'Isaac. Il appartient à la famtile d'Abraham.*"*

Napoleon then made some observations upon the formalities which the governor obliged Bertrand to go through, in order to get the bills which Las Cases had left upon London cashed, and the examination which every little bill, account, and receipt went

* Really he has the appearance of Isaac. He belongs to the family of Abraham

through. "Even the bills and salaries of the servants," said he, "are minutely examined, and every trifling sum obliged to be accounted for. Useless vexations; as every man of sense must know, that it would not be by means of any small sun that I could get here, that I could escape; and that though I have no money here, I have it at the extremity of my fingers. But this man *ha la rabbia di mischiarsi di tutto.** If he had his will, he would order me to breakfast at a certain hour, dine at another, go to bed at a time prescribed by him, and come, himself, to see it carried into execution. All will fall upon himself one day. He does not know that what passes here will be recorded in history, *ed è cosi imbecile che non sa che li ministri non hanno mai torto,* (he is imbecile enough not to feel that ministers are never wrong.) He sent a letter to Bertrand, in reply to the one written by him about the new restrictions, which convinces me more than anything he has ever yet done, that he is *un imbecile che non ha senso commune.*† If I had paid him for it, he could not have made a communication which would have pleased me more. There was nothing else wanting to verify and authenticate the tyranny under which I labor. *Il avoue des choses atroces.*‡ He says that he has authority to rip up the cover of a book, or to examine any piece of furniture in such a manner as to render it unserviceable either for ornament or utility, to search for letters. Next to his restrictions, I hold this letter precious.§ By his reasoning, he ought not to send up a loaf of bread, or a joint of meat, or a pair of shoes, as letters might be concealed in them, and frequently have been in the soles of the latter. What I said in ridicule of Lord Bathurst's speech, he writes in earnest to us. Nothing but the publication of that letter is wanting to convince the ministers that he is an imbecile. Ah, if I had only to do with such as him, I should not be here. Ah! poor country, that is obliged to employ such as him. If I were at the head of the

---

* Has the rage to meddle in everything.
† A simpleton who has not common sense.
‡ He acknowledges the most atrocious things.
§ This letter will be found in the Appendix, No. **XI.**

government, I should estimate his service to be worth an employment of 150*l.* a year."

He then made some observations upon a project mentioned in some papers to be contemplated by ministers, to lend two millions for the use of the poor, which he pronounced to be absurd ; England to recover herself must renew her commerce ; in a few words, she must no longer be a continental power. She must proceed in her proper sphere, as an insular power possessing the command of the sea. " You must not continue to be all *gentlemen,*" said he, " as Lord Castlereagh wishes. You must return to your ships. You want old Lord Chatham for a prime minister. You require able men. My opinion is, that if something be not soon done, you will be obliged to act as I did in Holland— reduce the interest of the funds to two per cent. So well assured and convinced am I that there will be a bankruptcy, more or less serious, that I would not place money in the English funds. This distress of yours is one of the consequences of the holy alliance. All the continental powers will endeavor to bridle (*raffrenare*) you, and unite against you as they have done against me, when I was more powerful than all of them put together. The only way to prevent it is by placing yourselves in such a situation as to command respect, and to make them court you, instead of you courting them ; which can never be the case as long as you have an army on the continent. As long as your ministers say, John Bull is not sick, so long will things go wrong. As soon as they come forward and say, ' Certainly there is deep distress. There wants a radical change. We have had great success which we have abused, and of which we have not availed ourselves,' then there will be some hope. But the manner in which they now act, is like a physician telling me, when I feel myself very ill and my legs swelling, that there is nothing the matter with me ; or like one replying to John Bull, when he complains that he has nothing to eat, ' Oh, you have too good an appetite. You must not indulge it. Repletion is a bad thing.' "

" Cipriani informs me," said he, " that the governor took great pains to make him comprehend that some Burgundy sent here some time back came from him. I ordered him never to bring me any more of it. I do not blush to drink the wine or eat the bread of John Bull, *mais je ne veux rien prendre des mains qui me sont devenues si odieuses* (but I will accept nothing from hands that are become so odious to me.")

He observed that he had contracted a catarrh by having sat for a quarter of an hour yesterday on the steps in front of the billiard room, and had been sneezing and coughing all the evening. Made some remarks on the *tempaccio*,* and told me, that since breakfast yesterday he had eaten nothing until the same meal this day.

He said that Count Montholon had met Madame Sturmer, and found that she was not so handsome as Betsy (Miss E. Balcombe); that she had *la tournure d'une grisette*.†

He afterwards made some observations upon Talleyrand "Talleyrand," said he, " maintained to me that assassination was sometimes justifiable, or at least that it ought to be winked at, and allowed to remain unpunished. He urged that such a practice was common to all revolutions or grand crises. That in revolutions, there were certain faults which the tribunals ought not to notice, and added, that if it had not been for *la lanterne*‡ of the constituent assembly, the revolution would not have succeeded. That some evils ought to be tolerated, because they prevented others that were greater."

4*th*.—The weather had been extremely wet for some days, and Napoleon ordered that a fire should be kept in the four rooms which he is accustomed to use himself. As he cannot bear the smell of coals, there was consequently a great deficiency of wood. Found Novarre breaking up a bedstead and some shelves to burn. Cipriani applied to Captain Blakeney to send a letter to the purveyors requesting that they would send up three thousand weight of wood, to be paid for by themselves, as the governor would not allow more than three hundred weight daily, being about a third

---

* Badness of the weather.
† The appearance of a chamber-maid.
‡ Secret chamber.

of what was wanting, in consequence of the great humidity of Longwood.

Saw Napoleon at breakfast in his bath. Expected to have found him discontented on account of the occurrences of the morning, but he was in a very good humor. He was eating some lentils, of which he asked the English name, and if I had ever seen any before. I replied that I had seen some in Egypt, but none in England. "That arch libeller, Pillet," said he, laughing, "asserts that you have none in England, and, in fact, that you have no good vegetables (*légumes*)." I replied that it was equally true with the rest of Pillet's falsehoods. That in no country in Europe were there better vegetables or a more plentiful supply. Napoleon laughed at the warmth with which I expressed myself, and said, "Oh, that atrocious libeller, Pillet. You English do not like to hear anything bad of your own country, though you are so fond of abusing other nations. I fancy that if Pillet had gone to England after the publication of that book, he would have had his brains beaten out by you." I said that he would certainly have been treated with the contempt which he deserved. Napoleon then remarked, that the northern people required the bottle to develop their ideas; that the English appeared in general to prefer the bottle to the ladies, as was exemplified by our allowing them to go away from table, and remaining for hours to drink and intoxicate ourselves. I replied, that although we did sit sometimes for hours after the ladies withdrew, it was more for the sake of conversation than for wine, of which last there was not so much drunk as formerly; that moreover, it was optional to retire immediately after the ladies or to remain. He appeared to doubt this, and made me repeat it. After which he said, that were he in England, he would always leave with the ladies. "It appears to me," said he, "that you do not pay regard enough to the ladies. If your object is to converse instead of to drink, why not allow them to be present? Surely conversation is never so lively or so witty as when ladies take a part in it. If I were an Englishwoman, I should feel very discontented at being turned out by the men to wait for two or three hours while they were guzzling their wine. Now in France society is nothing unless ladies are present. They are the life of conversation."

I endeavored to make it appear that our conversation after dinner frequently turned upon politics, and other matters, with which ladies seldom meddled; moreover, that in well-regulated societies, the gentlemen soon followed them. This did not, however, satisfy him. He maintained that it was a custom which could not be justified, that women were necessary to civilize and to soften the other sex.

He spoke about Maréchal Jourdan, of whose military talents he had a poor opinion. I observed, that I had been told by some English officers, who had been present at the battle of Albuera, that if Maréchal Soult had advanced after the attack made by the lancers, he would have cut the English army to pieces. Napoleon acquiesced in this, and said that he had censured Soult for having neglected to do so. He then adverted to the English mode of besieging towns, and said that Lord Wellington, at sieges, was *le bourreau des hommes ;** that the immense sacrifice of men at Ciudad Rodrigo and Badajoz was by no means compensated by the capture of those places. He observed, that the storming of Bergen-op-Zoom was a most daring attempt, but that it ought not, or could not have succeeded, the number of the garrison being greater than that of the assailants. I observed, that the failure was in part to be attributed to one of the generals not having taken the precaution to communicate the orders which had been given to him to any one else; so that when he was killed or mortally wounded, the troops did not know how to act. Napoleon replied, that even if no accident of the kind had occurred, the attempt ought not to have succeeded, unless the party attacked became, as sometimes happened, panic struck. Graham, he observed, had been commissary with the army at the time of his first career of arms at Toulon. "A daring old man," said he, and asked if he were not the same who had commanded in **the** affair near Cadiz.

* The executioner of men.

6th.—Had some conversation in the morning with Napoleon, relative to the deficiency of fuel at Longwood, and with General Montholon on the same subject.

Went to Plantation House by order of Sir Hudson Lowe, to whom I communicated the particulars of the deficiency of fuel, and the observations I had been desired to make upon the subject. Had a long discussion with his excellency, and explained that there were twenty-three fires in all at Longwood, which he thought much too numerous. He answered in his accustomed manner, " that they had no business with so many." I explained to him that Longwood was very damp, and that the French ladies and children required constant fires. He said that " Lady Lowe had no fire in *her* room." I observed, that the French were natives of a more southern climate than ours, and consequently more susceptible of cold, and that there could be no comparison made between the comfort of such a building as Plantation House and Longwood. His excellency said, that " he did not see any necessity for so many fires, and that he had seen a fire burning in the Countess Bertrand's room in the middle of summer." I told him I had no observation to make upon that circumstance. I observed, that it was necessary to regulate the quantity of wood by the seasons, as what was too much in summer was too little in winter, and explained to him that I had done everything in my power to explain to the French, that he thought the allowance which he had ordered for Longwood was sufficient, as he had made it nearly double of what was consumed at Plantation House. I also told his excellency that Napoleon could not bear the smell of coals; and suggested, that instead of sending wood to the soldiers in camp, coals might be furnished, and the wood sent to Longwood; to which he replied, that " he did not like to humor any person's whims."

Saw Napoleon in his bath. After some conversation respecting the deficiency of fuel, he said that he had seen Admiral Plampin, who had brought him a book, which he (the admiral) said had been sent out by Lord Bathurst, which, added Napoleon, " I suppose his lordship has sent in order to discover the author, as in the letter which the admiral said he saw, it was attributed to Benjamin Constant, or Madame de Staël."

Napoleon then observed, that he had spoken to the admiral about ships of war, and their interior economy. "The admiral says that a seventy-four gun ship will take about eighty tons more water by means of the tanks. Had I known this in 1806 or 1808, I would have sent an army of thirty thousand men to invade India. I had made several calculations about the possibility of sending so large a body of men to India, but always found that they would have been short of water for a month." I asked what his plan was? "In Brest," said the emperor, "I had at one time as many as fifty-six sail of the line, and often forty-six. In forty of these line-of-battle ships I intended to have dispersed thirty thousand soldiers, eight hundred in each, and only four hundred sailors. There were to have been a proportionate number of frigates, and other smaller vessels. Ten of the line-of-battle ships would have been old and of little value. They were also to take on board six or eight hundred dismounted cavalry, and a portion of artillery, with every thing necessary for an army to take the field, and be provisioned for four months. They were to make the best of their way to the Isle of France, where they would have watered and provisioned afresh, landed their sick, and taken on board some other troops to replace them, with three thousand blacks to form colonial regiments. From thence they were to have proceeded to India, and to have disembarked in the nearest possible place, so as to have allowed the Mahrattas, with whom I had an understanding, to join them. They were to form the cavalry of the army. A few of the French were also to be mounted, and all the horses they could procure purchased. After landing, they were to have burnt the ten old ships, and divided their crews amongst the rest, who would have been thus full manned. They would then proceed in different directions, and do you all possible mischief in your settlements. I had," continued he, "an understanding with the Mahrattas and others, in India, by the way of Bassorah, Bagdat, Mocha, and Surat; their communications were made to the consuls at Aleppo, through the ambassador in Persia, &c. I had frequently earlier intelligence from India than you had in England. The king of Persia was favorably disposed towards us. All this plan, however, was fustrated by the calculations I had made, which showed me that the ships must fall short of water by a month. Had I known of those tanks, I certainly would have made the attempt."

Napoleon then calculated the number of tons which would have been gained by the tanks, and found that the ships would have had more than sufficient water: " For a power which is inferior by sea," said he, " is an invention of great importance, as it will prevent the necessity of their going into harbor to water."

I mentioned Toussaint Louverture, and observed, that amongst other calumnies, some of his enemies had asserted that he had caused him to be put to death privately in prison. " It does not deserve an answer," replied Napoleon. " What possible interest could I have in putting a negro to death after he had arrived in France? Had he died in St. Domingo, then indeed something might have been suspected; but after he had safely arrived in France, what object could have been in view?"

" One of the greatest follies I ever was guilty of," continued the emperor, " was sending that army out to St. Domingo. I ought to have prevented the possibility of its being effected. I committed a great oversight and fault in not having declared St. Domingo free, acknowledged the black government, and before the peace of Amiens, sent some French officers to assist them. Had I done this, it would have been more consonant to the principles under which I was acting. It would have done you incalculable mischief. You would have lost Jamaica, and your other colonies would have followed. Having once acknowledged them, I could not have sent an army out there during the peace. But after the peace, I was continually beset with applications from proprietors of estates in the colony, merchants, and others. Indeed, the nation had *la rage** to regain St. Domingo, and I was obliged to comply with it; but had I, previous to the peace, acknowledged the blacks, I could under that plea have refused to

* A strong desire.

make any attempts to retake it; in doing which, I acted contrary to my own judgment."

6th.—Informed Count Montholon, by direction of Sir Hudson Lowe, that the latter had regulated the quantity of fuel necessary for Longwood, by a comparison with that consumed at Plantation House; and thought, that by giving twice as much coal as was used there, and three hundred weight of wood daily, he had allowed a sufficiency. That however, if any application had been made, he would have increased the quantity. I also showed him a letter from Major Gorrequer, stating the quantity used at Plantation House. Count Montholon replied, that they were not bound to regulate the quantity of fuel they thought it necessary to burn at Longwood by that consumed by Sir Hudson Lowe at Plantation House, where there were only four or five fire-places, and there were twenty-three at Longwood. That, moreover, they were natives of a warmer and a drier climate than the English, and stood in need of more heat; that the dampness of Longwood rendered fires absolutely necessary for the preservation of their health. That both his own and the countess's clothes were spoiled by the damp, in spite of the fires which were used. As to asking for more, he did not like to subject himself to slightings or refusals. Napoleon for some days has eaten no dinner. Told me, that he intended to accustom himself to only one meal a day. Mentioned in the course of conversation, that he once had it in contemplation to have sent five thousand men to invade Surinam; and asked me, (as I had been there,) if I thought it would have succeeded? I replied, that I thought not. First, on account of the difficulty of approaching the coast, as large ships could not come nearer than seventeen or eighteen miles, and the channel for vessels (not drawing more than eighteen feet water) was only practicable at high water, was very difficult, intricate, and required the aid of a skilful pilot. Besides, that the country itself was full of marshes and very inaccessible. That there was a garrison of three regiments, besides the colonial militia. Fort Amsterdam was strong, and could for some time sustain a regular siege.

The weather has not been so bad this day as for some time past. Napoleon went out as far as Count Bertrand's. "*Veramente*," said he yesterday, when speaking of the weather, "*non è paese Cristiano.*"*

7th.—Napoleon complained of rheumatic pains and slight head-ache, which he attributed, and with reason, to the dampness of the climate and the house. "Every evening," said he, "when I leave my little sitting-room, where there is a fire, and enter my sleeping-room,† where there is none, I experience a sensation as if I were going into a damp cellar. If it were not for the room that Cockburn built, which is light, airy, and built of dry wood, where I walk about and exercise, I should have been under ground before now. But that is, I suppose, what your oligarchy wants, and is of a piece with their treatment of the prisoners in the *pontons*, an act the most cruel as well as the most impolitic that was ever practised. Nothing ever done by your ministers enraged the French and other nations against them so much as their system of *pontons*. If humanity were out of the question, good policy ought to have made them treat prisoners well. It is incredible what effect the good treatment of prisoners in France had upon other nations, especially the Russians and Germans. I often experienced it to my advantage, as thousands of them threw down their arms, who otherwise would have fought desperetely, saying, 'We will go into Bourgogne to drink good wine.'"

I observed, that latterly in the prison-ships in England there was less mortality than amongst those confined in the depôts on shore, which was a proof that they were not ill treated, because sickness and deaths always followed the ill treatment of prisoners. Napoleon replied, "The most barbarous and unnatural measure ever adopted by one nation against another, was that of putting poor wretches who were not brought up to the sea, on board of ships, there to remain ten or twelve years without stirring out or walking upon the grass, exposed to the stink of the mud at low water, and huddled up as they were. It was a crying injus-

---

* Really it is not a Christian country.
† Napoleon had changed his bed-room some time before.

tice, and one which, mark me, will yet be revenged upon the English nation. Of the prisoners in France, I, with their own consent, formed battalions of pioneers, who labored on the fortresses and other public works, for which they were paid a certain sum daily Amongst them, there were some English. Directly afterwards, a letter was sent by order of the English government, to know if it were true that Englishmen were made to work as pioneers, expressing great anger, and desiring that it might be immediately put a stop to. I ordered an answer to be returned, stating, that an offer had been made to all the prisoners in France, that a certain number of them would be permitted to volunteer to work as pioneers, for which they would receive so much pay daily. That it was not made to the English in particular. No force was employed, and that some English, amongst others, had volunteered to work, for which they were paid; that I begged the English government would do the same with any prisoners of mine who would volunteer. However, they would not allow the Frenchmen to work; I suppose your oligarchy was afraid they would disseminate their principles of equality amongst the people of England."

He then made some remarks upon the Manuscrit venu de Sᵗᵉ Hélène, and observed, that there was such an ignorance of chronological events displayed in it, such as putting the battle of Jena after Tilsit, and others of a similar nature, and so many mistakes as to time and place, that it would make a corporal in the old French army laugh. "Notwithstanding this," added he, "it was written by a man of *esprit*,* though in several passages he appears not to have had *sens commun*.† In some places, his assertion of the motives which actuated me is correct. What he says on the subject of my nobility is correct. What he says about my intentions and wishes to do away with everything which had been established since Charlemagne, is also right. That the nobility I formed was that of the people is true, as I took the son of a peasant, and made him a duke or a marshal, when I found that he had talents. That I wanted to introduce

* Genius. † Common sense.

a system of general equality, is true, and that every person should be eligible to every situation, provided he had talents to fill it, whatever his birth might be. That I wanted to do away with all the ancient prejudices of birth is also correct. That I labored to establish a government of the people, which, though *dur*,* was still that of the people, is also true. That I ought to have deposed for my own security, when I had it in my power, the house of Brandenburgh, and all the ancient orders of sovereigns; and that they almost always combined against and attacked me, is also right. Probably I ought to have done so, and I should have succeeded. It is true that I wished to establish a government of the people. It is a work which will much displease the oligarchy, because they do not wish that any person, except one of themselves, should be eligible for any important situation. With *their* will, birth and not talents or capability should regulate the choice. A worse, a more despotic or unforgiving government than an oligarchy never existed. Offend them once, you are never pardoned, and no treatment can be too cruel for you when in their power. The pamphlet is written with that lightness peculiar to Frenchmen, and consequently contains many mistakes. The Edinburgh Review will find out directly that I am not the author of it. *La Revue d'Edinburgh le coulera en bas.*† They will take it to pieces as I have done. The editors of it will probably make similar remarks to those in the notes‡ I made yesterday, probably not so strong, in consequence of not being so well acquainted with the secrets as I am. I see by the sketch§ they have published of my life, that they take pains to ascertain the truth. Most of it is true; and it is difficult for me to imagine from whence they had their information on some parts of my early life, which were very little known to any except to my own family."

* Hard.   † The Edinburgh Review will sift it closely.
‡ Those notes were given by Napoleon to me, and published in the appendix to the ninth volume of the Memoirs of Napoleon dictated by himself.
§ The sketch alluded to came from the classical pen of John Allen, Esq. Napoleon had read it with great attention in my presence, and made some pencil marks upon particular passages.

"That work," continued he, "was not written by Madame de Staël, or if it be, it was the work of a few hours, and was sent to the press without any correction. But there are in it *fautes trop grossières** for Madame de Staël. The sentiments expressed in it are such as Madame de Staël would *talk*; and though new in England, were for several years the subjects of discussion in France."

"The author," continued he, "has made a great mistake in saying, that after Jena, I never did any thing worthy of my former actions. The greatest military manœuvres I ever made, and those for which I give myself most credit, were performed at Eckmuhl, and were infinitely superior to Marengo, or to any other of my actions. It is the work of some young *homme d'esprit*,† who has hurried it to the press without having submitted it to the revision of any of his friends. It is, however, composed with good intentions towards me. If I had written a work of the kind, it would indeed be different. Every line of it would be a subject of discussion for nations."

"Freeing the work from its mistakes and errors," added he, "it would be valuable. The author says that there will be a revolution in Europe. That is not at all improbable. He says, that it was perhaps necessary to place a Bourbon on the throne in 1814; but that it would have been advisable to have left me after my return from Elba. Perhaps he is right in both." He added, that such a work, really written by him, would make a great noise. "It will be, or perhaps is written," added he, "but it will be for my son and for posterity."

"It only rested with me," said he, "to have deposed both the King of Prussia and the Emperor of Austria. When I was at Scoenbrunn," (I think he said) "the Duke of Wurtsburg frequently insinuated to me that the only means to secure the good faith of Austria would be to depose his brother Francis, and place the crown on his head. These offers were repeated to me afterwards through a minister, with an offer of his son as hostage, who should be placed as my aid-de-camp, with every other pos-

---

* Faults too great. † Man of genius.

sible guarantee. I reflected upon it for some time ; but the marriage with Marie Louise put a stop to any further consideration on the subject. I was wrong in not having accepted of it. Nothing would have been easier to execute."

I asked, if he believed it to have been written by the Abbé de Pradt. "No," replied the emperor, "I do not think that he is the author. De Pradt," continued he, "may be said to be *une espèce de fille de joie qui prête sons corps** to all the world for payment. Once, when he was giving vent to his customary *bavardage*† and extravagant projects in my presence, I contented myself with humming a part of the air :

> Où courez vous donc monsieur l'Abbé
> Vous allez vous casser le nez,‡

which disconcerted him so much, that he had not another word to utter."

Speaking about the badness of the house, and the offer said to have been made by Sir Hudson Lowe to build a new one, Napoleon observed that he had only refused the offer of making additions to the present wretched old house of Longwood, and the design to build another on that miserable situation. "The governor," said he, "asked me if I had heard that wood had arrived to build a new house, but that I must not believe that a house had been sent out ; that I might perhaps have seen such an assertion in the papers ; but that only materials had come out. I told him that I did not believe what I saw in the papers; more especially any thing relating to myself. He said, that if I made choice of a spot to build a house upon, I might have it; but on condition that it was approved of by him ; without which I could not have it where I pleased. I was not so silly as not to have known this before. He then made an offer of building additions, but with a very bad grace. I told him, that I did not wish to

---

* Like a common prostitute who lends her body.
† Impertinence.
‡ Whatever course you may propose,
'Twill only be to break your nose.

subject myself to the inconvenience of having workmen continually to annoy me with their noise. That the English government ought to provide me with a house already built, and not one to be built. After this, he wrote a letter to Montholon on the same subject, who replied by my desire, that if he intended to build a new house for us, let it be built in a place where there was shade and water. Nothing could be more plain than this. It is a fine prospect certainly that he now holds out. With all the activity of Cockburn, the construction of a new house would take three years, and with this man, I dare say six; and that a house might be healthy, it ought not to be inhabited for eighteen months after being built. I shall be dead long before that time. This I also told him. Plantation House is the only one in the island fit for me. The governor having a house himself in town, could easily retire there for six months, until the improvements were made here, and having the command of every thing himself, without being obliged to ask permission from any body, he could soon render this habitable for some months in the year, which is all that it is adapted for. He could retire to town in the winter season."

Napoleon then said, that the English servants in the house had laughed at the French for eating lentils, and asserted, that in England they fed horses with what the French eat here. He laughed very heartily while saying this; and at an anecdote which I related about Dr. Johnson, who, I informed him, had, in the first edition of his English dictionary, defined oats to be "food for horses in England, and for men in Scotland."

Count Montholon called Captain Blakeney* and myself this day to look at the state of his apartments. The rooms, especially the countess's bed-room, the children's room, and bath-room, were certainly in a shocking state, from the extreme humidity of the place. The walls were covered with green fur and mould; damp and cold to the touch, notwithstanding the fires which were constantly kept

---

* Captain Blakeney had replaced Captain Poppleton as orderly officer on the departure of Captain P.'s regiment from St. Helena.

in them. I never saw a human habitation in a more mouldy or humid state, in which opinion the orderly officer agreed.

8th.—Saw Napoleon, who informed me, that after I had left him yesterday, he had found himself very unwell with head-ache and general pains in his limbs ; and had taken a warm bath, which had been very beneficial to him.

He was in very good spirits, spoke for a long time about the Manuscrit de Ste Hélène, and observed, that it must have been written by a person who had heard him reason, and was acquainted with his ideas. He added, that he thought he knew the author, whom he supposed to be a man who had figured in the revolution, and now lived retired.

He asked many questions about the number of bottles of wine we had drunk at our party the night before last. Blamed Mr. Boys's conduct, for having preached in allusion to the admiral.* Said that a man's conscience was not to be amenable to any tribunal ; that no person ought to be accountable to any earthly power for his religious opinions. " Had you not persecuted the Catholics in Ireland," added he, " in all probability the greatest number of them would before now have become Protestants ; but persecution strengthens them in their belief. Even Pitt himself was aware of the necessity of giving the Catholics equal privileges with the Protestants."

9th.—Races at Deadwood. The commissioners all present. None of the French from Longwood attended, except the children and some of the domestics.

During the interval between the heats, Sir Hudson Lowe sent for me, and asked if "some of General Bonaparte's horses were not on the race-ground ?" I replied in the affirmative. His excellency asked how they came there ? I replied, that I had borrowed the horses from General Gourgaud, one of which I had lent to Miss Eliza Balcombe, and the other to the surgeon of the Conqueror. Sir Hudson immediately broke out into not the most

* Mr. Boys had thought it a duty to mention something from the pulpit, in censure of an official person, for having set an example of immorality to a small colony, by publicly living with a woman not his wife, and for absenting himself from church.

moderate expressions, and his gestures attracted the attention of many of the spectators. He characterized my having dared to lend any of General Bonaparte's horses without his (the governor's) permission, to be the greatest piece of presumption he had ever witnessed I observed, that I had come to St. Helena to learn that it was a crime to borrow a horse for the use of a young lady; neither had I known that it was necessary to go to Plantation House to ask permission from him to borrow a horse belonging to the Longwood establishment. Sir Hudson replied, that " I had no business to form any opinion about it."

This was evidently only a pretext to have an opportunity of venting his pitiful vengeance, as not a week passed that horses were not sent down to town, and frequently to Sir Thomas Reade's, for Dr. Livingston and others to ride up to Longwood, without it having ever been signified that it was necessary first to apply to Sir Hudson Lowe for permission. Besides, Gen. Gourgaud always directed that a horse should be in the stable at my command.

A little before the conclusion of the races, the three commissioners, Madame Sturmer, and Captain Gor, came in as far as the inner gate of Longwood, where they remained for some time, during which the governor approached and looked in at the outer gate. Shortly afterwards Count and Countess Bertrand, Count and Countess Montholon, and General Gourgaud, went out to walk, and met the commissioners outside of the gate, with whom they had a long conversation. They afterwards proceeded together to Hut's Gate. It was nearly dark before they returned.

Napoleon in high spirits; looked out of a window at the races, with which he was much pleased. Told me that he had done everything in his power to establish the same in France.

12*th*.—Went to Plantation House, in consequence of orders communicated to me by Captain Blakeney. After some conversation relative to the late discussions respecting the quantity of fuel allowed to Longwood, Sir Hudson Lowe entered again upon the heinous crime I had been guilty of in lending one of the horses of the Longwood establishment to a young lady; to which I replied as I had done before, which he said was quite in the

Longwood style. He then asked in an abrupt manner if I had not received some books from Dr. Warden? I replied, that I had received seven or eight monthly publications, containing reviews of his work. "Did you not receive one, sir, with a view of Longwood?"* I replied, yes. "It is very extraordinary," said Sir Hudson, "that you did not inform me of it." I replied, that I was not bound to tell him of any or every book I received or purchased; that I was in the habit of having books and pamphlets of various descriptions from England, which I was not obliged to give any account of. Sir Hudson said, that I ought to have done so, and asked if I had lent any of them to the French, or if they had seen them. I replied, that to my knowledge the French had not seen them; that they were at present in my inner apartment. He said, that "it was very extraordinary I should have had those pamphlets for two months, without being able to tell whether the French had seen them; and that I might have books in my rooms, to be shown to them, of a very improper tendency, which they might read in my absence;" and after harping for a long time on those unlucky pamphlets, he said he supposed I had no objection to lend them to him. I replied, certainly not; that they should be sent to him on my return. They consisted of the Monthly Review, Gentleman's Magazine, Eclectic Review, British Ladies' Magazine, European Magazine, and New Monthly. His excellency then said, that Count Las Cases had given a pretty strong hint in the letter he had sent to Longwood from the Cape, that he was in want of the money which he had lent them, which it did not appear to be *convenient* for them to understand. After which he made a long and abusive harangue upon the "Character of Bonaparte," extracted from the Quarterly Review, which publication his excellency appeared to consider as a sort of political gospel.

14*th*.—Napoleon in very good spirits. Asked many questions about the horses that had won at the races, and the manner in which we trained them; how much I had won or lost; and about the ladies, &c. "You had a large party yesterday," continued

* A few days before I had lent this pamphlet to an officer of the staff.

he. "How many bottles of wine? *Drink, your eyes look like drink,*" which he expressed in English. "Who dined with you?" I mentioned Captain Wallis amongst others. "What, is that the lieutenant who was with Wright?" I replied in the affirmative. "What does he say about Wright's death?" I said, "He states his belief that Wright was murdered by orders of Fouché, for the purpose of ingratiating himself with you That six or seven weeks previous, Wright had told him that he expected to be murdered like Pichegru, and begged of him never to believe that he would commit suicide; that he had received a letter from Wright, about four or five weeks before his death, in which he stated that he was better treated, allowed to subscribe to a library, and to receive newspapers. Napoleon replied, "I will never allow that Wright was put to death by Fouché's orders. If he was put to death privately, it must have been by my orders, and not by those of Fouché. Fouché knew me too well. He was aware that I would have had him hanged directly if he attempted it. By this officer's own words, Wright was not *au secret*, as he says that he saw him some weeks before his death, and that he was allowed books and newspapers. Now, if it had been in contemplation to make away with him, he would have been put *au secret** for months before, in order that people might not be accustomed to see him for some time previous, as I thought this * * * intended to do in November last Why not examine the jailers and turnkeys? The Bourbons have every opportunity of proving it, if such really took place. But your ministers themselves do not believe it. The idea I have of what was my opinion at that time about Wright, is faint; but as well as I can recollect, it was, that he ought to have been brought before a military commission for having landed spies and assassins, and the sentence executed within forty eight hours. What dissuaded me from doing so, I cannot clearly recollect. Were I in France at this moment, and a similar occurrence took place, the above would be my opinion, and I would write to the English government, 'Such an officer of yours has been tried for landing brigands and assassins on my ter-

* Secreted.

ritories. I have caused him to be tried by a military commission. He has been condemned to death. The sentence has been carried into execution. If any of my officers in your prisons have been guilty of the same, try and execute them. You have my full permission and acquiescence. Or if you find hereafter any of my officers landing assassins on your shores, shoot them instantly.' This affair of Wright's," added he, " made so little impression upon me, that when Lord Ebrington spoke about it at Elba, I did not recollect it. My mind was so much occupied with grand objects, that I had little time to think of a poor English captain. Had the Bourbons, Moreau, or the Vendean chiefs been put to death, then indeed I might have been suspected. I might have tried and executed the Vendean chiefs for having carried arms against the country. They are all alive. My opinion is, if I had known Wright had been one of Sidney Smith's officers, and that he had fought against me at Acre, I would have sent for him and questioned him about the siege and released him. I recollect perfectly well seeing an officer wounded and carried off at Acre, whose bravery I admired at the time. I think that I should have released him, if I had found him to be that officer. It appears also that he killed himself when he was upon the point of being released, as I see that the Court of Spain had interceded for him. When you first spoke to me on the subject, I imagined that Wright had killed himself purposely to avoid giving evidence against your ministers; and I attached a degree of heroism to the act, which I gave him great credit for; but since I see that it was a long time after, and when I was at Ulm, at the head of a hundred and fifty thousand men, and three hundred leagues from Paris. It requires but a trifling circumstance to make you English kill yourselves."

Napoleon then rallied me upon my supposed attention to Miss * * *, and said, I ought to marry her. I replied, that I was neither rich enough, nor young enough, to have pretensions to so fine a lady. He now recounted some of his own love adventures. " The most beautiful female I ever saw," said he, " was an Irish girl, Mademoiselle G * * s; whether she had been born in

Ireland, or was only of an Irish family, I am not certain. It was during Josephine's time, and long before I married Marie Louise. One day, when I was hunting in St. Germains, some of the Court intriguers threw her in my way, and contrived it so, that she came with a petition in her hand to deliver to me. When she presented herself, and said she had a petition, every one made way for her, as I had given orders, that persons bringing petitions should invariably be allowed to approach me. She fell at my feet, and presented it. She was covered with a veil, that did not conceal the beauty of her countenance, which was really heavenly. Certainly I was taken with her charms, and although I suspected there was some intrigue, I was not displeased. Three or four times afterwards, I saw and conversed with her. I used to take little liberties with her, such as patting her cheeks. At this time a letter from her mother to her was brought to me from the secret post-office. This mother was an old intriguer, and gave her daughter directions which elucidated her character. There were instructions relative to her conduct towards me in many particular instances. I was now convinced that it was not proper for me to countenance this proceeding, and although I was assuredly smitten with her, for she was as beautiful as an angel, I gave such orders as prevented her ever having the means of being again admitted to my presence. Since that time, I have been informed, she really had a regard for me, and would have been faithful. She is now married to M. * * *, a very rich man, but still, I am led to believe, preserves an affection for me."

"The evening before I left Paris for Waterloo," continued Napoleon, "a beautiful Englishwoman came to the palace, and asked to see me. She saw Marchand, who told her that it was impossible. She said, she was an English lady, and a friend of Mademoiselle G * *'s, whom I well knew, and that she was persuaded I would see her; that I could not refuse to see a young lady who loved me, and admired my character. Marchand told her that I was to leave Paris the next morning, and could not be disturbed. At hearing this, she appeared to be much afflicted, and with some reluctance she went away. Perhaps she was some beautiful intriguer, or one who had *la tête montée** for me. When once a woman has *la tête montée*, all the world will not prevent her from attempting to succeed in her designs. Soon after I had taken Vienna, the Austrian Princess * * * got her head full of me, from hearing me so much talked of. She was one of those princesses of whom you know there are so many in Germany. Nothing would * * * * * * *.† For this purpose she came to Schoënbrunn, and insisted upon seeing me. Murat, who was a fine handsome fellow, tried to gain her affections, but she rejected him with disdain. I ordered her to be admitted, and represented myself as Maréchal Duroc. She could speak very little French or Italian, and I could not converse in German. I told her not to speak so loud, as the emperor would hear her, and pointed out Duroc as emperor; but she was not to be deceived. She had seen me pass by a house where she was, and cried, no, no, *vous, vous, empereur.*‡ She was extremely handsome, and very candid in her confessions."

Napoleon then spoke about the assertion, said to have been made by Lord Castlereagh, in the House of Commons, respecting him: viz., that he had made out a list of the richest heiresses in France, whom he was in the habit of ordering to marry such of his generals as he pleased. That none of them could marry without his leave, and were obliged to espouse any persons, to whom he thought proper to give them. These assertions he declared to be wholly false. "So far from being true," added Napoleon, "it was not in my power to get even Caulaincourt married to a lady to whom I wished to see him united. She was the daughter of * * *, who was president of the chamber, a banker, and enormously rich, which he had chiefly acquired, it was supposed, by a * * * * * * *. She was a beautiful girl, and he intended giving her a large portion. I asked the father myself, as a favor, to give her in marriage to Caulaincourt, but he gave me a positive

* The head turned.
† The following quotation from Douglas will sufficiently explain the designs of this *innamorata*.
      " As ladies wish to be, who love their lords."
‡ You are the Emperor.

refusal. At that time, Caulaincourt was one of my greatest favorites. So much for Castlereagh's veracity."

19*th*.—Went to Plantation House, in obedience to directions to go there, received from Sir Hudson Lowe through Captain Blakeney, and to take with me a report of the state of health of Napoleon. On my arrival, Sir Hudson Lowe asked for the report, which stated, that with the exception of a few slight catarrhal attacks, his health had been tolerable. Sir Hudson Lowe asked if they had been of any consequence, to which I answered in the negative. The governor observed, that others besides me had made reports relative to General Bonaparte's health. That Madame Bertrand had told the commissioners that he was extremely unwell; that because they saw him standing in the veranda, they must not believe that he was in good health. I repeated, that he had suffered some indisposition, but not of a serious nature. Sir Hudson Lowe then said, that he had heard a great deal, though not all of the conversation which had passed between the French and the commissioners, and that all of the former, except one, had abused the opportunity. That every time Count Bertrand had had an opportunity of speaking to them, he had abused it; that this last was the only time that Montholon had had an opportunity of speaking to them, which he (Sir Hudson) asserted, he had fully availed himself of by cramming them with misrepresentations.

20*th*.—Saw Napoleon in his bath. At first he was rather dull and out of spirits. Complained of pain in the right cheek, shooting from the diseased tooth. Gums spongy, and bled upon the slightest touch. Ankles and legs a little swelled. Great want of sleep at night. Explained to me several reasons which convinced me that Corvisart had been right in prescribing to him exercise on horseback, which I strongly recommended myself, and in as forcible a manner as possible. Napoleon replied, that under the present restrictions, liable to be insulted by a sentinel if he budged off the road, he could never stir out; neither did he think that I myself, or any other Englishman placed in his situation, would avail himself of the privilege to ride, fettered with such restrictions. To this observation of his I made no reply; for if I had expressed my real sentiments as a man, and not as a surgeon, I must have said that I agreed with him in opinion; and contented myself with recommending antiscorbutic vegetables, &c. "*Di qua un poco non mi vedrete più, Dottore; vorrei che fosse questa sera, una maniera d'* * * * * * as certain, but more barbarous than the stiletto. *Senta che la macchina sene va giornalmente.*† However, that is what he was sent for. In succeeding ages the * * * * will pay for it. *Sur le rocher le plus affreux dans le monde,*‡ they send out a man to impose restrictions which never have been practised in the revolutionary tribunals under Marat. Even there, the condemned, while permitted to live, were allowed newspapers and books. They did not expire in agonies, protracted so long as to make it appear a natural death. *That* refinement of cruelty was unknown to Billaud de Varennes, or Collot de Herbois.

"I ask you," continued Napoleon, "can *you* lend me a newspaper or a book? Can you *even* lend me a work upon science?"

Shortly afterwards, he spoke about Catholic emancipation, which, if effected, he pronounced would be of great benefit to the English on the continent, and be a most wise and politic measure for our ministers to adopt.

He then made some observations about Mr. P———es having sold his wife,§ which he said would reflect but little credit on the governor, and that, had such a circumstance occurred in France, the Procureur Général would have prosecuted the offending parties. That it appeared to be a most disgraceful circumstance, especially when, as it appeared to be, it had been sanctioned by the two organs of communication of the governor, civil and military.

Napoleon then observed that he was at a loss to conceive from whence the Edinburgh Review had obtained so much accurate information respecting him. "That circumstance," said he, " of the

---
* After a little you shall not see me, Doctor. I would wish to have this evening a kind of———
† I perceive that my machine is wearing daily.
‡ Upon the most frightful rock in the world.
§ This circumstance actually happened at St. Helena.

déjeûné de trois amis,* I never told to any person. It is true that I was the author, and that it produced great effect in France, but I do not recollect ever having disclosed it to any one. There are, however, some mistakes in the Review. I never knew Barras at Toulon. My first acquaintance with him commenced at Paris after the siege of Toulon.

"My marriage with Marie Louise," added Napoleon, "produced no change in me. I was precisely the same as before. Never was woman more astonished than Marie Louise was after her mariage, when she observed the few precautions that I took to ensure my safety against any attempts upon my life. When she perceived that there were no sentinels except at the outer gates of the palace; that there were no *lords* sleeping before the doors of the apartments, that the doors were not even locked, and that there were no guns or pistols in the rooms where we slept, 'Why,' said she with astonishment, 'you do not take half so many precautions as my father, who has nothing to fear.' I am," continued Napoleon, "too much of a fatalist (*trop fataliste*) to take any precautions against assassination. When I was in Paris, I used to go out and intermingle with the populace without my guards, receive their petitions, and was frequently surrounded by them so closely that I could not move."

I inquired of the emperor in what engagement or engagements he considered himself to have been in the greatest danger? He replied, "In the commencement of my campaign At Toulon, and particularly at Arcola. At Arcola, my horse was shot under me: rendered furious by the wound, the animal seized the bit between his teeth, and galloped on towards the enemy. In the agonies of death, he plunged into a morass and expired, leaving me nearly up to my neck in the swamp, and in a situation from which I could not extricate myself. I thought at one moment that the Austrians would have come and cut off my head, which was just above the surface of the morass, and which they could have done without my having been able to offer the least resistance. However, the difficulty of getting at me, and the approach of my soldiers, who rescued me, prevented them."

* Breakfast of three friends.

I asked, if he had not been frequently slightly wounded? He replied, "Several times, but scarcely more than once had 1 occasion for surgical assistance, or any fever in consequence of a wound. At Marengo, a cannon shot took away a piece of the boot of my left leg, and a little of the skin," said he, showing the mark to me, " but I used no other application to it than a piece of linen dipped in salt and water." I asked about a wound of which there was a deep mark in the inside of the left thigh, a little above the knee. He said, that it was from a bayonet. I asked if he had not had horses frequently killed under him, to which he answered, eighteen or nineteen in the course of his life.

"The regiment de la Fère," said Napoleon, "in which I had commenced my career, behaved so badly to the inhabitants of Turin, that I was obliged to reduce them. I accordingly had them marched to Paris, assembled on the parade, ordered the colors to be taken from them by some colonels, and lodged in the church of," (the Invalids, 1 think he said,) "covered with mourning. I divided the officers who had not behaved so badly as the principal actors, amongst other regiments. Some months afterwards, I formed the regiment again under different officers, and the colors were taken from the church with great pomp, by a number of colonels, each tearing a piece off, which they burnt, and new ones were given in their stead."

"When I was about seventeen years of age," said he, " I narrowly escaped being drowned in the Seine. While swimming, cramp seized me, and after several ineffectual struggles, I sunk. I experienced at that moment all the sensations of dying, and lost all recollection. However, after I had sunk, the current carried me upon a bank of sand, on the edge of which it threw me, where I lay senseless for I know not how long, and was restored to life by the aid of some of my young companions, who by accident saw me lying there. Previous to this, they had given me up for lost, as they saw me sink, and the current of the river had carried me down to a considerable distance."

While looking over a number of papers (chiefly Portsmouth), he observed an article stating that * * * had made large purchases in the north of Ireland. "Ah," said Napoleon, "some of my money has gone to pay for those estates. After the abdication at Fontainebleau, upwards of forty millions of francs, my private property, was seized and taken from the treasurer near Orleans. Of this money, about five and twenty millions were divided amongst T * * *, M * *, H * *, and C * * *. The money thus seized included the marriage portion of the Empress Marie Louise, which had been paid in sovereigns of gold, and old German coin. The remainder was placed in the French treasury. The whole of these sums had been guaranteed to me by the treaty of Fontainebleau. The share which C * * obtained was very large, and the exact amount of it is known to me."

The talents requisite in a good general then came under his observation. "The mind of a general ought to resemble and be as clear as the field-glass of a telescope, *et jamais se faire des tableaux*. Of all the generals who preceded him, and perhaps all those who have followed, Turenne was the greatest. Maréchal Saxe, a mere general *pas d'esprit*; (no genius) Luxembourgh, *beaucoup; le grand Frédéric, beaucoup*, (much; Frederick the Great, much) and a quick and ready perception of every thing. Your Marlborough, besides being a great general, *avait aussi beaucoup d'esprit*, (also had much genius.) Judging from Wellington's actions, from his despatches, and above all from his conduct towards Ney, I should pronounce him to be *un homme de peu d'esprit sans générosité et sans grandeur d'ame*, (a man of little genius, without generosity, and without greatness of soul.) Such I know to be the opinion of Benjamin Constant, and of Madame de Staël, who said, that except as a general, he had not two ideas. As a general, however, to find his equal amongst your own nation, you must go back to the time of Marlborough, but as anything else, I think that history will pronounce him to be *un homme borné*," (a contracted man.)

21*st*.—At about six minutes before ten o'clock at night, three distinct shocks of an earthquake were felt at Longwood. The whole of the house was shaken with a rumbling, clattering noise at first, as if some heavy body, like a loaded wagon, was **dragged along the upper apartments, succeeded by an evident tremulous** motion of the ground, the glasses rattling on the table, and the pictures receding from the walls. The duration of the whole might have been from sixteen to twenty seconds, as Captain Blakeney and myself, who were sitting together at the time that it occurred, had sufficient time from its commencement until it was over, to reason and reciprocally ask from what it could proceed, before we guessed at the right cause, which we discovered simultaneously before it ceased. No mischief was done.* Generals Montholon, Gourgaud, all the household attendants and English servants came out. No alarm appeared to exist amongst them. General Montholon informed me, that his son Tristan, who was asleep, was awoke by the shock, and exclaimed that somebody was endeavoring to throw him out of the bed. General Gourgaud also felt three distinct shocks. Upon inquiry being made of some of the sentinels about the house, they replied, that they had not experienced any thing extraordinary. This may be accounted for by the fact of the wind having been so strong at the time, that they were obliged to use considerable exertion in walking against it. The sensation was very strongly felt in our kitchen, about forty yards from the house, and at the guard-room, about five hundred yards distant, particularly by those men who were lying down on the ground.

Very little mischief was done in the island. It appeared that the direction of the shocks was perpendicular. Had it been lateral, Jamestown must have been overwhelmed with immense masses of rock.

22nd.—Saw Napoleon in his bed-room. When I entered it, he was employed in making some calculations. He raised his eyes, looked at me, and said, smiling, "Well Mr. Doctor, *tremblement de terre* (earthquake) last night." I observed that I had experienced three distinct shocks. After he had remained a short time at his calculations, he got up, and said that he was in bed at the time it occurred. " At the moment of the first shock," continued

* Although Napoleon was in bed, which he did not leave during the time of the shocks, some veracious person wrote to England that " Bonaparte endeavored to escape out of the house, but was stopped by the sentinels," which falsehood was eagerly inserted in some of the ministerial papers.

he, "I imagined, and said to myself, some accident has happened to the Conqueror; she has taken fire and is blown up,* or else some powder magazine on the island has exploded. At the second shock, however, I immediately perceived what it was, and said it was an earthquake." I asked if he had heard the rumbling noise which accompanied it, and that I thought the duration of it had been from sixteen to eighteen seconds. Napoleon replied that he thought it had lasted altogether about twelve seconds. He mentioned that he had felt the shock of an earthquake once before at Ferrara, at break of day. Some more conversation about earthquakes then took place, during which I mentioned that a shock had been felt in St. Helena in the year 1756, and another in 1782. I said, that it was likely the fanatics and the superstitious in the island would attribute the earthquake to his presence; for the Portuguese had said that the strong and destructive southeast wind which prevailed at Madeira in 1815, when the Northumberland arrived off Funchal, and had done so much mischief, had been produced by his arrival. He laughed very heartily at this, and observed, that to make a good tale of it (the earthquake), it ought to have occurred immediately upon his arrival, or a few days after.

Napoleon then said that he had been informed, Lord Moira had commanded twenty thousand additional European troops in India. "I do not believe it," said he, "but if there is any necessity to send troops to India, it is owing to the imbecility of your ministers, in having given up any possession beyond the Cape to the French If true, it has been most probably caused by some intriguing French adventurers, of whom there are now so many thousands without employment, who, joining necessity to their hatred of you, have stirred up the Mahrattas against you. Instead of having given up Pondicherry and the Isle de Bourbon to the French, you ought to have acted as the Romans did to the Carthaginians, and said, ' You shall not stir beyond such a lati-

* When this surmise was mentioned a short time afterwards to Admiral Plampin, the following remark was made : " Ay, ay, the d——d rascal supposed so, because he wished it !"

tude, not forever, because that would be an injustice, but **for ten years or longer**, until your fears for the safety of the Indies are over. My opinion is, that you having given up Pondicherry and Bourbon to the French, will cost you ten thousand more Europeans in India, without benefiting France in the position she is, under those imbeciles the Bourbons. Even when I was in power, I would not have given a *quattrino* (a farthing) for those possessions, had it not been for the hopes that I always entertained of driving you out of India; to effect which and to maintain a correspondence, the Isle of France or of Bourbon was so necessary. Every year I received ambassadors from the Nabobs and other Indian princes, especially those of the Mahrattas, imploring help from me, and offering to drive you from India, provided I would assist them with fourteen or sixteen thousand infantry, artillery, and officers. They offered to find all the cavalry if I would send officers to instruct their troops. The hatred they expressed against you was astonishing. Every year I had those proposals through different channels. Very frequently by the Isle of France, *mercantuzzi* (petty merchants) came with letters for me, in Danish vessels, and sometimes over land, which they had concealed about them. Several came in disguise by * *. Possibly you may have some interested views in giving up Pondicherry, thinking that thereby you may smuggle some of your India goods by French tenders into France. But this cannot be of sufficient weight against the great injury arising from the proximity to your Indian possessions of a rival nation like the French. Your having given up that colony, will also excite envy and a desire to recover all they formerly had, whereas, if they had none, they would forget that they ever had any possessions in India. You ought not to have allowed the French or any other nation to have put their nose (*metere il naso*) beyond the Cape. You ought to monopolize the whole China trade to yourselves. Instead of going to war with the Chinese, it were better to make war with the nations who desire to trade with them. You ought not to suffer the Americans to send a ship there. You give up Batavia to the Dutch, who, next to the French, it was your interest to shut out from India. The Dutch use a large quantity of tea, which should be supplied by you. The first and grand object of every nation is to consider its own interests, especially when every other country gains something. After my fall, you might have had anything you liked to ask for, but whilst other nations were acquiring territory, you abandoned your first interests, and even neglected to make a treaty favorable to your commerce, for which you are now suffering, and will suffer, and the expedients you have put into execution will only procrastinate the evil day."

25*th*.—Napoleon sent for me in the evening about eight o'clock. Found him in his bed-room. He complained of slight head-ache and pain in the right side of the face, which he said he had felt immediately upon going into the garden, in consequence of the effect of the wind, and which had prevented him from staying out more than a quarter of an hour. He had some nausea, and eat scarcely any thing at dinner. After I had recommended him what I thought advisable, he asked me (as he had done sometimes before) of what kind of temperament I took him to be, what was necessary to be done to keep him in a state of good health? I replied, that I conceived him to be of a temperament which required much activity; that it was necessary for him to employ both his physical and mental faculties almost constantly, and that without the exercise of both the mind and the body, it was my opinion he could not long remain in health. That he was a man who required to stir much about. "You are right," replied the emperor, "such has been necessary to me through my life, such is now, and such will be as long as the machine holds. Exercise of the mind I almost daily take in my writings and otherwise; and exercise of the body I should take even in this island, were I not in the hands of a *boja* (hangman.) But under the present system it can never take place. Never can I put myself in the way of being insulted by sentinels, or receiving a *fusillade* (a volley,) if I stirred off the high-road."

26*th*.—Saw Napoleon at nine o'clock. He complained of the sensation of soreness in the lower extremities. His legs, especially the left, swelled, and the ankles pitted upon pressure. Appetite deficient. Some nausea at times. Gums spongy. In addition to exercise, &c., I recommended the continuance of a greater quantity of antiscorbutic vegetables. He objected to taking a dose of physic, which I advised, not on account of any dread which he had of it, or of its bad taste, but because he was of opinion that the more medicine was administered, the more one stood in need of it. "Take a dose of medicine once," said he, " and in all probability you will be obliged to take an additional hundred afterwards."

He then eat his breakfast before me, which consisted of two or three radishes, a little toast and butter, followed by a little *café au lait*, (coffee.)

28*th*.—Saw Napoleon at eleven, A.M. Appeared to be in nearly the same state as yesterday. Ankles œdematous; appetite bad; eat nothing since breakfast yesterday. His body has been rendered so extremely sensible to external impressions, that the slightest exposure to wind or cold produced a catarrhal or rheumatic affection. I proposed to call in Mr. Baxter, giving as a reason, that when a person of so much consequence, and in such peculiar circumstances, was even slightly indisposed, it was proper to call in the first medical advice. Napoleon replied, "There is no necessity for it. If all the colleges of medicine in France and England were assembled, they would give the same advice that you have done, viz., to take exercise on horseback. I myself know as well as any physician what is necessary for me. It is exercise. Calling in Baxter to me would be like sending a physician to a man who was starving with hunger, instead of giving him a loaf of bread. I have no objection to your making known to him my state of health if you like, and I am well aware that he will say *exercise*. As long as the present system is in force, I will never stir out." When I again urged the subject, "What," said he, " would you have me render myself liable to be stopped and insulted by a sentinel, as Madame Bertrand was some days ago, at ten minutes past six in the evening, and while it was still daylight? If I had been in her place, it would have occurred, as the sentinel had orders to stop every body. It would have been a fine subject for this governor to have written upon to London, and to have stuck a caricature in the print shops, of Napoleon Bonaparte stopped at the gate, with a sentinel charging his bayonet upon him. It would have been very amusing to this * * *, and the Londoners would have laughed. Until matters are put on the footing they were in Cockburn's time, which were approved of by his government, or an equivalent given, I shall never stir out. The hill is posi ive; no alterations ought to have taken place, except such as were ordered by the Prince Regent and the privy council, and signed by the Regent or Lord Liverpool; not by Lord Bathurst. I consider all restrictions not made by them as null. Force certainly can execute any thing, and to avoid the possibility of being insulted, I have shut myself up; and until I know to a certainty what restrictions there are, and by whom made, I shall not venture out, or expose myself to the caprice of my enemy By prohibting me to speak to such persons as I might meet, he offered to me the greatest insult which could be given to man. It is true that he has since taken it off; but if he has the power to make restrictions as he pleases, he may renew it to-morrow upon some pretext To a man who has the power of doing what he likes, a pretext will never be wanting. You may tell him what I have said, and that I believe the intentions of * * * * * and * * * * * were and are to put and end to me, by inducing disease from confinement, and that such are not the intentions of the Prince Regent, of Lord Liverpool, or Lord Sidmouth. For the restrictions *sur la morale* (moral) imposed by him upon a man, like me, have the same effect in imprisoning me, as chains and irons on the legs would have upon galley slaves. To robbers and galley slaves, phyiscal restrictions are imposed—*aux gens éclairés*, (to enlightened people) moral ones. There is not a little lieutenant in that regiment who would go out if subjected to the restrictions imposed upon me. I asked the ambassador, ' Would you, my lord, go out under the restrictions of not speaking more to any person you met than, How do you do? unless in the presence of an officer? (It is true that he has taken this off, but he may put it on again according to his caprice.) Would you go out under the restriction of not being able to move to the right or to the left of the road? Would you stir out under the obligation of coming in again at six o'clock in the evening, or otherwise run the risk of being stopped by sentinels at the gates?' He replied instantly, '*Non, je ferais comme vous, je resterais dans ma chambre,*' (no, I would do as you do, I would remain in my chamber.) There are different ways of assassinating a man; the pistol, the sword, poison, or morally assassinating, as * * * * * * and * * * * * are doing to me. It is the same in the end, excepting that the latter is the most cruel. When the admiral, who was a man *d'un caractère aur* (of an austere character,) was here, you recollect what a different kind of life I led. I rode out four or five times a week, saw company, and even invited English officers, ladies, and others to dine. In the admiral I had confidence. His word I believed, and not the slightest suspicion of sinister design ever entered my head, *parcequ'il avait la marche droite et sincère, rien de tortueuse ou de tracassante,* (because he pursued an even and sincere course, nothing vexatious or perplexing.) Though I disagreed with him, and thought he was *un homme dur*, (a hard man) still I felt confidence in his character and in his integrity. Had I any intention of committing suicide, as this *geolier* (jailer) insinuates, I should have done it in the beginning, when, from not having been accustomed to it, I must have felt it most oppressive. Besides, if I intended it, a pistol would be my resource. *Je n'aime pas la longue guerre,* (I do not like a long war.) What inconvenience ever occurred during Cockburn's time by my riding out? The intentions of * * * * * * are to impose restrictions of such a nature, that I, without degrading my character, and rendering myself an object of contempt in the eyes of the world, must imprison myself; thereby in the course of time to bring on disease, which, in a frame impaired by confinement and the blood being decomposed, must prove mortal, and that I may thus expire in protracted agonies, which may have the appearance of a natural death. This is the plan, and is a manner of assassinating just as certain, but more cruel and criminal than the sword or the pistol."

"The only one of us," added he, "who goes out, I may say, is Gourgaud, and he has been stopped upwards of fifty times. Had I been in his place, the same thing would have happened to me. Once during the admiral's time I was stopped, but he instantly *metteva l'isola sotto sopra*, (turned the island topsy turvy,) on account of it; and I clearly saw that he was really displeased, and that he took every precaution to prevent the recurrence of a similar circumstance. Now this brute would, on the contrary, be pleased with it, or with anything else that would have a tendency to lessen or to degrade my character."

"I am well convinced," added Napoleon, "that the barbarous manner in which I am treated will be revenged by the blood of some innocent Englishman. By the arguments and doctrines of your ministers, that it is *useful* to keep me here, every act, however atrocious, may be justified. Would it not have been *useful* to me to have procured the assassination of Nelson or Wellington? Would it not now be *useful* to the French nation to get rid of all the allied troops by poisoning the bread and the water? Would it not be *useful* to them to assassinate Wellington? It is not the *utility* of an act which is to be considered, it is its justice; for by the former principle, every species of crime may be apparently justified, as being useful, and *therefore* necessary. It is the doctrine of Talleyrand."

Soon after this, Sir Hudson Lowe came to Longwood, and having made some inquiries respecting Napoleon's health, asked if I had had any particular conversation with him upon the subject of his complaint? In reply, I communicated to him the foregoing conversation, avoiding the repetition of the epithet *bourreau*. His excellency called Major Gorrequer to be a witness to some parts of it, viz., that about Lord Amherst, which he said he did not believe, and the intentions which Napoleon attributed to certain persons, and asked if I had made any reply? I said, No. He observed, that a reply might easily have been made, if I had been disposed to do so, but that it appeared I was of the same way of thinking as General Bonaparte asserted Lord Amherst had been; and asked, if such were the case? I answered, that as a medical man, I had strongly recommended Napoleon to take exercise on horseback. This did not satify Sir Hudson Lowe, who, in an angry tone and manner, repeated his question. I replied, that as my opinions, when given in reply to his questions, had latterly caused so much anger, I must beg leave to decline giving any, unless upon medical subjects: that, moreover, my opinion was of little consequence, adding, that as a medical man, I had strongly recommended exercise. This reply greatly displeased Sir Hudson Lowe, who observed that it was in vain to expect any thing good from a person possessed of such sentiments; that he had no confidence in any person about General Bonaparte. After a tolerable long harangue, in which he accused Napoleon of having crammed the ambassador's head with calumnies, and purposely delayed seeing him until the day before his departure, in order that he (Sir Hudson) might not have an opportunity of refuting them; he concluded by saying, " Do you not think, sir, that General Bonaparte has treated me most shamefully in that business?" I replied, that Napoleon had been so unwell as not to be in a situation to receive strangers; that until the last moment, he had been undecided whether to receive his lordship or not; and that Lord Amherst had been at his (Sir Hudson's) house for several days, during which he must have had ample opportunities of making his lordship acquainted with every particular. That if I was rightly informed, Lord Amherst had seen and conversed with him for some hours after his lordship had with Napoleon, with whom he had been only about two hours. This reply excited his excellency's wrath, who, looking at me with an expression of countenance I shall never forget, said, " If it were not that it would be made a subject of complaint, I should immediately, and without waiting the orders of government, send you off the island, sir. I have received no official intelligence from government concerning your appointment; you are not of my choosing; you are only permitted to visit General Bonaparte as a medical man." I observed that I was acting according to his own instructions, by confining myself to medical subjects. He repeated his threat of sending me off the island;

to which I answered by telling him that a dismissal from St Helena would not give me the smallest uneasiness. After this, Sir Hudson went down to Count Bertrand's, where he remained about half an hour. On his return he sent for me, and after saying, that General Bonaparte had been represented by Count Bertrand to be in a much worse state of health than I had mentioned, ordered me to send him a written report of his health.

About four o'clock, Count Balmaine, with Baron and Madame Sturmer, came as far as the inner gate of Longwood, where they met General and Madame Bertrand, who with the little Arthur, and a maid-servant, were walking out. Shortly afterwards, General Montholon joined them. They remained together for nearly an hour, walking between the guard-room and the inner gate. It was amusing to observe the gestures of Sir Thomas Reade, who was all the time standing at or moving before Captain Blakeney's door with a telescope in his hand; especially at a time when a thick fog came on, which completely obscured them from the knight's view, who was vainly endeavoring to penetrate it with his glass.

Sir Hudson Lowe's visit to Count Bertrand, I am informed, was to offer that a soldier's barrack should be put up at Longwood for Napoleon to walk under, as a substitute for the deficiency of continuous shade. Some conversation also took place about the restrictions, in which observations of a nature similar to those of Napoleon to me in the morning, were made to Sir Hudson Lowe by Count Bertrand, who also informed his excellency of the opinion expressed by Lord Amherst.

Saw Napoleon in the evening. He was in much the same state as in the morning. Told me that he had seen Madame Sturmer through his glass, and passed some commendations upon the rosy bloom of her cheeks.

20*th.*—Signal made for Captain Blakeney to proceed to Plantation House. Sent my report of Napoleon's health by him, and made application for some sea-water, to be sent to Longwood for a bath for the use of Napoleon.

Saw Napoleon, who was in much better spirits. He had eaten

freely of antiscorbutics. His gums were a little better. The lower extremities nearly the same in point of size, but not so painful.

Had a jocular conversation with him about patron saints. He asked who was my patron saint,—what was my Christian name? I replied, that my first was a family name; that I was called after Barry, Lord Avonmore, an Irish peer. "But," said he, laughing, "you must have some patron saint to befriend you, and plead your cause in the next world?" I mentioned my second Christian name. "Ah!" said he, "then *he* will plead for you. St. Napoleon ought to be very much obliged to me, and do everything in his power for me in the world to come. Poor fellow; nobody knew him before. He had not even a day in the calendar. I got him one, and persuaded the Pope to give him the fifteenth of August, my birth-day. I recollect," continued he, "when I was in Italy, a priest preaching about a poor sinner who had departed this life. His soul appeared before God, and he was required to give an account of all his actions. The evi. and the good were afterwards thrown into opposite scales, in order to see which preponderated. That containing the good proved much the lightest, and instantly flew up to the beam. His poo soul was condemned to the infernal regions, conducted by angels to the bottomless pit, delivered over to devils, and thrown into the flames. 'Already,' said the preacher, 'had the devouring element covered his feet and legs, and proceeded upwards even unto his bowels; in his vitals, oh! brethren, he felt them. He sunk, and only his head appeared above the waves of fire, when he cried out to God, and afterwards to his patron saint. 'Oh! patron,' said he, 'look down upon me; oh! take compassion upon me, and throw into the scale of my good deeds all the lime and stone which I gave to repair the convent of ————.' His saint instantly took the hint, gathered together all the lime and stone, threw them into the scale of good, which immediately preponderated; the scale of evil sprung up to the beam, and the sinner's soul into paradise at the same moment. 'Now you see by this, brethren, how useful it is too keep the convents in repair, for had it not been for the lime and stone bestowed by this sinner, his poor soul would even now, children, be consuming in hell-fire; and yet you are so blind as to let the convent and the church, built by your forefathers, fall to ruin.' At this time," continued he, laughing, " these *canaglie* wanted to get a new convent built, and had recourse to this expedient to procure money, which, after this, poured in upon them from all quarters."

Napoleon then began to rally me about my profession. " You medical people," said he, " will have more lives to answer for in the other world than even we generals. What will you say for yourself," said he, laughing, " when you are called to account for all the souls of poor sailors you have despatched to the other world ? or what will your saint say for you, when the accusing angel proclaims, ' such a number you sent out of the world, by giving them heating medicines, when you ought to have given them cooling ones, and vice versa ; so many more, because you mistook their complaints, and bled them too much ; others because you did not bleed them enough, numbers because they were *canaille*, and you did not pay them as much attention as you could have done to the captain or the admiral, and because you were over your bottle, or at the theatre, or with a fine girl, and did not like to be disturbed, or after *drink* (in English) when you went and distributed medicines, *a dritto ed a torto* (right and wrong). How many because you were not present at the time a change in the complaint took place, when a medicine given at the moment might have saved them ? How many others because the provisions were bad, and you would not complain for fear of offending the *fournisseurs* (contractors) ?"

I replied by observing, that on the score of conscience I was perfectly easy in my mind ; that human nature was liable to err ; that very likely I had made mistakes, but not intentional ones ; nor had I ever paid less attention to the *canaille* than to the officers ; and endeavored as much as possible, as I perceived that he was half in earnest, to uphold the honor of my profession. I also explained to him, that in our service, the surgeons could gain nothing by not complaining of the *fournisseurs*, &c. Napoleon answered, that certainly a man ought always to be judged by his intentions; but that there were abuses in all departments, which were principally kept up by people being either interested, or afraid to complain: that he had endeavored to eradicate them as much as possible, in which he had effected much; but had not been able perfectly to succeed. "My opinion," continued he, "is, that physicians kill as many as we generals. When they despatch a number of souls to the other world, either through ignorance, mistake, or not having properly examined their complaints, they are just as cool and as little concerned as a general with whom I am acquainted, who lost three thousand men in storming a hill. Having succeeded, after several desperate attempts, he observed, with great *sang froid*, ' Oh, it was not this hill I wanted to take, it was another; this is of no utility,' and returned back again to his former position." I remarked, that it appeared he thought physicians to be as bad and as ignorant as they are described to be in Molière or Gil Blas. He laughed, and said, "I believe that there are a great many of Molière's physicians. Of surgery, I have quite a different opinion; as there you do not work in the dark. There you at least have daylight, and your senses to guide and assist you. You recollect having heard of Sieyes?" I replied in the affirmative. "Sieyes," continued he, "before the revolution, was almoner to one of the princesses. One day, when he was performing mass in the chapel before herself, her attendants, and a large congregation, something occurred which made the princess get up and retire. Her example was followed by her ladies in waiting, and by the whole of the nobility, officers, and others, who attended more out of complaisance to her than from any true sense of religion. Sieyes was very busy reading his breviary, and for some time did not perceive it. Lifting up his eyes, however, from his book, lo! he observed that the princess, nobles, and all the others *comme il faut* (very properly), had disappeared. With an air of displeasure and contempt he shut the book, hastily descended from the pulpit, exclaiming, '*I* do not say mass for the *canaille* ;' and went out of the chapel, leaving the service half finished. Now," said he, laughing very heartily, "many of you physicians would leave a patient half cured, because he was one of the *canaille.*"

He then spoke of Larrey. " Larrey," said he, " was the most honest man, and the best friend to the soldier, that I ever knew. Vigilant and indefatigable in his exertions for the wounded, Larrey was seen on the field of battle, after an action, accompanied by a train of young surgeons, endeavoring to discover if any signs of life remained in the bodies. In the most inclement weather, and at all times of the night and the day, Larrey was to be found amongst the wounded. He scarcely allowed a moment's repose to his assistants, and kept them eternally at their posts. He tormented the generals and disturbed them out of their beds at night, whenever he wanted accommodations or assistance for the wounded or sick. They were all afraid of him, as they knew he would instantly come and make a complaint to me. He paid court to none of them, and was the implacable enemy of the *fournisseurs.*"

Speaking about service on board of ships of war at sea during the winter, especially of a certain class, I remarked, that the seamen were better off in point of being able to warm themselves at a fire than the officers. " Why so ?" said Napoleon. I replied, " Because they have the advantage of the galley fire,* where they can warm and dry themselves." " And why not the officers ?" I said, that it would not be exactly decorous for the officers to mix in that familiar way with the men. " *Ah! la morgue aristocratique, la rage aristocratique,*" (Oh ! the aristocratical haughtiness, the aristocratical rage,) exclaimed Napoleon. " Why, in my campaigns I used to go to the lines in the *bivouacs,* sit down with the meanest soldier, converse, laugh, and joke with him. I always prided myself on being *l'homme du peuple,*" (the man of the people.) I observed, that a man in his exalted situation might do without impropriety that which, if done by an inferior officer, especially on board of a ship, might produce too much familiarity, perhaps contempt, and thereby relaxation of discipline

* The galley is the kitchen on board of a man of war.

"*La morgue aristocratique,*" cried Napoleon again, "you are the most aristocratical nation in the world. Had I been one of those *principiotti* (princes) in Germany, your oligarchy would never have sent me here. But because *je suis l'homme du peuple ;* (I am the man of the people,) because I may say that I raised myself from the *canaille* to the greatest height of power without the aid of the aristocracy or hereditary rights ; because a long line of nobles or of petty princes did not distinguish my name ; because, in fact, I was not one of them, they determined to oppress and humiliate me when in their power. Lords Bathurst and Castlereagh, *la canaille de l'aristocracie,* (the refuse of aristocracy,) are the persons who have ordered all these attempts. John Bull will comprehend that I am oppressed, *parceque je sors du peuple,* (because I am one of the people,) in order to prevent any of them from presuming to elevate themselves to a level with the aristocracy."

He concluded by observing, "that the governor always took a witness with him to Bertrand's, for the purpose, he supposed, of testifying to every thing that he thought proper to assert. That in all probability he made a *procès verbal* as he liked, and got the other to sign it. That therefore, to prevent his *making* conversations, he had ordered Bertrand to write an official letter* to him, stating their grievances and what they wanted."

30*th.*—Napoleon much in the same state. Went to Plantation House to report. Found that Sir Hudson Lowe had gone out. Met him at Longwood on my return. Informed him of the state of Napoleon's health ; and in reply to some of his observations, told him that there was nothing immediately dangerous, but that œdematous swellings of the extremities taking place with a man of Napoleon's time of life, and of his temperament and present habits, were always to be looked upon with a suspicious eye, as such were frequently the primary symptoms of dropsy.

His excellency said, that his principal object in coming to Longwood had been to obtain an answer from Count Bertrand, to an offer which he had made on the 28th of the month, to put up a

* Appendix No XII.

soldier's barrack seventy feet long, which might be formed into a temporary gallery to walk in, until an answer arrived from England relative to building the new house. That he could get no reply from Bertrand, but a shrug of the shoulders. That Count Bertrand had been very violent in his language, and had not merely asked for one or two things, but had insisted " that every thing should be put upon the same footing as during Sir George Cockburn's time. That the emperor would not stir out unless permission were given to him (Bertrand) to admit persons by his pass into Longwood. That he should write and hold correspondence with whoever he liked, go where he liked, enter what houses he liked, in fact do what he liked in the island without any restriction." He then asked if I had heard anything from him of the conversation which they had held with the commissioners? I replied, that " I had not heard him mention even their names." His excellency said, that " it was very extraordinary, as General Bonaparte had made some very strong remarks about them to Mr. Balcombe."

Saw Napoleon again in the evening. He complained of pain in his teeth and cheeks, which he attributed to having taken a walk in the garden for ten minutes. Proposed to him that the barrack should be erected. He replied that " he stood in need of exercise in the open air, and not in a covered gallery. That he had caused a gallery of a league in length to be built at ——, in France, but that it had not answered the purpose. Moreover, that in summer the billiard-room became so hot at five o'clock in the afternoon, from the rays of the sun penetrating through it, as to render it impossible to remain there; that a wooden barrack would be worse; that it would therefore be useless to erect it, as the shade of the trees was what was desired."

October 1st.—Saw Napoleon in his bed-room at eight, A.M. He complained of a dull pain (*dolore sordo*) in the right hypochondriac region, immediately under the cartilages of the ribs, which he said he experienced yesterday morning for the first time. Sensation in the right shoulder, which he described to be more of numbness than of pain. Slight inclination to cough. Want of rest at night. He said that he felt as if he wanted to lean or press his side against something (*vorrie appoggiar mi contra qualche cosa.*) Gums spongy, and his legs a little swelled. Pulse 68. Appetite tolerable. Said he felt something in the right side which never was there before. Told him that it might probably be owing to costiveness, and recommended a dose of physic, which I said would also be proper if it were the commencement of a liver complaint, the prevailing disease of the island. That if it increased, and were accompanied by other symptoms, there could not be a doubt of it being hepatitis; in which case it would be necessary to have recourse to proper remedies, which I specified, together with abstinence from wine and a suitable diet. He shook his head at the proposal of physic. I told him that if it were hepatitis, it must not be neglected, as if not taken in time, it would terminate fatally. He replied, "*Almeno avrò questa consolazione, che la mia morte, sarà un disonore eternale alla nazione Inglese,* (I shall at least have this consolation, that my death will be an eternal disgrace to the English nation,) which has sent me to this climate to die under the hands of a * * *." I observed, that he ought not to accelerate his own death by refusing to take proper remedies. He replied, "*Ce qui est écrit, est écrit,* (what is written, is written,) from above," looking up. "*Nos journées sont comptées.*" (Our days are numbered.) I answered, that according to that doctrine, all medical aid was useless. He made no reply.

With respect to diet and abstinence from wine, he observed, that he was a man who had never committed any excesses either in eating or drinking. That he drank very little wine; however, that he found the little he took was absolutely necessary, always finding himself better after it, and was convinced that if he left it off, he should sink rapidly. He then went into a salt-water bath, and had a long conversation with me upon medical subjects.

2*d.*—Napoleon felt relieved by the salt-water bath yesterday. Continued much in want of rest. Recommended exercise on horseback, &c.

Saw him again at ten in bed. His legs were a little **more** swelled than in the morning. He would have taken another bath, but there was no water. Had eaten scarcely any thing. Slight head-ache

3d.—Examined the right side, and perceived that it felt firmer to the touch than the opposite one. There was also a tumefaction evident to the sight, which when pressed hard, gave a little pain. Napoleon said, that this was observed about two months since. That he had thought nothing of it, and attributed it to obesity, but that now, from its being attended with pain, he imagined it might be connected with enlargement of the liver.*

I recommended calomel, frictions to the extremities, diligent use of the flesh-brush, hot salt-water bath, a continuance of antiscorbutics, a gargle, exercise on horseback, &c. Napoleon said that the governor had written to Count Bertrand yesterday, stating that he (Napoleon) might go off the road, and down into the valley, but that the same privilege was not to be extended to his officers, unless with him. " Mere *tracasserie*," (vexation) said he, when I recommended him to profit by it. " It would only expose me to more insults; for the sentinels do not know me, and every old soldier who wished to fulfil his duty, so as to clear himself of all responsibility, would say, ' *Halte là*, (halt there) is General Bonaparte amongst you? Are you him? Oh, then, if you are him, you may pass.' Thus should I be exposed to daily insults, and be obliged to give an account of myself to every sentinel who thought it right to fulfil his duty properly. Besides, he has no right to impose more restrictions upon *questi signori*, (those gentlemen) than upon me. By the paper which they have signed, they only agree to subject themselves to such restrictions as are or may be imposed upon me. Moreover, I do not recognize his right to impose any other restrictions than those made by Admiral Cockburn, which were approved of by his government, unless he shows that they are signed by the Prince Regent or by the ministers. For if he has the power to impose

---

* As it is not the intention of the author to tire the reader with the detail of a medical journal, the enumeration of the symptoms will, for the future, be discontinued, unless where absolutely necessary.

what restrictions he likes, he may according to his caprice, or upon some pretext, which, to him, would never be wanting, lay them on again or make them worse than before. This is one of the reasons that I have not taken exercise, in order to leave nothing in his power to inflict. I do not choose to subject myself to the caprice of a man whom I do not trust, and who is my personal enemy. Besides, I never would go out without sending Gourgaud to ascertain that there was no danger of being stopped and insulted by sentinels."

I asked permission to call in Mr. Baxter to see him. He said, that if the symptoms increased, he probably would, as I wished it, provided that the governor did not interfere with it, *se sene mischia, mai,* (if he did interfere, never.)

4*th.*—Went to Plantation House, according to order, and gave Sir Hudson Lowe a written report of the state of Napoleon's health. After having read it, he said, that there were too many details in it, and that I must make out one which could be made public. Said that he had received a long letter from Count Bertrand, containing arguments similar to those which I was in the habit of using, and in which there was an allusion to Lord Liverpool, which when coupled with circumstances that had taken place some time ago, looked as if there were some correspondence in that quarter. I said, that Napoleon had always declared, that he believed Lords Liverpool and Sidmouth to be better disposed towards him than any others of the English ministers. That, indeed, I had never heard him speak ill of any of the English ministers nominatively, excepting Lords Bathurst and Castlereagh.

5*th.*—Saw Napoleon in the morning, who was much in the same state as before.

Count Montholon, Count Balmaine, and Captain Gor had a long conversation together.

6*th.*—Napoleon nearly the same. Again recommended him exercise most strongly, and told him that if he deferred it much longer, the swellings in his legs might increase so much, as to render him incapable of taking it. That if he mounted on horseback, and **rode**, I was convinced all the swellings in the lower extremities would soon disappear. He assented to this, but declared, that until things were put on the footing they had been in Sir George Cockburn's time, or equivalent, he would not go out. That he was determined to leave nothing in the power of a man who had been mad enough to prohibit him from speaking, and who, at his caprice, might order him to be blindfolded, to prevent his making a *reconnaissance*. That the restrictions were chiefly upon the *morale*, and not physical; as he might go into the wood when he liked, but that considering the person he had to deal with, he was convinced that if he did, he (the governor) would find some pretext to insult him, and he would leave nothing in his power, unless matters were put as they had been before, which would be an acknowledgment, that he was not to be subject to his caprice."

I took the liberty of observing, that he was like a man tumbling down a precipice, who would not lay hold of a rope within his grasp, by which he might save himself from inevitable death.* He laughed at this comparison, and said, "*Que le sort se fasse, nos journées sont comptées.*" (Lest fate should force itself, our days are all numbered.)

7*th*.—Napoleon nearly the same. Observed, that the governor had insinuated that he (Napoleon) wanted to kill himself. "Had I intended this," continued he, " I would have fallen upon my sword long ago, and died like a soldier. But to purposely kill myself by the slow agonies of a lingering disease, I am not fool enough to attempt. *Je n'ai jamais aimé la longue guerre.* (I never loved tedious warfare.) But there is no death, however slow and painful, that I would not prefer to dishonoring my character. A man who was once capable of imposing the restrictions of the 9th of October, and the 14th of March, is capable of laying them on again, or even worse, according to his caprice or his fears, real or imaginary. If I were to go out and be once insulted by a sentinel, it would have the effect of doing more in-

---

* The reader will, I trust, agree with me in opinion, that I was bound, as his medical adviser, to endeavor to prevail upon my patient to use any *remedy* I thought would be beneficial to his malady; for this purpose only I recommended exercise.

jury to my health than six months confinement. But this man is insensible to any moral feeling. He thinks that he has got some Corsican deserters or corporals to deal with. *C'est un mélange d'imbécilité et d'astuce.* (He is a compound of imbecility and craft.) Before I had gone out a week, he would make some insinuations, as he perpetually does, to the commissioners, and say that I had abused the permission he had given."

A large sealed packet addressed to the Earl of Liverpool, given by Count Bertrand to Captain Blakeney, for which a receipt was taken.

Communicated the substance of what Napoleon had said to Sir Hudson Lowe, to whom I repeated, that whenever Sir George Cockburn made any regulations relative to the French, he was accustomed to discuss the matter with Count Bertrand or Montholon, by means of which they were enabled to make arrangements in a manner likely to give the least offence. Sir Hudson said, that *his own measures* had been approved of by the British government, and that most of the letters which he had received, commenced by stating, that the Prince Regent approved of, and had commanded, that such and such measures should be adopted.

8th.—Napoleon walked out for a short time in the garden. Being so little accustomed to exercise, this fatigued him so much that he was obliged to sit down on the steps before the veranda. He was, however, in better spirits than yesterday, and felt benefited by the salt-water baths, and such of the other remedies as he would consent to use.

9th.—Not so well. Got cold yesterday, and complains of pains in the lower extremities, and had been very unwell in the night. " I was going to send for you early in the morning," said he, " but then I considered this poor devil of a doctor has been up all night at a ball, and has need of sleep. If I disturb him, he will have his eyes so heavy, and his intellect so confused, that he will not be able to form any correct opinion. Soon after this, I fell into a perspiration, and felt much relieved."

Immediately after I had left him, he went to bed again, where he remained for some hours.

7*

10th.—Napoleon in rather bad spirits, legs somewhat less swelled, &c.

"The governor," said he, "was at Bertrand's yesterday, and professed his wish to accommodate, but he has already done the same so often, without having come to any conclusion, that he will probably end as before. I ordered Bertrand to send for the little Major (Gorrequer), talk the matter over with him, and explain what we want. I conceive, that the only guarantee I have for my life consists in having some communication with the officers of the army and navy, and the inhabitants. For had communication existed before, this governor would not have been able to have continued his absurd restrictions so long as he has; although the place is small and wretched, and the inhabitants nearly slaves to arbitrary power, still the public opinion would have had some weight. Rumor would have reached England, and John Bull would not have suffered conduct so disgraceful to his country. What I want is to have no mystery or secrecy used about me. Whenever there is mystery, there are always bad intentions. Every thing ought to be conducted so that it might be printed, and then nothing would be printed. I care not if the house I live in were made of glass. So ought the proceedings with respect to me to be conducted. You recollect, that during the admiral's time, no attempts were made to send letters to England, nor ever would, had he remained, because the situation was tolerable. One could live then. I have explained to Bertrand my wishes relative to the receiving of visitors, and told him to communicate to the governor that he may easily arrange the matter by sending up a list himself of such persons as he will permit to visit Longwood, and to require that no insinuations shall be made to prevent them from coming, as has been the case hitherto. We can send every thing we please to Europe, and always could. With respect to the commissioners, as policy enters into that, I leave it to him. I have told him already, that I would with pleasure receive the Austrian, his wife, and the Russian, as private persons. If, however, political reasons oppose it, I care not for it, though nothing can be more ridiculous than to see those commissioners unable to come inside of the inner gate of Longwood, when they are permitted to come as far as it, and hold conferences with us as long and as often as they please, which must excite for the author of such absurdities the ridicule and contempt of every beholder. All that I desire is, that it may be clearly understood and explained to those commissioners, that political reasons alone prevent their being received at Longwood, and that they may not be crammed with such lies as have been told to them up to this day. They say they have been informed by the governor that it is all my fault; that I have refused to see them; that there does not pass a week in which this man does not make insinuations to them; and that such is the mystery and secrecy observed, that they thought themselves in Venice or Ragusa, instead of an English colony. Every week produces hints and insinuations that they have abused this or that privilege. There is nothing in the world makes a man hate another so much as insinuations; especially when they come from one in power, because he cannot repel or answer them. With respect to strangers, let him, when a ship arrives, send a list of such as he will allow to come here—I mean of the greater number, and not pick out one or two favorites. If he suspects any of them, let him say so, and no notice will be taken of them, or let him not place their names on the list. If I see strangers at all it shall be from my own will, and not because *he* likes it. Let him do this—let him leave off his insinuations, and above all, let there be no mystery, and I shall be contented."

Had some conversation with the emperor afterwards about Talleyrand. "When I returned from Italy," said he, "I went to live at a small house in the Rue Chantereine (I think). A few days afterwards the municipality of Paris ordered that it should be called *Rue de la Victoire*. Every one sought to manifest the national gratitude to me. It was proposed to give me a fine hotel in Paris, and a magnificent estate. Although I had maintained and paid the army for two years, and even paid the arrears for some time posterior, and sent more than thirty millions to the treasury of France—I was scarcely worth three hundred thousand francs. The directory, however, influenced probably by jealousy, would not consent, and said that my services were such as could not be rewarded by money. Every description of persons tried to see me. The enthusiasm was *au comble*, (at its height.) I rarely, however, associated with others than Kleber, Desaix, Caffarelli, and some *savans* The directory gave me a splendid fête. Talleyrand, who was minister of foreign affairs, gave another. I remained but a short time at either. I was afterwards nominated to the command of the army of England, which, in fact, was named so to deceive your ministers as to its real destination, which was Egypt."

" Talleyrand had been bishop of Autun during the revolution, and was one of the three bishops who swore to the civil constitution of the clergy. He was afterwards sent to England, but becoming suspected during the fury of the revolution, he fled to America, where he remained until after the 13th Vendémiaire, when his name was erased from the list of emigrants. He insinuated himself into the confidence of the directory, and was made minister of foreign affairs, and as such had constant communication with me. It was then customary to celebrate the anniversary of the execution of Louis the Sixteenth, at which Talleyrand wished that I should attend. I replied, that I had no public functions; that I did not like the ceremony; that fêtes were celebrated for victories, but that the victims left on the field of battle were lamented with tears; that celebrating the death of a man, was not the policy of a government, but that of a faction. Talleyrand maintained that it was just, because it was politic; that all countries had rejoiced at the death of tyrants, and that my presence was expected. After a long argument, it was arranged that the Institute should attend, which I was to accompany as a member of the class of mechanics to which I belonged. Although I avoided public notice, the multitude, which paid no attention to the directory, but had waited to see me go out, filled the air with cries of ' *Vive le général de l'armée d'Italie.*' (Long live the general of the army of Italy.) Never yet," added he, " was there a general who was more beloved by his troops.

"To show you the confidence that I had in the disposition of the army," said he, "I need only recount to you an event which will be consecrated by history. Five or six days after my landing at Cannes, the advanced guard of my little army met the advance of a division marching from Grenoble against me. Cambronne, who commanded my troops, wanted to address them, but they would not listen to him. They also refused to receive Raoul, whom I sent afterwards. When I was informed of this, I went to them myself, with a few of my guard, with their arms reversed, and called out, 'The first soldier who pleases may come forward and kill his emperor.' It operated like an electric shock, and '*Vive l'empereur*' resounded through the ranks; the division and my guards fraternized, all joined me, and advanced together to Grenoble. Close by Grenoble the brave Labedoyère, a young man, animated by the noblest sentiments, and disgusted by the conduct of the *misérables*, against whom France had fought and bled for so many years, joined me with his regiment. At Grenoble, I found the regiment, in which, twenty-five years before, I had been captain, and some others, drawn up on the ramparts to oppose me. No sooner did they see me, than enthusiastic cries of *Vive l'empereur* were heard, not only from them, but from the whole of the national guard and the populace; the gates were torn down, and I entered in triumph. What is singular, and which strikingly shows the sentiments of the troops, is, that in a moment the six thousand men by whom I was thus joined, mounted old tri-colored cockades, which they had kept as a treasure, when the army had been obliged to adopt the Bourbon antinational flag. I advanced to Lyons, where I was joined by the troops charged to defend it against me, and the Count d'Artois was happy to escape, escorted by a single dragoon, from the city he had commanded a few hours before. To all his entreaties, offers, and prayers, *Vive l'empereur* was the reply."

While sitting on the steps of the veranda this day, Napoleon observed Mr. Stokoe walking with me in the garden, and ordered him to be called. He asked him several questions in Italian.

Sir Hudson Lowe and Major Gorrequer were for some time at Count Bertrand's this day.

Sir Thomas Reade told me that Sir Hudson Lowe had received a sealed parcel from Bertrand, addressed to Lord Liverpool, which he would forward, although he knew that it contained complaints against himself. That he did not care what complaints they made. That if it were not for the d—d commissioners, things would be better. He then asked me if I had much conversation with them? I said, very little, that I had observed a marked alteration in their conduct towards me latterly; instead of asking me numerous questions as before, they rarely spoke, except upon common-place subjects. He observed, that "it was very likely they (the commissioners) would tell the French the tenor of my reports on Bonaparte's health, as the French had represented him to be worse than I had described him to be."

Major Gorrequer came to Longwood by signal, and had a long conference with Count Bertrand.

11*th.*—Saw Napoleon in bed at seven A. M. Complained of having been restless all night, and of increase of pain in his side and shoulder. Had a return of palpitation, &c., which he attributed, and probably with reason, to his having sat in the sun for some time yesterday. I recommended such remedies as were proper, some of which he put in practice.

Saw him again at three. He had been in the hot bath, and found much relief from it. His appetite was considerably diminished.

Sir Hudson Lowe at Longwood, very busy in measuring the distance at which the sentinels were posted.

A ship arrived from the Cape with stores, and a mail from England.

12*th.*—Saw Napoleon with his legs in a tub of hot water. Told me that he felt uneasy, and *di cattivo umore* (in bad humor.)

Sir Hudson Lowe had a long interview with Count Bertrand; the latter endeavored to explain to him the point in dispute, viz. that being obliged to send all letters through him open to such persons resident on the island, as he (the governor) might allow to visit them, was considered a useless humiliation. If he wished to forward a letter privately to England, or to carry on an improper correspondence with an individual or individuals in the island, he (Bertrand) having the power of inviting a certain number of persons to visit Longwood, and to retain them there some hours (as the governor said he would grant,) would surely embrace *that*, as the proper moment to give them such letters, or otherwise to communicate improperly with them, rather than hazard the compromising of himself and them, by sending a sealed letter containing improper communications through the orderly officer, which, should suspicions arise, might be opened, and ruin the person to whom it was addressed. Sir Hudson Lowe, however, would not understand this. Count Bertrand also mentioned to him that the emperor considered a free intercourse with the inhabitants as the only guarantee he had for his life.

When Major Gorrequer was at Count Bertrand's on the 10th, the latter informed him that the governor's proceedings had been so illegal, and involved in such mystery and obscurity, that some of the officers of the 53d regiment, conceiving that there might be criminal intentions in view, had signified to them not to be afraid, for that in the 53d regiment there were neither assassins nor executioners to be found. Also, that Sir George Cockburn had said, soon after the arrival of Napoleon, " If I put sentinels in such a manner, and insist upon such and such measures, this man will shut himself up and never stir out. He will not live six months. I will not be the means of assassinating any body. I will arrange matters so that he shall have liberty, and at the same time not afford the least chance of escaping from the island which is all that I can effect or indeed care about."

14*th*.—This morning, on presenting myself according to custom to call upon Napoleon, I was informed that he was asleep, and had left word for me to go down to Count Bertrand. Had a conversation with the latter, the purport of which was, that the emperor had been given to understand that I was in the habit of writing bulletins of his health, daily, or at more distant periods, and that it was his desire that every bulletin should be shown to him, the emperor, before being sent. That any person acting as his physician must necessarily have a portion of his confidence; and that he would not consent to be styled General Bonaparte in reports made by him, as such would appear in Europe to be an acquiescence on his part in the use of such a title, which he would sooner die than consent to; that the words *l'empereur* must be used, and that I had better make the governor acquainted with it. I observed, that with respect to the title of *l'empereur*, I knew that it would be inadmissible.

Saw Napoleon afterwards, who told me that he had always thought I might be required to make out reports of the state of his health, especially when laboring under indisposition; that, however, as it was only a surmise, he did not take any notice of it; but that some days ago, Generals Montholon and Gourgaud were asked how were certain symptoms (palpitations), which they were totally ignorant he had ever been afflicted with, as he (Napoleon) had only made me acquainted with them, and had professed their surprise; that a reply was made, stating that such symptoms were described in the bulletins of health sent to the governor. I informed Napoleon that I had often made out reports of his state of health. He asked to see one. I immediately brought him one of the 10th. Looking over it, he observed the word "general," and said that he would never consent to be so styled by me, or by any other person acting as his physician; that as such, I must possess a certain share of his confidence, without which I could not be acquainted with the symptoms; that a physician was to the body what a confessor was to the soul, and was bound to keep such confession equally sacred, unless permitted to divulge it. For the future, therefore, he insisted I should submit to him all reports which I should make of his health, previous to sending them to the governor. That he did not wish to influence me in their compilation; on the contrary, if I conceived any observations made by him to be incorrect, I was not to insert them, but that I should not render an account of such symptoms as delicacy or other motives, might induce him to wish should be kept secret. That after this warning, if I were to send any more bulletins without having been previously shown to him, it would be acting the part of a spy and not that of a physician, which, he added, was what the jailer of St. Helena wanted, and had done everything in his power to make me. That my reports were transmitted to the commissioners, and by them to their courts. That, therefore, he could not consent to allow a person in my situation to style him "general," in reports which might be sent to France, where he had once been sovereign; or to the courts of Vienna and Petersburg; as coming from me, it would appear to be an acquiescence on his part in such title, which he would rather die than consent to. Therefore I must give my word of honor not to make any more reports without complying with what he thus required, and leaving the original in Bertrand's possession; if I did not consent to this arrangement, that I must not write any more; if I did, he would never see me again as a physician.

I replied, that I never should be permitted by the governor to style him *l'empereur*, and suggested that I might use Napoleon or Napoleon B. That as to showing the reports to him, I must first communicate with the governor, which he consented to, but not to the appellation. In my verbal reports, he said he cared not if I called him *generale*, *boja*, or *tiranno Bonaparte*.

Communicated the purport of the above to Sir Hudson Lowe at Plantation House. As I had foreseen, he decidedly refused to consent to the use of the title required; that he was willing he should be styled Napoleon Bonaparte. As to showing the reports to Napoleon previous to their being sent to him, he said that he saw no objection for the present; however, it was a matter he could not decide upon directly, that it required some consideration, &c. He added, that it was some deep-laid scheme of the commissioners.

Informed Napoleon in the evening of the answer made by the governor. He observed, that he could not think of allowing himself to be insulted by his physician. That after the proposal he had made to the English government to assume the *incognito*, to which no answer had been given, it was the height of insult to insist upon naming him as they liked. That the more they endeavored to humiliate, the more tenacious would he be of the title. "*Ho perduto il trono,*" said he, "*per un punto d'onore, e perderei la vita cento volte, &c.*" ("I lost my throne for a point of honor, and would lose my life a hundred times rather than allow myself to be debased by consenting to be denominated as my oppressors please.")

After some time, I proposed dropping all titles and using the word *personage*, which, I said, I thought might remove all difficulties. He approved of my suggestion, but said that *patient*, (*la malade,*) would answer better, and satisfy him, provided the bulletins were first shown to him, and his consent obtained to send them.

It was signified to Count Bertrand this day by Sir Hudson Lowe, that Sir George Cockburn used to cause the notes and papers which were sent by the French to town, to be shown to him before they were allowed to be transmitted to the persons to whom they were directed.

15*th*—Communicated the proposal of yesterday to Sir Hudson Lowe, who refused his consent, saying, that he must be styled Napoleon Bonaparte, or General Bonaparte, in any bulletins or reports made of the state of his health.

16*th*.—Had a conversation with Napoleon upon the subject of the refusal of the governor to comply with the suggestion of calling him *the patient* in the bulletins. He observed that the governor evidently wanted to destroy the confidence which existed between him (Napoleon) and me as his physician. "When a man has not confidence in his physician," said he, "it is useless to have one. Confidence cannot be commanded. You ought to consider yourself as of no nation. A physician and a priest ought not to belong to any particular nation, and be divested of all political opinions. Treat me as if I were an Englishman. Chance gave you to me; and that is the reason I had confidence in you. If I had not taken you, you know that I should have had a French physician, who would not have made bulletins without my permission; therefore I insist that you shall not,

Would you, if you attended Lord Bathurst, write bulletins of the state of his complaints, to be printed, or sent to any other than members of his own family, without having first obtained his consent? I insist upon being treated in a similar manner; and that you drop all political considerations as to what I am, or what I was; and when I consult you, act as you would do to one of your own countrymen who was ill."

17*th.*—Napoleon was lying on his sofa, looking low and melancholy, with a cup of chicken-water before him. Marchand told me that he had been very unwell in the morning, and that he was obliged to chafe his temples and forehead with *eau de Cologne*. Napoleon would not answer the inquiries which I made relative to his complaints.

The Griffon sloop arrived this day, bringing the intelligence of the loss of the Julie sloop of war, on the island of Tristan d'Acunha, on the 2d, with all the officers, except Captain Jones and two midshipmen.

18*th.*—Napoleon in his bath. Still persisted in refusing to consult me on his complaints. Told me, that I had been remarked to go regularly every Tuesday and Saturday to Plantation House; and that, were it not for the confidence he had in me, he would, the moment it had been noticed, have dispensed with my services; as it was evident from the regularity of the periods, that I went by order of the governor. "The fact," continued he, "is, that all this is only an artifice to deprive me of medical assistance, *e d'arrivare piu presto alla fine ;* (to arrive sooner at the end,) for it was well known, that as soon as I found it out, I would not submit to it, or that no man of feeling or honor would do so. But this man has no *morale*, no feeling. He has been always accustomed to deserters and galley-slaves; and nature never intended him for any higher situation than a keeper of convicts. I shall not gladden his heart with a picture of my malady, in order that he may glut his enmity by calculating how long I may suffer before the last agony. You may tell him that I conceive his object to be to deprive me of all medical aid, and by that to arrive sooner at the end which he proposes. That I do not esteem life so much as to allow my physician to be made a spy. Tell him, that I said his views are directed to lessen the confidence I had in you, and to make you a spy, or to make me suspect that you are one. In fact," continued Napoleon, " had it not been for the confidence which I have in you, from the character Captain Maitland gave of you, and from my own observation, the measures of this governor would long ago have induced me to tell you, that I had no longer any occasion for your services."

Communicated part of the sentiments thus expressed by Napoleon to Sir Hudson Lowe, at Plantation House, who after some hesitation authorized me to say, that for the future no more bulletins would be demanded, without first having made him (Napoleon) acquainted that such were asked for.

Some conversation then passed about the permission which had been granted by Sir George Cockburn to the French of sending sealed letters to persons residing in the island. His excellency maintained, that Sir George Cockburn had never authorized such a practice ; that he had only *tolerated* it, and had greatly exceeded his powers in many respects.

19*th*.—Communicated this reply of the governor to Napoleon ; after which, and after having assured him that I would not send any bulletins without having shown them to him, he entered into a communication with me touching his malady. He was never free from dull pain, or an uneasy sensation in the right side ; his appetite was diminished ; his legs still swelled, especially towards night ; occasional nausea ; great want of sleep, &c. There was some degree of anxiety evident, and a cast of melancholy, probably caused by his complaint, and increased perhaps by the information in the last paper sent him by Sir Hudson Lowe, containing the decision of the allied powers, that his son should not succeed to the duchies of Parma, &c.

22*nd*.—Napoleon very unwell last night with an attack partly of a nervous nature.—Asked me if there was a witness present during the conversation which I was obliged to hold twice a week with the governor ? I replied in the affirmative. " Then," said he, " Doctor, you will be made to speak as he likes. I will venture to say, that he has a *procès verbal* made out every time you go there, and such conversations as best suit his views made and signed by his witness, which will be produced against you hereafter. It would not surprise me if he had a conversation ready made before you arrive there. It places you in a very dangerous situation."

28*th*.—Went to Plantation House, where Sir Hudson Lowe, after some inquiries touching Napoleon's health, demanded if I had any remarkable conversations with General Bonaparte, what length of time they lasted, and on what subjects? This led to a discussion in which his excellency was more than ordinarily violent and abusive. Amongst other elegant expressions, he said, that he conceived me to be a jackal, running about in search of news for General Bonaparte.

In reply to this expression, I said that I would neither be a jackal, nor a spy, nor informer, for him or for any one else. "What do you mean, sir," said he, "by a spy, nor an informer?" I said, that if I complied with his directions, to inform him of the conversations which passed between Napoleon and myself, I should conceive myself to be both. In a paroxysm of rage, he said, that I was to consider myself as prohibited from holding any communication whatsoever with Napoleon Bonaparte, except upon medical subjects. That I was to have no sort of communication with him upon other points. I asked him to give me this order in writing, which he refused, and after some abuse, told me to wait outside of the room for some time. In about a quarter of an hour, I was called in again, and informed by Sir Hudson Lowe, that I was to conduct myself as before, observing, however, that he (Sir Hudson) only authorized me to hold medical communication with General Bonaparte; that as to other subjects, I was myself responsible;* that I was not to refuse to answer General Bonaparte upon a subject that he questioned me

---

* It may be necessary to remind the reader that the governor, in one of his proclamations, which will be found in the appendix, had pronounced the holding of " any *unauthorized* communications with General Bonaparte," to be felony.

on, but that I *was not to ask him any questions other than medical ones, &c.*

Afterwards he asked me what I thought myself bound to divulge? I replied, as I had formerly done when similar questions had been put to me. He asked if I did not think myself bound to communicate to him any abusive language made use of by General Bonaparte, respecting him? I answered, certainly not, unless ordered by Napoleon. He asked, "Why so, sir?" I replied, that I did not choose to act the part of an incendiary. His excellency then denied that he had ever asked me to tell him *all* the conversations which passed between General Bonaparte and myself. I put him in mind of his having told me, at Longwood and elsewhere, that it was necessary he should know every thing that was said, as he might draw conclusions and inferences which I would not, and therefore that it was essential for him to know every thing. After this, I demanded permission to take the last directions he had given to me in writing, from his own dictation, to prevent the possibility of a mistake, which he refused. He then told me that he would in future dispense with my attendance twice a week; but that he expected me to confer with Mr. Baxter every week on the state of Napoleon Bonaparte's health; to which I consented, as Napoleon had no objections to verbal communications being made, and I need not say that I was heartily glad that my presence at Plantation House was dispensed with.

November 2nd.—Napoleon reclining on the sofa, with some newspapers lying before him, and his snuff-box in his hand.* He looked very melancholy and low. After the usual inquiries about his health, my advice was given as usual, in as forcible a manner as I could, especially as to exercise on horseback. He

---

* It has been asserted that Napoleon took snuff in such immoderate quantities, that he was in the habit of cramming his waistcoat pockets full of that article, as no snuff-box could contain a sufficiency for his consumption.—The reader may form his own opinion upon the correctness of this assertion, when he is informed, that twelve pounds of the only kind of snuff he used, were brought by Marchand from Paris in July, 1815, of which rather more than one half remained when I left St. Helena, in July, 1818.

replied that he felt no confidence in the governor, who, he was convinced, would find out some pretext to insult him, or make some insinuations before he went out four times. "That letter," continued he, "which you saw at Bertrand's the other day, came from him, and contained a paper, with the account that my son had been disinherited from the succession to the duchies of Parma, &c. Now, this coming from another person would be nothing; but as he invariably culls out all the news that might prove agreeable, which he retains at Plantation House, and sends whatever may wound my feelings, it is easy to see the motives by which he is actuated."

"You see," added he, with an emphasis, "that he lost no time in sending that news to me. I was always prepared to expect something of the kind from the wretches who compose the congress. They are afraid of a prince, who is the choice of the people. However, you may yet see a great change; that is, provided they continue to give him a good education, or that they do not assassinate him. If they brutify him by a bad education, there is little hope. As for me, I may be considered as dead, as already in the sepulchre. I am certain that before long this body will be no more. *Sento che la macchina lutta, ma che non può durare.* (I feel that the machine struggles, but cannot last.")

"I," added he, "could listen to the intelligence of the death of my wife, of my son, or of all my family, without change of feature. Not the slightest sign of emotion, or alteration of countenance, would be visible. Every thing would appear indifferent and calm. But when alone in my chamber, then I suffer. Then the feelings of the man burst forth."

"I suppose," added he, "that Montchenu is very glad to hear of my illness. By what channel does he send his letters to France?" I replied, that he sent them through the governor and Lord Bathurst. "Then, they are all opened and read in London by your ministers." I replied, that I was ignorant of their having recourse to such practices. "Because," said Napoleon, "you never have been in a situation to know anything about it. I tel. you, that the despatches of all the ambassadors and other diplomatists, that pass through the post office, are opened. Otto told me, that when in London, he ascertained this to be a fact beyond a doubt." I said, that I had heard that in all the states on the continent, official letters were opened. "Certainly they are," answered Napoleon, "but they have not the impudence to deny it, like your ministers, though it is carried to as great an extent amongst you as any where else. In France," continued the emperor, "an arrangement was made, so that all the letters sent by the ambassadors, or other diplomatic characters, all the household and all persons connected with foreign affairs, were sent to a secret department of the post-office in Paris, no matter in what part of France they were put in. All letters or despatches, in like manner, for foreign courts or ministers, were sent to this office, where they were opened and deciphered. The writers sometimes made use of several different ciphers, not continuing the same for more than ten lines, in order to prevent their being understood. This, however, did not answer, as in order to decipher the most ingenious and difficult, it was only necessary to have fifty pages of the same cipher, which from the extent of the correspondence, was soon to be had. So clever were the agents employed, and so soon did they read the ciphers, that latterly only fifty louis were paid for the discovery of the means of deciphering a new one. By opening all the letters addressed to the diplomatic persons, the post-office police got acquainted with their correspondents, to whom all letters addressed subsequently were treated in a similar manner. The ambassadors suspected that there were some infidelities committed upon their correspondence, and to prevent it used generally to change their cipher every three months. But this only gave a little additional trouble. They sent their letters sometimes to a post-office town a few miles distant from where they actually resided, thinking that they were very cunning, and would thus escape observation, not knowing of the arrangement I have mentioned to you. The ambassadors of the lesser powers, such as Denmark, Sweden, and even Prussia, used, through avarice, to save the expense of couriers, to send their despatches through the post-office in cipher, which were opened and deciphered, and the most important part of their contents copied and communicated to me (never to the ministers) by * * * * *. By these means, I knew the contents of the despatches that Bernstorf, * * * *, and others, sent to their courts, before they arrived at their destination; for they were always sealed up, and sent on after we had done with them. Several of them, especially those of Bernstorf, were full of injurious reflections upon me, censures on my conduct, and fabricated conversations with me. How often have I laughed within myself, to see them licking the dust from under my feet at my levee, after having read in the morning the *bétises* they had written of me to their sovereigns. We used, also, frequently to discover very important matters which they had communicated to them in confidence from the ambassadors of Russia and Austria, and of your country, (when you had one in Paris,) who always sent their despatches by couriers of their own, which prevented me from being acquainted with the nature of them. Through the correspondence of the lesser powers, I became acquainted with the opinions of the greater. The cleverness of those who conducted this machinery was astonishing. There was no species of writing which they could not imitate perfectly; and in the post-office were kept seals similar to those used by the ambassadors of all the powers of Europe, independent of an immense number of others, belonging to families of different countries. If they met with a seal for which they had not a fac-simile, they could get one made in twenty-four hours. This arrangement," continued he, " was not an invention of mine. It was first begun by Louis the Fourteenth, and some of the grandchildren of the agents originally employed by him, filled in my time situations which had been transmitted to them from their fathers. But," added he, "Castlereagh does the same in London. All letters to and from diplomatic persons, which pass through the post-office, are opened, and the contents forwarded to him, or some other of your ministers, and they must be aware that a similar practice is followed in France."

I asked if it was a general rule to open at the French post-office letters addressed to persons not diplomatic. "Rarely," said he, "and never, unless when a man was strongly suspected. Then the first thing that was done, was to open every letter directed to him, by means of which his correspondents were discovered, and all letters addressed to them inspected; but this was an odious measure, and very seldom resorted to with Frenchmen. As to foreigners, enemies of France, it was proper to adopt every means of becoming acquainted with their secret machinations."

Napoleon then told me that he had resolved for the future only to have one regular meal daily, at about two or three o'clock. For some time past he has eaten very sparingly.

3rd.—Napoleon much the same. According to his general custom, when newspapers were before him, he asked me now and then the meaning of any word which he did not comprehend. He strongly censured the conduct which the allied powers had practised in persecuting his brother Lucien, who was a literary character, a man who had never commanded, and who had endeavored to withdraw himself from political affairs. "It is," added he, "from a consciousness of their own tyranny, and the fears resulting from a knowledge that they have violated the rights of nations, and have acted contrary to the spirit of the age, and the will of the people. For persecuting me, they might allege some reason. They might say that I had been a sovereign and a tyrant, and that it was necessary for the repose of the world; but nothing can justify such acts of oppression and barbarity towards him. The principle of utility, upon which they act, once established, God knows to what length it may be carried Upon a similar pretext the French might justify the assassination of Wellington and his whole army. It is a principle which will make kings tremble upon their thrones."

Some conversation now took place about Lord Cochrane, and the attempt which his lordship had made to capture or destroy the ships in the Charante. I said that it was the opinion of a very distinguished naval officer whom I named, and who was well known to him, that if Cochrane had been properly supported, he would have destroyed the whole of the French ships. "He could not only have destroyed them," replied Napoleon, "but he might and would have taken them out, had your admiral supported him as he ought to have done. For, in consequence of the signal made by L'Allemand," (I think he said) "to the ships to do the best in their power to save themselves, *sauve qui peut* (save themselves who can), in fact, they became panic-struck and cut their cables. The terror of the *brulots* (fire-ships) was so great, that they actually threw their powder overboard, so that they could have offered very little resistance. The French Admiral was an *imbécile*, but yours was just as bad. I assure you, that if Cochrane had been supported, he would have taken every one of the ships. They ought not to have been alarmed by your *brulots*, (fire-ships,) but fear deprived them of their senses, and they no longer knew how to act in their own defence."

When asking the emperor some medical questions, he recounted the following anecdote. "About seven years ago, the Persian ambassador in Paris fell sick, and ordered a physician to be sent for. The messenger, not properly comprehending what he meant, thought that he wished to see a minister of the treasury, to whom he went and informed him that the Persian ambassador desired to speak to him. The minister, surprised, said, 'This is a curious mode of acting, but those barbarians know nothing of etiquette, and perhaps he has something important to communicate.' On his arrival, the ambassador held out his wrist, that he should feel his pulse, whilst another great fellow with a turban brought a chamber utensil, which he held up to his nose for inspection. You may judge how the minister was confounded at such a reception."

5*th.*—Napoleon remained in bed very late, not having had any sleep during the night. Found him not risen at eleven.

Saw him once more in the course of the day, and had some more conversation about his brother Lucien. He observed again on the cruelty and injustice of persecuting a literary character who did not meddle in politics, and who had even quarrelled with him. To persecute a man from whom no danger was to be apprehended two years after he (Napoleon) had been sent to St.

Helena, was the height of injustice. Such fear of an individual shows that they are conscious of acting contrary to the will of the people. "*Les tyrans tremblent pour leurs seuils.*" (Tyrants tremble for their thresholds.) Here he made a quotation about Pluto trembling lest the earth should open and expose to view all the horrors of the infernal regions.

"What a degradation," added he, "to see the ambassador of one of the greatest powers in Europe persecuting an individual who has never been, nor ever desired to be a sovereign. *Quando io sarò morto e forse il giorno non è lontano John Bull mi vendichera.* (When I am dead, and perhaps the day is not far off, John Bull will revenge me.")

Napoleon then recounted to me some private anecdotes of Lucien.

He also told me, that one Ignatio Lorri, (I think was the name,) a Corsican and a foster brother of his, had early in life embraced the English party, and entered their sea-service. He was ignorant, though *un bravissimo uomo*, and an excellent seaman. He commanded an English store-ship, and landed in ———,* where he went disguised as a peasant to see the French consul. "When he came into his presence," continued Napoleon, "he threw off his *cappotto*, showed the English uniform, and told who he was. He made many inquiries concerning me, without however offering to enter my service. The consul did not believe him, and wrote a long history to Paris of an impostor who had presented himself to him, and asserted himself to be the emperor's foster brother. He was much astonished to find that I admitted it to be perfectly true. It is surprising that during all the height of my power, this man never asked a favor of me, although in his childhood he lov♥d me, and knew, that since my elevation, I had loaded his mother with favors and money."

6th.—Napoleon in rather better spirits, otherwise much the same. Spoke to me about an article which he had seen in the papers, stating that Talma had paid a reckoning for him at a tavern once, when through the want of money he had offered his

* The name of the place is illegible in the manuscript of my journal.

sword in pledge. This he declared to be untrue, and that he did not believe Talma had ever said so. " I did not know Talma personally," continued he, " until I was first consul. I then favored and distinguished him very much, as a man of talent and the first in the profession. I sometimes sent for him in the morning, to discourse with me while I was at breakfast. The libellers said that Talma taught me how to act the king. When I returned from Elba, I said one morning at my breakfast to Talma, who was present with some other men of science, ' *Eh bien, Talma,* (Well, Talma,) so they say that you taught me how to sit upon my throne. *C'est un signe que je m'y tiens bien.*' " (It is a sign that I shall sit well on it.)

Count Balmaine and Baron Sturmer had a long interview with General Montholon yesterday. They rode up to the inner gate, where they remained for some time looking in. Signals are made to Plantation House whenever they come near Longwood, and a spy is generally sent to dog them from the town; but no direct attempts are made to prevent their intercourse with the inhabitants of Longwood.

8*th.*—Napoleon observed that I walked lame, and asked me if I had the gout. I replied in the negative, and said, that it had been caused yesterday by a tight boot; that I never had the gout, and never had been confined to my bed a day in my life by illness. He then asked if my father had ever had that disease, and said that he would prescribe for my present complaint, by ordering me to eat nothing, drink barley-water, and keep my leg up on a sofa during the day. He then made some observations about his son, and said, that his having been disinherited from the succession to Parma gave him little or no uneasiness. " If he lives," added he, " he will be something. As to these contemptible little states, I would rather see him a private *gentleman,* with enough to eat, than sovereign of any of them. Perhaps it may, however, grieve the empress to think that he will not inherit after her; but it does not give me the smallest trouble."

" The Emperor Francis," added he, " whose head is crammed with ideas of high birth, was very anxious to prove that I was descended from some of the old tyrants of Treviso; and after my marriage with Marie Louise, employed divers persons to search into the old musty records of genealogy, in which they thought they could find something to prove what they desired. He imagined that he had succeeded at last, and wrote to me, asking my consent that he should publish the account with all official formalities. I refused. He was so intent upon this favorite object, that he again applied, and said, '*Laissez moi faire,*' (Let me do it,) that I need not appear to take any part in it. I replied, that this was impossible, as if published, I should be obliged to take notice of it; that I preferred being the son of an honest man, to being descended from any little dirty tyrant of Italy. That I was the Rodolph of my family."

"There was formerly," added he, "one Buonaventura Bonaparte, who lived and died a monk. The poor man lay quietly in his grave; nothing was thought about him until I was on the throne of France. It was then discovered that he had been possessed of many virtues, which never had been attributed to him before, and the Pope proposed to me to canonize him. '*Saint Père,*' said I, '*pour l'amour de Dieu épargnez moi le ridicule de cela ;*' (Holy Father, for God's sake spare me the ridicule of that,) you being in my power, all the world will say that I forced you to make a saint out of my family."

25th.—Signal made for me to go to Plantation House, where I found Sir Hudson Lowe, who interrogated me upon various matters that had taken place at Longwood, and the conversations I had with Napoleon. I replied that I had formed a determination not to meddle with what did not concern me, and only troubled myself about my professional pursuits. He said that I must have had some conversations not medical with him, and demanded to be informed of the subject of the conversations I had with General Bonaparte. I replied, that in the first place, nothing important had taken place; that in the next, I did not think myself bound to repeat the subject of such conversations as I had with Napoleon, unless permitted, or unless matters came to my knowledge connected with my allegiance, or of great importance to my own government. Sir Hudson replied, " You are no judge, sir, of the importance of the conversations you may have with General Bonaparte. I might consider several subjects of great importance, which you consider as trifling or of no consequence." I observed, that if I was not at liberty to use my own discretion or judgment, I must necessarily repeat to him every thing I heard, which would place me in the situation of a man acting a most dishonorable and disgraceful part. The governor replied, " that it was my *duty* to inform him of what circumstances came to my knowledge, and of the subject of my conversation with General Bonaparte; for if I did not, it was easily in his power to prohibit me from holding any communication with him, except on medical subjects, and then only *when sent to* for that purpose. That it was a duty I owed to the English government." I answered, that it would be acting the part of a spy, an informer, and a *mouton*. That I never understood the government had placed me about him for other than medical purposes; that my duty did not require me to commit dishonorable actions; and that I would not do so for any person. Sir Hudson remained silent for a few moments, eyeing me furiously, and asked what was the meaning of the word *mouton*. I replied, "*Mouton* means a person who insinuates himself into the confidence of another, for the purpose of betraying it." Sir Hudson then broke out into a paroxysm of rage; said that I had given him the greatest possible insult in his official capacity that could be offered, and concluded with ordering me to leave the room, saying that he would not permit a person who had made use of such language to sit in his presence. I told him that I did not voluntarily come into, nor ever would have entered his house, unless compelled to do so. He walked about in a frantic manner, repeating in a boisterous tone, " Leave the room, sir," which he continued bawling out for some moments after I had actually quitted it.

The following narrative may convey some idea of the manner in which Lieutenant-General Sir Hudson Lowe, K.C.B., &c. &c., was duped, when he had the command of an important fortress.

It was communicated to me at Longwood, principally by the *maître d'hôtel*, Cipriani, whose name was also Franceschi, but which latter he never assumed at St. Helena, for reasons which will be seen hereafter.

In 1806, Sir Hudson (then Lieutenant-Colonel Lowe) was intrusted with the command of the island of Capri, which is situated in the bay of Naples, and with the secret service, or, in plainer terms, the espionage of the continent, at least as far as regarded the Mediterranean. In the island he commanded, he generally received intelligence from the city of Naples, from which it is distant only a few miles. It was most generally brought to him by means of a fishing boat, commanded by a man named Antonio, who went out at night under pretence of fishing. Sir Hudson employed as a spy Antonio Suzzarelli, a Corsican, and a man of talent, who had been educated as a lawyer, along with Pozzo di Borgo, and Saliceti, the then minister of police at Naples. Suzzarelli had formerly been an officer in the English service. Maresca, a Neapolitan, and Criscuolo, another Neapolitan, were also employed by him on a similar service; and Cassetti,* a Neapolitan lieutenant-colonel of dragoons, was spy for Queen Caroline of Sicily. Suzzarelli remained faithful to Sir Hudson Lowe for about twenty days, viz. from the 19th or 20th of January, to the 10th of February, when some despatches of his were taken, in a boat going over to Capri. At a tavern, he met Cipriani Franceschi, who was then in the confidential service of Saliceti, supposed to be his natural son, and generally known by the name of Franceschi. Being countrymen and intimate acquaintances, Suzzarelli confided to Franceschi the nature of his employment, informing him also, that he received a certain sum monthly from the English government. Cipriani proposed to him to apparently continue to furnish information to the governor of Capri, and receive his salary, but at the same time really to communicate everything to Saliceti, and obey his directions; adding, that he then would be paid

---

* All those respectable persons, I believe, are now in existence, **and one of them I have reason to believe enjoys a pension from his majesty's government for his** *services.*

double what he received from the English; and insinuating, that should he refuse, in all probability he would in two or three weeks be discovered and shot. Suzzarelli, who was no novice, took the hint immediately, closed with the proposal, and was brought before Saliceti, from whom he received instructions how to act. Suzzarelli also brought over Maresca and Criscuolo to the same mode of acting, partly by promises and partly by threats. Cassetti also became a spy on the queen for Saliceti. All of them were paid double what they received from the other parties. Matters were ordered so, that whenever Suzzarelli received a despatch from Sir Hudson Lowe, it was immediately brought to Saliceti in the state in which it had been received; who, after reading it, dictated such answers as he thought proper. Sometimes Suzzarelli was permitted to tell the truth. For example, while the French troops were in great force in Naples, he was directed to mention their number. Whenever it related to an affair which Saliceti did not like to answer directly, he caused the master of the boat and his crew to be arrested and thrown into confinement for some days, when, after some forms of examination had been gone through, they were released. This also gave an opportunity for Suzzarelli to exercise his talents in obtaining more money from Sir Hudson, by inventing tales of the trouble he had been at, and the expenses he had incurred in paying bribes to save those poor devils, who otherwise would have been shot. In this manner the whole of the information furnished to the British government, was only such as answered the ends of Saliceti, and consequently of the Emperor Napoleon, except what trifling intelligence Sir Hudson could glean from the master of the boat, and his sons, who were faithful to him, but were ignorant of every thing of importance. Commissions of the most difficult nature were frequently sent by Sir Hudson Lowe to Suzzarelli to execute, which, by order of Saliceti, were done with the greatest punctuality and despatch. Amongst others, there was one for some expensive French watches for Queen Caroline, scarce books, and all recent publications for Sir Hudson, particularly a copy of Les Cases' Atlas, (then called Le Sage's,) to obtain which he was very anxious. This also afforded honest Suzzarelli another opportunity of gaining money from Sir Hudson, for, although he was ordered by Saliceti to furnish the articles at prime cost, with a reasonable charge for expenses, in order to prevent suspicion, he never failed to lay on from fifty to a hundred per cent. under different pretences. He practised smuggling also to a considerable extent, Sir Hudson frequently paying for the articles he received in English or colonial goods, which Suzzarelli used afterwards to sell at Naples, at a large profit.

Sir Hudson, in his cunning, had recourse to an extraordinary mode of sending over the wages to Suzzarelli, Criscuolo, and Maresca, which last, in the fulness of his heart, he used to call his champion, (*suo campione*.) They were paid in gold, which was generally sent in loaves of bread, that the cautious Sir Hudson had baked in his own house, and put the money in with his own hands, lest his spies should be discovered by any spies of the Neapolitan police. The loaves had the appearance of bread for the use of the boatmen, while fishing at night. As soon as they were landed, they were brought up by Suzzarelli to Saliceti; the latter insisting that every kind of correspondence should be first submitted to him. By means of Suzzarelli the French government became acquainted with the real destination of the army under General M'Kenzie Fraser, and the fleet under Sir J. Duckworth.

Suzzarelli even offered to procure Sir Hudson some soldiers to recruit the Corsican regiment in Capri; and some I believe were actually despatched over to him, to corrupt the foreigners under his command. While the attack upon Capri was meditating, Suzzarelli had the art to persuade Sir Hudson Lowe that it was meant against the little island of Ponza; which the English frigate Ambuscade, and the greatest part of the gun-boats, were accordingly sent to defend; thus leaving the passage to Capri defended only by a small force. To encourage this belief, an embargo was laid upon all vessels in Naples; but some fishing boats, manned with persons in the employ of Saliceti, were sent out at night, purposely to fall in with some of Sir Hudson's boats, and to assure them that the expedition was meant for Ponza. In order to embroil the British government and Sir Hudson with Queen Caroline, letters were fabricated by a Neapolitan, called Don Antonio, as if from her to Cassetti; whilst others, purporting to be written by Sir Hudson, were forged by an English schoolmaster residing at Naples; these last confidentially stating, that the object of the English was to get the royal family out of Sicily, and send them to England on a pension, that they might subsequently take possession of the country; and the first containing complaints of Sir Hudson by the queen, and invectives against him and the English. Those wretches also, to afford amusement to Saliceti, and to themselves, used sometimes to create a quarrel between Sir Hudson and the Prince of Canosa, who commanded in Ponza, by means of forged letters, abusing each other, which they caused to fall into their hands. They usually assembled at night to enjoy themselves, drinking and laughing at their dupe, Sir Hudson, whose health they toasted out of derision, whilst, in the midst of their revels, they were hatching new means of deceiving him. Even Saliceti himself sometimes went to listen and laugh at their schemes.

Some time in 1807 or 1808, Suzzarelli was to go to Vienna, to execute a mission for Saliceti, and determined to make Sir Hudson Lowe pay the expenses of the journey. The chief object of this mission was to sound the English Ambassador, and Pozzo di Borgo, then at Vienna. Suzzarelli went to Sir Hudson Lowe, whom he persuaded that at Vienna he could procure information of the greatest importance, and obtained from him six thousand francs for the expenses of his journey, &c., with strong letters of recommendation. He then went to Vienna, where he was very well received by the English Ambassador, from whom he procured some important intelligence. He also obtained from him an order to have the salaries paid which were given to other English agents and officers who resided on the continent. With Pozzo di Borgo he did not succeed, as the wary Corsican could not believe that it was possible for him to deceive Saliceti, as he pretended to have done. Suzzarelli, in trying to ingratiate himself into Pozzo di Borgo's confidence, boasted of his influence over Saliceti, saying, *Io faccio intendere a Saliceti tutto ciò che voglio** (I make Saliceti believe whatever I like,) *.1 me tuconti questo?* (Dost thou tell this to me?) replied Pozzo di Borgo, bowing down to the ground. All the art of Suzzarelli could not extract a single secret from him, although the letter of recommendation given by Sir Hudson Lowe, represented him as a man in whom every confidence could be placed, and in the passport which he received afterwards from the English ambassador, he was styled *Il Signore Barone Suzzarelli.* On his return to Naples, he was asked by Saliceti, "*Ebbene cosa hai tirato da Pozzo di Borgo?*" (Well, what hast thou extracted from Pozzo di Borgo?) "Ah," replied Suzzarelli, shrugging up his shoulders, "*dui birbi insieme, non si guadagna niente,*" (two rogues together, nothing is gained.) He then told Saliceti, that Pozzo di Borgo had sent his compliments to him. Saliceti replied, " Suzzarelli, I know that thou has told me many lies, but this is the greatest that ever has escaped thy lips, accustomed as they are to lying. I well know Pozzo di Borgo; I have been the means of banishing him from his country, and of proscribing him; so that through my means, if caught in France, he would be shot. Thinkest thou, then, that so proud a man as Pozzo di Borgo, and a Corsican, would send his compliments to one who has done him so much injury? None but the meanest and vilest of men would be capable of it, and I well know Pozzo di Borgo to be one of the proudest on earth." In fact, Suzzarelli† acknowledged afterwards, that he had invented it.

Suzzarelli had, at one time, persuaded Sir Hudson Lowe to prom-

---

* The Italian in this narrative is given as delivered by Cipriani, who generally conversed in not the most pure or correct language.

† After Saliceti's death, Suzzarelli confessed that he had never succeeded in deceiving him but once, and even then not completely; as Saliceti, in giving him some money for the expenses of his journey to Vienna, told him that it was not given on account of the services he had then rendered the public, as he, in the bottom of his heart, believed that most of what he had told him was false, but because he knew that he must get money by some means, for the existence of his family and himself.

ise to come over to Naples, and meet him in a little house on the beach, belonging to Maresca, where he would have seen Saliceti in disguise, who had decided not to seize him, as he conceived that it would be difficult to find another governor, who would allow himself to be gulled so egregiously, and would, besides, have prevented them from deriving any more services from Suzzarelli. "*Vorrei vedere questo colonello tuo,*" said Saliceti, "*fammelo vedere. Un uomo può lasciarsi ingannere per qualche mese, ma di lasciarsi coglionare a questo segno per tanti anni, bisognà essere ben bestia.*" (I should like to see this colonel of thine. Let me see him. A man may allow himself to be deceived for some months, but he who suffers himself to be humbugged so grossly for so many years, must be a beast indeed.) "Oh," replied Suzzarelli, with an air of gravity, "*non è tanto bestia, è talento mio.*" (Not quite so great a blockhead, it is my cleverness.) Something, however, induced Lowe to change his intentions.

Murat being desirous of seizing all the English merchandise, of which there was a great quantity in Naples, under the name of American, and, at the same time, not wishing to quarrel with the Americans, employed Suzzarelli to find out the means of ascertaining what was really American, and what was not. Suzzarelli went to Sir Hudson Lowe, whom he persuaded that he should be able to render essential service to the British government, if he were possessed of the means of distinguishing the English passports from the real American ones. Sir Hudson gave him two, one real and American, and the other counterfeit and English, showing him how to distinguish between them, the only difference being in the stamp. In the English, the initial was exactly in the centre of the stamp; in the American, though the letter was the same, it was placed a little underneath. Furnished with these, Suzzarelli departed, and in the beginning of 1810, a general seizure of the ships was made by Murat, and all those found with passports in the manner described above, were confiscated. While Saliceti lived, but few were seized, as he wished to keep Suzzarelli on terms with Lowe.

It was by means of the money acquired by the seizure and confiscation of the above-mentioned vessels, that King Joachim in a great measure equipped and paid the expedition undertaken against Sicily in the year 1811. Saliceti became acquainted with almost every thing that passed at the court of Palermo, by means of the Duchess of C * * *, with whom he intrigued. She was daughter to the Princess C * * *, wife to the Sicilian ambassador in * * *, and *prima dama* to Caroline and her confidant. Her husband wrote her an account of every circumstance that took place at the court of * * *. She hated the French, and Saliceti pretended that he was a republican, and detested the French party. She established a correspondence with her mother, who communicated every thing to her, for the disclosure of which she received one thousand *scudi* per month from Saliceti.

In 1808 or 9, a Neapolitan named Mosca, and in rank a captain, was sent over from Capri by Queen Caroline to assassinate Napoleon's brother Joseph, at that time King of Naples. In order to stimulate him to the deed, she gave him a lock of her hair, and a letter in her own handwriting, engaging to make him a colonel as soon as what he promised was effected. Independent of this, he received a letter from the Princess V * * T * * *, confidant to Queen Caroline, specifically pointing out what he was to do; viz. *to rid his country of the usurper*, and giving him every assurance that the "*good queen his mistress, would fulfil all her promises to him.*"* He accordingly left Capri, in a felucca, provided with all the necessary passports; in one of which, signed by an English officer, there were instructions requiring that all British officers should afford every assistance to the bearer, who was proceeding on a *secret mission*, for the good of the service of King Ferdinand. He landed at Molino, near to a country house of Joseph's, and his intention was to have assassinated him while walking in the garden. While lurking about in expectation of his victim, he met with a girl, whose appearance struck him, and to whom he offered some pieces of gold to consent to his wishes. Not succeeding in this, he told her that he had come over from

---

* Those two letters, as well as the passports, I saw in the original since my return from St. Helena.

the queen to execute a grand object, and that if she would consent to his desires he would make her a great woman. The girl became alarmed, and would not consent, notwithstanding the sight of his gold, and the promises he made. Information was given to the police, who proceeded immediately to the spot. Two of Mosca's associates were killed, and he himself seized, after a desperate resistance. The letters, the lock of hair, the arms which were found upon him, and the girl, were produced against him before a military commission. He said, in his defence, that he merely had come over to throw himself at Joseph's feet, and ask pardon and permission to return to Naples. After condemnation, however, he confessed his real intentions. He died with great courage, and refused to disclose the names of his accomplices. Some time after this, Queen Caroline sent over a Neapolitan apothecary, named Gherardi, (or Visconti,) and his two sons to assassinate Saliceti. For this purpose he went to Ponza, from whence he proceeded to Capri, and from Capri to Naples, where he landed at night, taking with him a sort of catamaran, in shape and size similar to a ship's buoy. He managed matters so well, as to get admittance into Saliceti's house, and even to hire a room under the stairs as an apothecary's store, in which he placed his machine. Saliceti, who had been at a party at the house of the princess * * *, did not return until about twelve or one o'clock, alighted from his carriage, and according to his usual custom, bounded up stairs with great quickness: this saved his life: for the incendiary's machine did not explode until he had passed through four rooms of his suite of apartments. Cipriani was with him at the moment of the explosion. Upwards of thirty of the rooms were either blown to pieces or materially injured, and the palace nearly reduced to ruins, under which was buried one of Saliceti's daughters (now the Duchess of * * *,) where she remained for some hours, but at last was discovered by Cipriani hearing the moans of some person. While proceeding on in the direction of the voice, he tumbled through the floor down to the room below, for-

---

* This lady is now alive, and resides in Naples. In 1819, I saw and conversed with her sister at Rome.

tunately without sustaining any injury, which brought him nearer to the sufferer. An alarm was given, and after considerable difficulty, the young lady was extricated, half dead, from under the mass of ruins. Some of the rafters had formed a cross over her, which was the means of saving her life. Gherardi and his sons were arrested and tried, the sons shot, but the father, in consequence of his advanced age, escaped with perpetual imprisonment.

Immediately after this event, Sir Hudson Lowe wrote a letter to Saliceti, professing his entire ignorance of it, and his detestation of similar attempts.

Saliceti, suspecting the drum-major of the regiment of Vajro, then in Naples, to be an agent of Queen Caroline, employed Suzzarelli to discover it. Accordingly Suzzarelli, with whom the drum-major was intimately acquainted, embraced an opportunity of addressing him one day while he was walking about, looking very discontentedly, and commenced by inveighing against the tyranny to which they were subjected, and how happy he should be to get away from a place where no one's life was safe for a moment; professing his intention of effecting his escape as soon as he could do it without running the risk of being seized and shot by the police, of which he said he was in great dread. The poor drum-major heartily joined him, professed his own disgust at the government they were under, and his attachment to that of Caroline, adding, that *he* would also get away as soon as possible. Upon this Suzzarelli proposed to him to induce twenty or thirty of his regiment to enter into either Caroline's or the English service, telling him to make them sign a paper purporting their readiness to enter, and giving him two hundred dollars to forward his plans, with a promise that as soon as they were ready, he would procure them a passage over to Capri. The drum-major went amongst his friends in the regiment, and used all his endeavors to inveigle some to enter into his projects. He could not, however, succeed with more than ten or twelve, who were so illiterate that they could neither read nor write, and he was obliged to write their names himself, along with those of his two sons. He then met **Suzzarelli** according to appointment, acquainted him how far he had succeeded, and showed him the list of names. Suzzarelli communicated this to Saliceti, recommending him at the same time to wait until he had procured more victims. Saliceti rejected this, replying, that it was the business of the police by every means to discover traitors, but not to encourage or make them; on the contrary, that his duty was to nip everything of the kind in the bud, and not knowingly to allow such practices to be carried on. The drum-major and his associates were immediately arrested, the paper with the names found upon him, and, a short time afterwards, himself, his sons, and some of the others were hanged. Suzzarelli lay concealed for several days, and then went to see the widow of the unfortunate drum-major, told her that her husband had nearly been his ruin, that he had come to him to request assistance in getting away from Naples, which he in his friendship had promised to afford, but that all had been discovered; that he had been taken up, thrown into prison, and would have been hanged, if luckily for him a countryman of his had not been in Saliceti's office, who had interested himself to save his life. This he told so plausibly, that the poor woman implicitly believed what he said, looked upon him as a benefactor, and ever afterwards, when in trouble, used to have recourse to Suzzarelli for advice, who occasionally gave her a dollar or two. Two or three days after this abominable treachery, Cipriani said to Suzzarelli, " What a *scelerato* (miscreant) thou art, Suzzarelli. How canst thou reconcile to thyself being the cause of the death of these poor fellows who were hanged through thy deceit?" " Bah," replied Suzzarelli, " *Sono porci Napolitanacci*," (they are Neapolitan hogs.)

In 1809, Saliceti, wishing to discover when the packet from England was expected to arrive in Sicily, set Suzzarelli to work upon Colonel Lowe. Suzzarelli accordingly wrote to the colonel, stating that as the news they had received from England by the last English papers had been very distressing, and had produced bad effects, by discouraging those partisans' of the English who believed it; that even those who did not credit it to the full extent, thought that something unfavorable had occurred; he therefore requested the colonel to communicate immediately to him any news that he might have received, that he might be able to keep up the spirits of the party. Sir Hudson Lowe replied, that he was very right to use every exertion not to allow the loyal sentiments of the faithful subjects of King Ferdinand to be lowered; but at that moment he had no authentic intelligence to communicate; that, however, he expected to a certainty that the packet from England would arrive in a few days, when he would take care to forward to him forthwith every intelligence that was favorable. As soon as Suzzarelli made this known to Saliceti, a privateer, called *l'Ardito*, was despatched to cruise between Sardinia and ———, and in a few days actually fell in with the English packet, (which, I believe, was called the Success) which she took. The mail was thrown overboard, but in the hurry, it hung by one of the cords which attached it, and the privateer's men kept up such a fire of musketry, that the crew of the packet durst not approach to cut it away, and it was taken. In it were despatches giving some directions concerning an attack which was meditated upon Corfu; with some letters from the admiralty to the admiral relative to the blockade of that island. Cipriani described the packet as having been commanded by a young man about twenty, and manned with fourteen men.

Suzzarelli extorted large sums of money from Colonel Lowe under various pretexts; such as indemnifying his agents for their imprisonment, and as bribes stated by him to have been given to the police to prevent his own arrestation. He was a most debauched character, but a man of talent, of prepossessing appearance and manner. He tried at times to deceive Saliceti with wonderful stories, and invented schemes to obtain money from him. Saliceti on these occasions has been known to say, " *Vai a far credere questo al colonello tuo, che è un coglione; a me non puoi, che ti conosco.*"* " Canst thou not say at once that thou hast need of money?"

With a view to embroil the English government with the Sici-

* Go and make thy blockhead of a colonel believe this. It will not go down with me, who know thee fian, a letter was fabricated by Suzzarelli, in imitation of Colonel Lowe's handwriting. In the course of conversation with Cassetti, Suzzarelli observed that Queen Caroline was playing the devil in Sicily, and endeavoring to destroy all the English. This excited Cassetti's curiosity, and caused him to make many inquiries from Suzzarelli, who, after many seeming difficulties, replied that he had a letter from the colonel to that effect, which Cassetti, with great eagerness, asked to see. Suzzarelli, after much persuasion, allowed him too look at it. It stigmatized the Neapolitans as a set of wretches without faith; counselled Suzzarelli to beware of them; asserted that Queen Caroline had formed a plot to assassinate all the English in Sicily; that the barons had every thing ready to take up arms, and to massacre or drive them off the island; concluding with declaring that in consequence of this discovery, the English government had resolved to seize upon the queen, and take the island under their own protection. Cassetti begged hard to be allowed to retain the letter, which Suzzarelli refused, but gave him a copy, promising that he would consider of the propriety of giving him the original. He then went to Saliceti, to whom he related that Cassetti had taken the bait, adding, that he had promised to consider of the propriety of letting him have the original. Not to neglect taking every precaution, Saliceti desired Suzzarelli to send for the English schoolmaster in their employment, who counterfeited handwriting to perfection, to ascertain if the colonel's handwriting had been well imitated by Suzzarelli. On looking at it, he declared that the cheat would be discovered. He then was ordered to copy the letter, and imitated Sir Hudson Lowe's handwriting so perfectly, that the latter was subsequently deceived by it himself. The next morning Suzzarelli gave it to Cassetti, instructing him at the same time not to show or lose it, as he said his life depended upon it. Cassetti immediately hurried off to Palermo, and showed the letter to the queen, who, in a rage, sent for Sir John Stuart, who was then at Palermo, and presented him the counterfeit letter, insisting that a most summary punishment might be inflicted upon Colonel Lowe for having dared to make use of her name in such a manner. Sir John Stuart immediately sent to Colonel Lowe to demand an explanation. On being shown the letter, his handwriting was so well counterfeited that he acknowledged it to be his, but declared that he was not conscious of ever having written such a letter, neither could he find a copy of it in his private despatch-book. At the time that Suzzarelli forged the letter, the police purposely sent out some boats and seized the colonel's boat coming over from Capri. The next day, Suzzarelli wrote to the colonel to inform him that the boat had been seized, and that he did not know what intelligence he had forwarded to him, as all had fallen into the hands of the police, who had possessed themselves of the boat.

Maresca was usually the person employed to go over to the colonel in Antonio's boat. Sir Hudson styled both Suzzarelli and him *sui campioni*, (his champions.) Maresca had two sons, who, as well as Antonio, the boatman, and his sons, were faithful to Sir Hudson Lowe. About the middle of 1809, Sir Hudson Lowe began to suspect Suzzarelli, who in consequence went over to Capri, where he employed his eloquence so effectually as to convince Sir Hudson that he was the most trusty of mankind, and wholly devoted to his service. On his return Suzzarelli went to Saliceti, to whom he related the whole conversation that had taken place between them, accompanying it with divers strokes of wit, at the expense of the poor colonel. Saliceti, when he wished to unbend from state affairs, and divert himself, used sometimes to send for Suzzarelli to make him laugh, by recounting the gross manner in which he had humbugged the colonel.

Several plans were laid to induce the Prince of Canosa to land on the coast of Naples, but fortunately for himself, he did not agree to any of them, as he would have been seized and shot within twenty-four hours. While Suzzarelli was thus carrying on his game, a letter arrived from the police at Paris, stating, that information had been received that one Suzzarelli, a Corsican emigrant, in the pay of England, was at that moment in Naples, employed as a spy for the English, and desiring that Saliceti might cause him to be arrested, tried by a military commission, and the tentence executed directly. Saliceti sent for Suzzarelli, in whose hands he put the letter to read. He then wrote to the police in Paris, explaining the nature of Suzzarelli's connection with Sir Hudson Lowe, and that he was a *treasure* to them. This incident Suzzarelli turned to his own advantage, as it gave him an opportunity of extracting some money from Sir Hudson Lowe, under pretence of having been obliged to bribe largely some of the police; adding, that if it had not been for his friend and countryman, *Franceschi*,* who was in the service of Saliceti, and had great influence, he should infallibly have been arrested and shot

Information was sent to Saliceti that Cassetti intended to poniard him. Although he did not credit it, he nevertheless determined to take precautions. Accordingly, one night when Cassetti made his appearance, he was seized and minutely searched. Nothing, however, was found upon him to justify such a suspicion. After having gone through this ordeal, he was permitted to enter, and loudly complained of the ignoble treatment he had received. Saliceti pretended utter ignorance of it, and affected the greatest astonishment, sent for the officer of gendarmerie, and with an angry air asked how he dared to put such a measure in execution towards a man of honor like Cassetti.† The officer, who was prepared, pretended that it was a mistake, and by order of Saliceti made many apologies to the *man of honor*. "I saw," said Cassetti, who was himself deceived, great rogue as he was, "fire flashing from Saliceti's eyes with indignation, at the unworthy treatment to which I had been exposed."

Suzzarelli, while over in Sicily, had a conversation with one of the Roncos, a captain of brigands under the command of one Piccioli, a native of Cheti, and in the employ of Queen Caroline, who were in the habit of landing and committing depredations in the Calabrias. Piccioli was tired of her service, and was desirous of doing something to procure his pardon and admittance into

---

* This was the reason that Cipriani never assumed the name of *Franceschi*, at St. Helena.

† Cassetti had the rank of lieutenant-colonel in King Joachim's army, as well as in that of Queen Caroline.

that of Murat. He therefore proposed, through Ronco, to cause the gang to land at night in such part of Calabria as might be agreed upon, for the purpose of betraying them into the hands of the Neapolitan police. Suzzarelli mentioned this to Saliceti, and proposed to send a vessel to bring them to Calabria, under pretence of landing in some place where they would meet with a rich booty; which plan he hoped to effect through Ronco. Saliceti, however, who doubted Suzzarelli's courage, told him that he was clever at making proposals and projects, but not in executing such a one as he had suggested, and sent him away. At this proposal was present one Spadaccini, a Neapolitan, a lawyer by profession, and the secret spy of the interior for Saliceti. Ostensibly he was a partisan of Queen Caroline's, and in order the better to deceive the partisans of the exiled family, he procured himself to be arrested and thrown into prison by orders of Saliceti, where he was detained as a suspected person for four months, and apparently treated with great rigor; although in reality he was allowed to do what he liked, and every night went out of the prison in disguise, to make merry with his brother villains. He was a man of determined courage, and capable of any desperate enterprise. At night he returned to Saliceti, to whom he said that the project proposed by Suzzarelli was one of *straw*, and that he alone was the person who could succeed, as he was intimate with Piccioli, they having been brought up together at college, and their houses next to each other. Saliceti promised him six thousand *scudi* in case of success, but if he failed, he declared that he would not only not give him any thing, but would take his present pension from him; adding, that he would give him no money in advance, but would allow six companies of Corsican gendarmerie to be placed under his orders. This offer was immediately accepted by Spadaccini, who proceeded to Pescara, from whence he sent a messenger to Piccioli, who was then at Rocoli. On Piccioli's arrival they had a long conference together, during which they arranged their diabolical plans. A few days afterwards, Piccioli landed in the gulf of Tarento with his gang, consisting of between seventy and eighty ruffians, all *gente di riputazione*, (men of *reputation,*) who had signalized themselves by robberies and murders along the coast, and were the terror of the kingdom of Naples. These wretches marched forward to the mountains, and in their way took an escort with the contribution of the district for three months, which was on its road to the treasury. In the Abbruzzi, they were led by Piccioli at night into a defile, where, under pretence of ascertaining the way, their Judas proceeded in advance. The Corsican gendarmerie were disposed amongst the trees, and as soon as Piccioli got to a certain distance, he stepped in amongst them, when they commenced a fire upon the deluded villains, and massacred every individual of them, who certainly had merited death, but not through the treachery of their leader. After this exploit, Spadaccini and Piccioli returned to Naples, where the former received the reward of his enterprise, and the latter his pardon.—Saliceti, however, considered his treachery to be of so black and atrocious a nature, that he never would either see him, or allow him to be employed.

At the end of October, 1808, King Joachim, finding that the possession of Capri by the English was a source of continual annoyance to the trade of Naples, and also being alarmed by the attempts at assassination made by persons coming from that island, and in the pay of Queen Caroline; and considering it as a reproach to him to suffer the English to hold an island so near to his capital, determined to make himself master of it. Accordingly, great preparations were made for the attack, which Suzzarelli and his confederates persuaded Sir Hudson Lowe was destined for the island of Ponza. Every thing having been prepared, a council of ministers was held a short time previous to the attack. Some wished that Suzzarelli should continue to deceive Sir Hudson Lowe to the last; one,[*] however, gave his opinion that the success of the attack was uncertain, and should it fail, Colonel Lowe would perceive that he had been deceived by Suzzarelli, and would never trust him again. He thought there-

[*] This fact was related to me in 1819, by the minister himself, whose name, for obvious reasons, I shall not mention.

fore that to prevent this, it would be right to permit Suzzarelli to send information of the real destination of the expedition to Sir Hudson Lowe a few hours before it sailed. Until that moment Suzzarelli should continue to persuade him that it was intended for Ponza; thus, whatever might be the event, Suzzarelli would not be compromised. A number of scaling ladders were requisite for the attack of Capri, and it appeared difficult to cause them to be constructed without its coming to the knowledge of Sir Hudson Lowe, which would not only expose Suzzarelli, but point out at once the real object of the expedition. This appeared at first to be an insurmountable difficulty. The genius of the same person, however, who had proposed the above measure, suggested an expedient which perfectly answered. The day before the attack, an order was given by the police, that all the lamplighters in the city of Naples should assemble with their ladders at a certain hour on the following day. The same night, Suzzarelli sent over intimation to Lowe, that the island was to be attacked the next morning, and even enclosed him a copy of the proclamation which was to be issued to the troops who were to make the attempt. It was considered that this short notice would only tend to increase the confusion of the garrison. The expedition, consisting of sixteen or eighteen hundred men, under the command of General Lamarque, sailed from the bay of Naples on the 4th or 5th of October, and arrived under the rocks of Capri, without any molestation from the English squadron, consisting of the Ambuscade frigate and three or four sloops, or the flotilla of gun-boats; which, in the supposition of Ponza being the intended point of attack, had been sent to defend it. Capri had a garrison composed of the royal regiment of Corsicans, the royal regiment of Malta, and some English artillery. There is not perhaps in the world an island which presents more obstacles by nature to an attacking army than Capri. Nine-tenths of the circumference of the island consist of steep and perpendicular rocks, several hundred feet above the level of the sea. Every known landing-place was fortified, and there were about forty pieces of cannon mounted in the forts. In spite of all these natural and artificial obstacles, the French landed, being obliged in some places to climb the precipices by means of ladders, resting on the moving basis of the boats below. The regiment of Malta, whether through cowardice, or from having been corrupted by *the champion*, Suzzarelli, threw down their arms, and refused to fight, and were made prisoners, in spite of all the exertions of their officers, several of whom, including the commanding officer, were killed in the attempt. In this manner, the fort St. Barbe and Ana-Capri, the summit of the island, were taken. The only way of communicating with Capri itself, the citadel, and the forts, where Sir Hudson and the rest of the garrison were, was by means of a stair, or ladder, of four or five hundred steps, down which only one person at a time in front could descend, and was commanded by several pieces of cannon. Notwithstanding this, the French troops made the attempt, succeeded, and invested the town. Five hundred men were harnessed to some twenty-four pounder guns, which they dragged up in one night to Mount Solara, the most elevated point of Ana-Capri, and commanding the citadel. During the whole period of his government, Sir Hudson Lowe had neglected to fortify this part, in the supposition that it was impracticable to drag heavy cannon up the steep sides of the mountain. Breaching batteries were constructed facing the citadel, and others furnished with furnaces for red hot shot erected along the beach, in order to keep off the English squadron and flotilla which were seen beating up from Ponza. Some reinforcements also pushed off from Naples and landed near Tiberius's Bath, and in a few days, Sir Hudson Lowe capitulated, surrendering to the French the island, forts, artillery, ammunition and stores.

Capri was commonly called the Gibraltar of Naples, and the obstacles to its capture, or even to landing, appeared so insurmountable, as to draw forth from Saliceti the following remarks, on visiting it after it was taken. "*J'y ai trouvé les Français mais je ne puis pas croire qu'ils y soient entrés,*" (I found the French there, but I cannot believe it possible that they entered it.)

When the expedition under Lieutenant-General Sir John Stuart and Admiral Freemantle, consisting of about eighteen or nineteen thousand men, left Sicily in 1809, the advice and intention of the Admiral were, that the expedition should land between Portici and Castelamare, and attack the city of Naples. Sir Hudson Lowe was with the army. Reference was made to Suzzarelli for advice, who recommended that the English should at first secure some point of support and retreat, by taking the islands of Ischia and Procida, and then to land at Baja, the garrison of which he said was commanded by a Corsican colonel, a relation of his, who would for a certain sum of money, and an equal rank in the English service, betray the place, after making a show of resistance. That by this time the English party and that of Ferdinand would have time to arrange their plans to assist them, and collect their adherents. This advice was unfortunately followed. There were at this time only four thousand men in that city, as most of the French troops were upon their march towards Germany, it being a little before the battle of Wagram. Orders had been given to those troops who were in the city to abandon it if the English landed, and retire to Fort St. Elmo, there to remain until they were succored. They had even been ordered not to fire upon the town of Naples, if the English occupied it. All the treasure, all the king and queen's baggage and jewels were packed up, as well as those of the principal persons, and ready to depart the moment the English landed. Little or no resistance could have been made. There were several frigates and a seventy-four on the stocks, immense stores, between two and three hundred sail of merchantmen, and a very large flotilla, which must have been all taken, as Murat did not like to injure the city by attempting a useless defence. When the English first appeared, Saliceti was in Rome. Murat became imbecile, and thought of nothing but saving his treasures. The queen, however, who had much more firmness and talent in the cabinet than her husband, sent Cipriani with a note to Saliceti, entreating him to return without loss of time to Naples; that the king had lost his senses, and was incapable of commanding, and that everything depended upon him. This letter Cipriani concealed in the sole of his boot; and after some difficulty, and a narrow escape from robbers near Terracina, succeeded in arriving at Rome. If he succeeded in bringing back Saliceti, he was ordered by the queen to return with all possible celerity; and at a place agreed upon near the entrance of the town, to take out his handkerchief, and appear to wipe the sweat off his brows; if not, he was to continue his course. He saw Saliceti at about two in the morning, to whom he communicated everything. After reading the letter, Saliceti demanded what Suzzarelli and Maresca were doing. Cipriani replied, that they were in Naples, and endeavoring to persuade the English generals not to land between Portici and Castelamare, but to attack Ischia. "*Bravo Suzzarelli*," exclaimed Saliceti, "*son perduti*; but if they land between Portici and Castelamare, we are lost." Saliceti sent Cipriani on, who returned with a rapidity never before heard of, and made the signal agreed upon. He was soon followed by Saliceti, who on his arrival found Murat's horses saddled, and the king himself in the street, and on the point of abandoning the city to its fate. Saliceti in rather a harsh manner told Murat that he was unworthy of a kingdom if he did not defend his people; and concluded by assuring him that he would himself take the direction of everything in the name of the Emperor Napoleon, if he did not adopt the necessary measures for defence. Murat, confounded, returned to his palace. Orders were instantly despatched to recall the troops in the interior, and those on their march to Germany; the fourth regiment of dragoons was brought from the Abbruzzi, and every necessary measure instantly adopted. Cannon were placed in the streets, with trusty troops and matches lighted; and orders publicly given to fire upon any assemblage of the people. Saliceti sent for those whom he suspected, and told them that he could not trust to their bare words that they would remain quiet, and not meddle with what was going on; and concluded by asking, in a stern tone of voice, what guarantee they could give him for their conduct? Astonished at his manner, after a little hesitation, they asked to be confined in one of the forts until the business was over, which was accordingly done. While he acted publicly in this manner, and ordered that every means of defence should be put in practice to encourage those who were faithful, and dismay the disaffected, he had at the same time secretly continued the directions, that if the English disembarked, the troops were to evacuate the town, and retire to the forts, until a sufficient force had returned from the interior to afford some chance of success. In three days a respectable force was collected, and all fears at an end.

Saliceti was a republican in principle, and would have supported the establishment of that sort of government in Italy, had there appeared a probability of success. He died a few hours after having dined with an enemy, to whom he had been reconciled, which gave rise to a supposition that he was poisoned. Upon this, however, there was a difference of opinion; the French physicians asserting, and the Italians denying the fact. No traces of poison were discovered on opening his body. When Napoleon was informed of his death, he exclaimed, "*Son nom seul me valait une armée de cent mille hommes,*" (his name alone was worth an army of a hundred thousand men to me.)

Independent of the confirmation of the above account given to me by one of the then ministers of King Murat, and the fact of Sir Hudson Lowe's letters to Suzzarelli being now in existence, Napoleon, to whom I mentioned some of the circumstances, replied, that he was aware of the manner in which we had been betrayed by our spies at Naples; and added, that Cipriani, who had been a principal agent, could furnish me with all the particulars. He remarked that in general our spies betrayed us. That the French had a great advantage in the Roman Catholic religion, as the spies were induced to believe that it was not only not necessary, but even meritorious, not to keep faith with heretics.

December 4th.—Miss V * * *, a pretty girl, and *femme de chambre* to Lady Lowe, came to Longwood this day from Plantation House, mounted on one of the governor's horses, and furnished with a letter from Major Gorrequer, stating that Sir Hudson Lowe had forgotten to leave a pass for her before he went to town, and directing Captain Blakeney to admit her. She went to Longwood House, where she remained for near **two hours,** during which time she passed through almost every room in the building; the French domestics were so much enchanted with the apparition of a young and pretty girl, that their gallantry could scarcely refuse her any thing. She was very desirous of obtaining admission to Napoleon, and at one time had partly opened the door of the room where he was, for the purpose of going in to him, but was prevented by St. Denis. She persuaded them, however, to allow her to peep at him for some time through the key-hole.*

7th.—Communicated to Mr. Baxter, that Napoleon had at last agreed to take some medicine which I administered to him myself, and by which he had been temporarily benefited. Mr. Baxter agreed with me in opinion of the propriety of affording him some other winter abode, than the dreary and exposed situation of Longwood; where, in consequence of the bleak and eternal southeast wind, he very generally contracted a catarrhal affection whenever he went out. Mr. Baxter himself mentioned Rosemary Hall or Colonel Smith's, as being the most suitable.

9th.—Signal made for me to proceed to Plantation House. Soon after my arrival, Sir Hudson Lowe said, with a serious air, that he had sent to me on business not medical; that he had great occasion to censure my conduct, and then proceeded to ask, if I had not kept up a correspondence, or was not the medium of communication for the French at Longwood, with persons on the island? I felt surprised at the question, and replied, that I was ignorant of his meaning. He repeated his interrogations more than once, adding, that he did not mean communications to favor General Bonaparte's escape from the island, but of another nature. I replied, that if going into shops and buying articles for Countesses Bertrand and Montholon, or others at Longwood, could be

---

* A short time afterwards this young person left St. Helena, pregnant (if report be true) by one of the inmates of Plantation House. She was accompanied on board ship by Sir Thomas Reade, and every possible attention paid her by the governor. Various were the surmises at Longwood, as to the cause of this young woman's visit under *such* circumstances, some of which the intelligent reader will not fail to guess.

construed into carrying on communications or correspondence for them, I must certainly plead guilty. He then asked, if I had not written to town to a person to send up some articles for Madame Bertrand? I replied, certainly, that I had written to Mr. Darling to send up some basins, chamber utensils, and other articles of household use. The governor said that it was a breach of orders, as he had prohibited me from being the bearer of any message or communication not medical. "What business had I to do so? If Madame Bertrand wants any thing of the kind, let her apply to the orderly officer; and why had she not done so?"

I replied, that in the first place, cleanliness was necessary to prevent sickness, and consequently, every thing relating to it was medical. That, in the next place, the orderly officer was absent from Longwood when the request was made to me; that, even if he had been present, delicacy would prevent a lady from making demands to him for certain necessary articles, which she could with propriety mention to her surgeon; and that I did not conceive it to be a crime to desire a tradesman to purchase chamber utensils, (naming them,) or similar articles, either for Madame Bertrand or myself. His excellency, as usual, flew into a violent passion, and said that he would not allow me to insult him in his capacity of governor, and was otherwise very violent; asked me, "how dare I order articles to be sent out of the king's stores without consulting him? or to have them charged to those stores?" I replied, that I had said nothing about charging them to the king's stores. A reference was then made to my letter to Mr. Darling, which the governor had in his possession, and which confirmed my statement. Notwithstanding this, he continued his abuse, and made some common-place remarks upon the delicacy of *French* ladies.

I asked for written orders, in order to prevent the possibility of a mistake, which he refused to give. I then asked, if the ladies required me to purchase some articles for them in the shops, what reply was I to make? After some hesitation, he said, that "if they wished me to purchase any thing for them myself, I need not refuse; but that if they asked me to apply to another to purchase any thing for them, I was not to comply with it!!" He was very violent for a great part of the time, and I had much difficulty in repressing a smile at the serious manner in which he treated this *important* subject.

No alteration of importance has taken place in the state of Napoleon's complaint. Had some discourse with him upon the libels which had been published at his expense. "Of all the libels and pamphlets against me," said he, " with which your ministers have inundated Europe, not one will live to posterity. During the reign of Louis the Fourteenth, and even under Henry the Fourth, the press teemed with libels, not one of which is now to be found. The labors of those wretches employed by your ministers,* to dance over the ruins of their own country, will die in a similar manner. When I was asked to write, or cause to be written answers to them, I replied, ' *une victoire, un monument de plus est la véritable réponse,*' (one victory, one monument more, is the real answer.) Besides, it would have been said that I paid for the writing of them, which would have been discreditable.

---

* The acrimony still entertained towards the deceased Emperor Napoleon, is exemplified by a reply which I have been told escaped from the lips of an under-secretary of state, who, when informed that, a short time before his dissolution, Napoleon ordered that his body should be opened, his heart taken out, preserved in spirits of wine, and sent to the Empress Marie Louise ; replied, " *It ought to have been thrown into quick-lime.*" When Napoleon was sent to St. Helena, it was expressly stated, in the regulations for his safe custody, that should he die in that island, his body should be interred wherever he thought proper to order it in his will. This promise, however, has not been kept. In the codicil to his will, which was made known to the ministers, the following words are to be found :—

"*Avril le* 16, 1821. *Longwood.*
" *Ceci est un codicille de mon testament.* 1°. *Je desire que mes cendres repo sent sur les bords de la Seine, au milieu de ce peuple Francais que j' ai tant at· me.*"
(*Signe*) " NAPOLEON."

(April 16, 1821. Longwood.
This is a codicil of my will. 1st, I desire that my ashes may repose upon the banks of the Seine, in the midst of the French people whom I have loved so much.)

His remains were refused, at the end of last year, to the prayers of his aged mother.

Posterity will judge by facts; calumny has exhausted all her poisons on my person. I shall gain every day. *La première fureur passée, je ne conserverai pour ennemis que des sot ou des méchans*, (When the first fury shall have passed, I shall have only the wicked and foolish as my enemies.) When there is not a trace of those libels to be found, the great works and monuments that I executed, and the code of laws that I formed, will go down to the most distant ages, and future historians will revenge the wrongs done to me by my contemporaries."

I asked, if, in his own mind, he believed that * * * was privy to the death of * * ? "There is not a doubt," replied he, "that the attempt was made with his consent. The empress," added he, "never could bear the sight of any of the murderers afterwards, and never would receive them; but one is now aid-de-camp to * * *.

"After the execution of the Duc d'Enghien, * * * *," said he, "ordered a service to be celebrated for his death. I did not like this, and caused the conduct relative to the death of his own father, to be *served up to him in prose and verse*."*

"Lord * *," continued he, "was also privy to it. He was the most intimate friend of P * *, the principal contriver and actor. This was well known at Petersburg."

He mentioned that Talleyrand certainly had first suggested the attempt upon Spain, partly through hatred of the Bourbon family, and partly in hope of filling his pockets.

Conversing on the policy adopted by our ministers, "It would have been better for England," he observed, "to have left me on the throne, as Russia, Austria, and Prussia would, through jealousy of me, have given commercial advantages to England. There is nothing now to prevent their taking steps to promote their own commercial interests, by injuring those of England. Moreover, having great influence with the French nation, and being loved by them, I could have given you a favorable commercial treaty, which the Bourbons, who are hated, dare not propose. But, in truth, there was nothing really to be feared from France,

* An idiomatic expression.

under any sovereign. Until she has an army of five hundred thousand men, France is not to be dreaded. Besides, it was always for the allies, to grant peace. France was tired of war, and was frightened at the idea of new conquests. I succeeded in beating the allies, because I attacked them in detail, and destroyed one power before the army of the other could arrive to support it. Hundreds of years will probably elapse, before circumstances will arise similar to those which concentrated such a mass of power in me. I repeat, that there was nothing to be feared from me, for if I had attempted new conquests, the opinion which brought me back from Elba, would have thrown me to the ground again."

Massena, he observed, on a former occasion, had lost himself in the campaign of Portugal, which, however, he attributed to the bad state of his health, that did not permit him to sit on horseback, or inspect, himself, what was going on. "A general, who sees with the eyes of others," added he, "will never be able to command an army as it should be. Massena was then so ill that he was obliged to trust to the reports of others, and consequently failed in some of his undertakings. At Busaco, for example, he attempted to carry a position almost impregnable in the manner he attacked it; whereas, if he had commenced by turning it, he would have succeeded. This was owing to his not being able to reconnoitre personally." He added, "that if Massena had been what he was formerly, he would have followed Wellington so closely as to be able to attack him,* while entering the lines before Lisbon, before he could have taken up his position properly."

14th.—Sir Hudson Lowe at Longwood. Asked me several questions about Napoleon's health. Observed that it was very extraordinary he did not take exercise; that if he expected, by confining himself, to obtain any further relaxation in the system adopted, he was mistaken. He then inquired if the want of sleep

---

* Speaking of the Duke of Wellington on a former occasion, he observed, that all generals were liable to err, and that whoever committed the least number of faults, should be esteemed to be the greatest, and that he (Wellington) had committed them as seldom as most others.

was caused by mental, or by bodily disease. I said, that I thought it was chiefly caused by the want of exercise; that no man, leading such a life as Napoleon did, could possibly remain long in a state of health. The governor said, with a sneer, that *he* believed *laziness* was the cause of his not taking exercise. I replied, that when he first came to the island, he had taken a great deal. He then said, that he wanted to have information of his state of health more frequently, and desired me to mention anything extraordinary to Captain Blakeney. I said, that it would be very easy to arrange matters, by sending him bulletins, describing Napoleon as "the patient," giving copies to Count Bertrand at the same time. This he refused to allow, saying, that as long as verbal reports could be got, he did not think written ones of consequence. He also made some insinuations about his not naving seen Mr. Baxter.

In the course of conversation this day, Napoleon expressed his disapprobation of our custom of shutting up shops and prohibiting people from working on Sundays. In reply to what I said, he remarked, "For those who are at their ease, it may be very right and proper to discontinue working on the seventh day, but to oblige a poor man who has a large family, without a meal to give them, to leave off laboring to procure them victuals, is the height of barbarity. If such a law be enforced, provision ought to be made by your government to feed those who, on that day, have not wherewithal to purchase food, and who could obtain it, if permitted to labor. Or let your gorbellied priests (*panciuti*) give a portion of their dinners on that day to the starving poor, whom they will not allow to work. They would have an apoplexy, or an indigestion the less. Besides, it does not serve the cause of morality. Idleness is the mother of mischief, and I will wager that there is more drunkenness to be seen, that there is more vice, and that more crimes are committed in England on a Sunday, than on any other day of the week."

Speaking upon the possibility of cordially uniting the negroes with the whites, Napoleon observed, that it had occurred to him, that the only mode of effectually reconciling the two colors, would be to allow polygamy in the colonies. That every black or white man should be permitted to have a wife of each color. By such means, he thought, that in the next generation, nearly all would be alike, and consequently all jealousy and hatred done away. He added, that it would have been easy to have obtained a dispensation from the Pope to that effect. He also said, that he considered the negroes to be a race inferior to the whites.

Saw Napoleon again in the evening, who made some observations upon the governor, who, he observed, had passed by his windows. "I never see that governor," said he, " without thinking I view the man heating the poker (*échauffant le bar de fer*) for your Edward the Second in Berkeley Castle. *La nature m'a prévénu contre*, (Nature has prejudiced me against him,) and gave me a friendly warning the first day I saw him. *Comme Cain, la nature l'a bien cacheté*, (Like Cain, nature has set a mark upon him.) If I were in London, and Sir H. Lowe were presented to me *en bourgeoise*, and I were asked, whom do you conceive that man to be? I should reply, *c'est le bourreau de la municipalité*, (he is the common hangman.) For you cannot say," added he, " that it arises from prejudice against your nation, as I never have been so with Cockburn. Never did I for a moment, as you well know, suspect or distrust him in the slightest manner. From him I would readily have received a surgeon or any thing else. I had every confidence in him, even after we had differed. But I think that I see this * * * * * * * * heating the poker. He wanted to encircle the house with *grilles de fer*, (iron grates,) in order to make the second *cage de fer de Bajazet*, (Bajazet's iron cage,) for which purpose he put his government to the useless expense of sending out a ship load of iron bars to make his cage."

I recommended him to see Mr. Baxter, adding, that it would be a satisfaction to me, to have the assistance of the advice and opinion of another medical person. He replied, " *Il governatore sen è mischiato ; è vero che la sua fisono mia è buona, ma è troppo attaccato a quel boja*, (The governor has interfered ; it is true he has a good physiognomy, but he is too much attached to that hangman.) *Le gouverneur est* * * * * * *. *Il rend odieux tout ce qui se passe entre ses mains,* (He renders every thing disagreeable that passes through his hands,) therefore I think that he must have suffered by contact with him. Besides, he has been recommended by him, and that is sufficient to prevent me from ever seeing him."

"If I, *malheureusement,*" (unfortunately,) added he, "had such a physiognomy, the world would then believe the libellers. Look, they would say, oh, look at the countenance of the *scelerat*, (miscreant.) See the murders of Wright, of Pichegru, and of a thousand others stamped on the visage of the monster."

18*th*.—Summoned to attend at Plantation House by letter from Major Gorrequer. As the reader must be already disgusted with the details of the manner in which the governor took advantage of his situation to insult and oppress an officer inferior in rank, because the latter refused to be his spy; I shall not fatigue him with any further account of the conduct practised towards me on this day, than that my replies and refusals to disclose Napoleon's conversations, caused me to be treated in a more outrageous manner than on the 18th of last month. The governor followed me out of the room, vociferating after me in a frantic manner, and carried his gestures so far as to menace me with personal violence.

After this, orders again given me to attend interrogations at Plantation House twice a week.

27*th*.—A letter sent by Major Gorrequer, informing me that I had been expected yesterday at Plantation House, and ordering me there this day. On my arrival, I saw Mr. Baxter, to whom, after some conversation about Napoleon's complaint, I communicated my positive determination, never to come again to the governor at Plantation House, or attend him elsewhere, if a repetition of the scandalous treatment I had met with on the 18th again occurred; that this I was determined upon, whatever might be the consequences.

January 1*st*, 1818.—Napoleon nearly in the same state as yesterday.

Some conversation took place upon Mr. Hobhouse's book, which, as has been already stated, had been sent by the author, and detained by Sir Hudson Lowe. I said that it had been seen by accident in Sir Hudson's library, by the person who had acquainted him (Napoleon) with the circumstance. "It was a *bêtise* in the governor," said he, "after he had illegally detained it, to leave it where any person might see it. In Cardinal Richelieu's time, a nobleman who waited upon him about some affairs, and to ask some favor, was ushered into his private cabinet. While they were conversing together, a great personage was announced, and entered the room. After some conversation with Richelieu, the great man took his leave, and the cardinal, in compliment to him, attended him to his carriage, forgetting that he had left the other alone in the cabinet. On his return to his cabinet, he rung a bell, one of his confidential secretaries entered, to whom he whispered something. He then conversed with the other very freely, appeared to take an interest in his affairs, kept him in conversation for a short time, accompanied him to the door, shook hands, and took leave in the most friendly way, telling him that he might make his mind easy, as he had determined to provide for him. The poor man departed highly satisfied and full of thanks and gratitude. As he was going out of the door he was arrested, not allowed to speak to any person, and conveyed in a coach to the Bastille, where he was kept *au secret* for ten years; at the expiration of which time the cardinal sent for him, and expressed his great regret at having been obliged to adopt the step he had taken, that he had no cause of complaint against him; on the contrary, that he believed him to be a good subject to his majesty; but the fact was, he had left a paper on the table when he quitted the room, containing state secrets of vast importance, which he was afraid he might have perused in his absence; that the safety of the kingdom demanded that they should not be divulged, and obliged him to adopt measures to prevent the possibility of the contents being known. That as soon as the safety of the country permitted, he had released him, was sorry, and begged his pardon for the uneasiness he had caused him, and would be happy to make him some amends."

Some sentiments relative to the French revolution were also delivered by Napoleon, and arguments in favor of the validity of the imperial title. " The republic sent to and received from all the powers of Europe ambassadors. It was sanctioned by the will of the people, by victory, by religion, and by all the nations of Europe. Louis, driven from one state to another, was at last obliged to seek for refuge in England, but was received there as a private person, and on the express stipulation that he should only assume the title of the Count de Lisle. None of the powers ever acknowledged Louis the Seventeenth, or Louis the Eighteenth. Every legitimate government cancels the rights and the legitimacy of the governments which preceded it. The French revolution was a general movement of the mass of the nation against the privileged classes. The nobles retained the higher and the inferior justice, and other feudal rights, under various forms; enjoyed the privilege of being exempt from the burthens of the community, and exclusively possessed all honorable employments. The chief object of the revolution was to destroy those privileges and abuses, to abolish the manorial courts, suppress the remains of the ancient slavery of the people, and subject all citizens equally to bear the expenses of the state. It established equality of rights. Any citizen might succeed to any employment according to his talents. Before it, France was composed of provinces differently divided and unequal in extent and in population. They had a great number of legal customs and peculiar laws for the administration of civil as well as criminal justice. She was an assemblage of several states without an amalgamation. The revolution destroyed all those little nations, and formed a new one. There was one France with an homogeneous division of territory, the same civil and criminal laws, and the same regulations for taxes. There no longer remained any trace of the ancient privileges of the provinces, their ancient sovereigns, or ancient parliaments. One half of the territory had changed proprietors

France presented the spectacle of thirty millions of inhabitants circumscribed in natural limits, composed of one class of citizens, and governed by one law, one regulation, one order. Subsequently the French nation established the imperial throne, and placed me upon it. No person ever ascended a throne with more legitimate rights. The throne of France was granted before to Hugh Capet by a few bishops and nobles The imperial throne was given to me by the desire of the people, whose wishes were three times verified in a solemn manner. The Pope crossed the Alps to crown and anoint me. Kings hastened to acknowledge me. England acknowledged the republic, and sent ambassadors to the first consul. Before she violated the peace of Amiens, the English ministers offered, through Malouet, to acknowledge me as king of France if I would agree to the cession of Malta; and in 1806, Lord Lauderdale came to Paris to treat for a peace between the king of Great Britain and the *Emperor Napoleon*, exchanged his powers, and negotiated with the plenipotentiary of the *emperor*. If Fox had lived peace would have been made. Moreover, the imperial title was acknowledged by Lord Castlereagh, when he signed the *ultimatum* at Chaumont, acknowledging the existence of the empire, and me as emperor."

2nd.—Went to Plantation House by order of the governor, whom I saw in the library. He asked a great many questions concerning my appointment as surgeon to Napoleon, and concluded by asserting that I was not his surgeon, but only *tolerated to visit him*. I observed, that the bills which I drew for my pay on the Navy Board, the form of which had been ordered by Sir George Cockburn, were worded " as Surgeon to Napoleon Bonaparte and suite." I also took the liberty of asking him for what object I was at St. Helena.

He asked me, " If I conceived myself to be independent of him as governor, and of the government under whose orders I acted ?" I replied, that no British officer could be independent of the government of his country. He then asked, " whether I conceived myself independent of *him*, and if it were not in his power as governor, and having charge of Napoleon Bonaparte, if he thought that my conduct was not correct, to send me away if he pleased?" I told him that he could reply to that himself, as he best knew what the extent of his authority was. This answer did not please him, and after walking about the room for a little time, exclaiming against my conduct, he stopped, crossed his arms, and after looking at me with an expression of countenance which I shall never forget, said, "This is my office, sir, and there is the door leading to it. When I send for you on duty, you will come in at that door; but do not put your foot in any other part of my house, or come in at any other entrance."

I calmly replied, that it was not for my own pleasure, or by my own desire, that I ever set foot in any part of his house; and after suffering this paltry abuse of authority, departed.

Saw Napoleon afterwards, who was nearly in the same state as yesterday. Had some conversation relative to the capture of Rome by the French. "After the treaty which I had concluded at Tolentino with that imbecile and fraudulent court of old women at Rome," said Napoleon, "they endeavored by all means to assist the Austrians, and even placed an Austrian general at the head of their troops. Every where the populace were excited, by all the means generally put in practice by superstition and bigotry, to massacre the French. General Duphot, who was residing at Rome as a private person, was murdered at the door of my brother Joseph, who was ambassador there. However, under all the circumstances, and concluding that a rupture with Rome would infallibly lead to one with Naples, I was of opinion that we ought only to correct, and not destroy her. That we ought to demand that an example should be made of the guilty; that Provera, the Austrian general, should be obliged to depart, and an ambassador sent to Paris to beg pardon. The directory, however, decided that we should march against the Pope; and said that the time was come to overturn that idol. Berthier was sent with an army to revolutionize Rome, and establish a republic, which was done. The people at first were transported with joy at the thought of the re-establishment of the Roman republic, and fêtes were given, and a *te deum* celebrated with great pomp; at which last a number of the cardinals attended, although the act of re-establishment was the annihilation of the Pope's temporal power. Their joy, however, was of short continuance, as the troops, who were little restrained by their generals, and excited by agents of yours and of the Austrians, commenced a scene of robbery, and plundered the Vatican and the palaces of the nobles of their pictures and pieces of art of all kinds, and finished by mutinying against the *imbéciles*, who saw the error too late, and endeavored in vain to put a stop to their abuses."

"When the Venetians," continued Napoleon, "deceived by false reports that Joubert's army had been defeated and cut to pieces; and duped by the traitorous and Machiavelian policy of the court of Vienna, armed a number of Sclavonians and peasants, the priests preached destruction to the French, and another Sicilian vespers. All the French in Verona were massacred, and their bodies thrown into the Adige. Four hundred of the sick and wounded in the hospitals were barbarously murdered. In other towns in the Venetian territories similar cruelties were practised. As soon as they discovered that the army of Joubert was entire; that Augereau was marching against them, and finding that the Austrians, defeated every where, had sent to me to supplicate for peace, their fright knew no bounds. A deputation waited upon me, making the most submissive proposals; pledging themselves to agree to every thing I should require, and offering me millions if I would grant their prayers. Finding this useless, orders were despatched to their minister at Paris to corrupt the directory, in which they succeeded, as orders were sent of a nature favorable to their wishes. The despatches of their ambassador, however, were seized and brought to me, and the whole intrigue discovered, together with the amount of the bribes they had given. I commanded the French minister to quit their territories within twenty-four hours, and declared war against Venice, which Baraguez d'Hilliers entered with his division, upset the oligarchy, and the whole of the states were soon republicanized."

Received the letters which are inserted in the preface.

6th:—Interrogated by Sir Hudson Lowe whether Napoleon

Bonaparte had directed or commanded me to make a communication which I had done to him, viz. that he, Napoleon, had told Lord Amherst, "neither of your houses of parliament can oblige me to see *mon bourreau*, &c.," (my executioner,) or whether I had repeated it without having had authority to do so from Bonaparte? I answered, that Napoleon had said, if I were asked any questions about the conversation with him, I was permitted to mention it. This did not satisfy Sir Hudson Lowe, who wished me to answer it as best suited whatever purposes he had in view; and on my persisting in the above reply, he became very violent and abusive, and ordered Major Gorrequer to write down, "Mr. O'Meara refuses to reply to the question of, 'Did Bonaparte or did he not desire you to communicate the above-mentioned expressions to the governor?'" I said that some persons would consider it as a desire, and others only as a permission, and therefore it was best to put down Napoleon's words, which, however, his excellency would not allow.

7th.—Sir Hudson Lowe sent for me at six o'clock in the evening, when after having made some inquiries about Napoleon's state of health, which I told him was not so good as the last time I had reported; he said, that if General Bonaparte thought he should gain any further relaxation in the restrictions by confining himself to the house in the manner he did, he was mistaken, as he, (Sir Hudson,) without an order from government, would not make any more alterations in the regulations, even if he were worse in health. I asked if he wished this to be communicated to Napoleon? He said, that he did not *desire* it; but that it ought to be known.

9th.—Another series of interrogations at Plantation House, partly about Lord Amherst, during which the governor said, that "General Bonaparte would not have dared to make use of the insulting expressions he did before any other persons than Lord Amherst and myself; that General Bonaparte had so expressed himself, because he (Napoleon) knew that his lordship had received the governor's permission to listen to any complaints which he might make · that a listener was as bad as a **repeater; and** that Count Bertrand had told him (Sir Hudson) in October last, that General Bonaparte was influenced by the persons about him, amongst whom I formed one." I could scarcely help smiling at the supposition that *I* could have influenced such a person as Napoleon, and contented myself with replying, that as far as I knew him, he was not a man to let himself be guided by the opinion of others. Sir Hudson, however, insisted that Count Bertrand had confessed it, and said that I should be responsible for a great deal of what might happen, &c., &c.

13*th*.—More interrogations at Plantation House. Sir Hudson Lowe took out of his pocket a Morning Chronicle of the 17th of September, 1817, (I think,) containing a detail of a conversation stated to have taken place between Napoleon and some English gentlemen, and was desirous, he said, " to know from me whether such a conversation had ever taken place between General Bonaparte and myself, or if I had ever communicated it to other persons. That he inferred from the commencement of the article, viz., *after the usual salutations*, that the conversation had taken place between General Bonaparte and some person who was frequently in the habit of seeing him; that Admiral Malcolm, and myself, were the only persons who had *tête-à-tête* conversations with him; therefore that it must have been communicated by one of us." I replied, that I had neither written nor communicated it, and reminded him, that others besides the admiral and myself had communications with Napoleon. His excellency appeared to be very anxious that I should assist him to saddle it upon the admiral; in which, however, he did not succeed. Indeed, on the first glance I had of it, I saw that it must have come from Mr. Ellis; it however contained some misrepresentations.

15*th*.—Saw the governor at Plantation House, to whom I reported that Napoleon's indisposition had rather increased, and that I had been that morning under the necessity of giving him physic. Communicated the same to Mr. Baxter.

16*th*.—Saw Napoleon, who felt somewhat relieved by the effect of the physic administered yesterday. Had a conversation with him upon some of the early periods of his life, and the manner in which he had obtained the command of the troops of the convention against the sections. "When Menou," said he, "was repulsed in his attempt to disperse the sections, through the imbecility of the representatives who were with him, and his own incapacity, the convention was in the greatest alarm, as the *comité* of the section had declared itself sovereign in the exercise of its functions, and permanent, refusing to obey the orders of the convention, and had even sent deputations to the other sections to assist them. Their numbers amounted to above forty thousand. I was in a box at the theatre Feydeau when informed of this, and proceeded to the assembly. The convention were in the greatest dismay; Menou was accused of treachery—the danger was imminent. Each member of the assembly proposed the general in whom he had confidence. The members of the committee of public safety, and some who had known me at Toulon, proposed me as the person best calculated, by the energy of my character, to save them in the present crisis. A deputation was sent to offer the command to me. I balanced, however, for some time before I would accept of it. It was a service that I did not like; but when I considered that if the convention was overturned, *l'étranger* (the stranger) would triumph; that the destruction of that body would seal the slavery of the country, and bring back an incapable and insolent race, those reflections and destiny decided that I should accept of it. I went to the *comité*, pointed out to them the inconvenience of having three representatives with the troops, who only served to impede all the operations of the general. The *comité* perceiving that there was no time to be lost, proposed Barras to the convention, as general-in-chief, and gave the command of the troops that were to protect the assembly, to me. The measures that I adopted, as I explained to you before, saved the convention, with a very trifling loss of men* on both sides."

---

* I was informed by the Duke of Rovigo, and by many other officers who had served with him, that the humanity displayed by the emperor to his soldiers was exemplary on all occasions. That in particular he was frequently in the habit of riding over the field of battle after an action, accompanied by numbers of his staff, and by persons carrying restoratives of different kinds for the purpose of resuscitating any of the wounded, in whom signs of life appeared. That Napo-

20th.—Went to Plantation House, according to orders. While speaking to Mr. Baxter in the library, the governor came in looking very angry, and asked in a rough and abrupt manner, what communications I had to make respecting General Bonaparte's health? I replied that no permanent relief for the better had taken place. "Has he been out of the house?" "He has not." "Has he been in the billiard-room?" "He spends a considerable portion of his time there every day." "How does he employ his time there?" "I cannot tell, sir." "Yes, you can, sir," replied the governor, regarding me in his customary manner, "you well know what he does there; you do not do your duty to government."

His excellency then walked about the room, stopping occasionally, and regarding me with his arms crossed over his breast in a manner which it is difficult to describe, and bursting out into furious exclamations. I contented myself with taking out my watch to ascertain the length of time he contemplated me in this manner. I thought more than once that he meditated some act of violence. This composure and silence appeared not to be what he wished, and he began another series of interrogations in his usual manner, relative to the name of the person who had given me information about twelve months ago, that Lord Liverpool had interfered and prevented my removal from St. Helena. I answered that I had, at the time I had first mentioned it to him in July last, offered to show to a third person that part of the letter which stated

---

leon has often spent hours in this pious employment. Amongst other strong instances, the Duke of Rovigo mentioned, that after the battle of Wagram, Napoleon, accompanied by him and several others, rode over the field, and pointed out for assistance many of the wounded from whom life had not yet departed. While employed in this manner, the body of a colonel named Pepin, who had fallen under his displeasure for some misconduct several years before, and had not been actively employed until a short time before the battle of Wagram, attracted his attention, though he had not seen him for a number of years. He was on his back, a ball had perforated his head, and life was not extinct, though he was insensible. "Ah, Pepin! poor fellow," said Napoleon, in a feeling manner, "I am sorry to see him here, and still more so, that, before he met his fate, I had not an opportunity of letting him know that I had forgiven him, and forgotten his conduct."

that application had been made to Lord Liverpool, that his lordship should prevent my being removed. The governor renewed in a violent tone his demand that I should forthwith give him the name of the person who had communicated the information to me, and that the offer I had then made of showing it to a third person, was an insult to him; and advanced towards me in a menacing manner, evidently with an intention to intimidate me to a compliance. I answered as before, which drew forth another demand of the name with an increase of violence. I said then, that as my replies only brought upon me abuse, bad language, and bad treatment, I must decline giving him any more answers on the subject. "Put down, Major Gorrequer, that Mr. O'Meara refuses to answer," was the governor's reply. After listening to a long and abusive harangue, about my improper conduct since he had catechised me about a newspaper, (*id est*, since I had refused to be an instrument to calumniate Admiral Malcolm,) I was permitted to depart.

28*th*.—Saw Napoleon, who was rather better than on the preceding day. Had some conversation about Chateaubriand. "Chateaubriand," said he, "is an old emigrant, who was appointed secretary to Cardinal Fesch, when the latter was ambassador to the court of Rome, where he contrived to render himself disliked by the Pope and the cardinals, notwithstanding the *galimathias*, (nonsense,) which he had published upon Christianity. While he was there, he endeavored to persuade the old king of Sardinia, who had abdicated and turned *religieux*, to renew his claims to the throne of Sardinia. The king, suspecting him to be a *mouton, le mit à la porte*, (spy, turned him out of doors,) and made a complaint to me of his conduct, which caused his disgrace. While I was in power, he was one of the most abject of my flatterers. *C'est un fanfaron sans caractère, qui a l'âme rampante, et qui a la fureur de faire des livres,*" (he is a miserable boaster without character, with a grovelling soul and an itch for writing.)

I asked some questions about Bernadotte's conduct. "Bernadotte," said he, "was ungrateful to me, as I was the author of his greatness; but I cannot say that he betrayed me; he in a manner became a Swede, and never promised that which he did not intend to perform. I can accuse him of ingratitude, but not of treachery. Neither Murat nor he would have declared against me, had they thought that it would have lost me my throne. The wish was to diminish my power, but not to destroy me altogether. Murat's bravery was so great, that the Cossacs used to express their admiration of him with cries. They could not restrain their feelings, at seeing a noble figure advancing like a knight of old, and performing such prodigies of valor."

"Labedoyère," said he, "was a young man animated by the noblest sentiments, and the most sovereign contempt for a race that had surrounded themselves with all that was most foreign to the manners and rights of the French; and with a set of *misérables*, who to avoid starvation, had vegetated for twenty-five years in inferior and disgraceful situations. His attachment to me was enthusiastic, and he declared himself at the moment in the greatest danger."

Drouot he described to be one of the most virtuous and unassuming characters in France, though possessed of talent rarely to be met with. Drouot was a man who would live as contentedly, as far as regarded himself personally, upon forty sous a day, as if he had the revenues of a sovereign. He was charitable and religious; and a man whose morals, probity, and simplicity, would have been honored in an age of stern republicanism.

30th.—Went to Plantation House. After some questions relative to Napoleon's state of health, Sir Hudson Lowe said, that he had heard, in an indirect manner, which it was not necessary for him to explain to me, that General Bonaparte was in a much worse state of health than I had reported him to be; that he desired, therefore, whenever I went to town, that I would mention to Mr. Baxter or Sir Thomas Reade the state of his health, which might prevent the necessity of my coming to Plantation House to report on the day I made them. That I might now mention to Major Gorrequer what I had to say about his health. Accordingly, I told the major that, since the 26th, Napoleon had not suffered so much from head-ache, especially in the right side of the head, as I had extracted the tooth from that jaw; that the swelling in his cheeks was considerably less; that his bowels were very costive; that he had some symptoms of dyspepsia, such as nausea and flatulence; that the pain in his side was not increased, nor were his legs diminished in size; that on the whole, though the local complaint in his cheek was better, there was no amelioration in his general state of health. I also applied for a small still, or alembic, in order to make some orange-flower water, as there was none to be had on the island; which to Napoleon would have been very grateful, and indeed necessary.*

February 3rd.—The Cambridge store-ship arrived, bringing the melancholy news of the death of the Princess Charlotte.†

Communinated this intelligence to Napoleon, who expressed his affliction at the unfortunate event; as, independent of the feelings which naturally arose at the fate of a princess, cut off in the prime of youth and beauty, and with such prospects before her; he said, that he had not been without hopes that she would have caused a more liberal policy to be adopted towards himself. He inveighed against the accoucheurs, and expressed his surprise that the populace had not stoned them to death. He observed, that the business had a strange appearance, and that precautions appeared to have been taken to deprive the princess of every thing necessary to support and to console her in her first accouchement. He urged, that some old married women, who had frequently borne children, ought to have been at her bed side to comfort her. Had they been present, they would have perceived that matters were going on wrong, and would have insisted upon further assistance being rendered. It was unpardonable in the old queen not to have been on the spot. "What signified Leopold," said he, "he is a *garçon*, (boy,) and knew not what to do. Had it not been for me," added he, "Marie Louise would have

* This request was never complied with, although frequently repeated.
† I have suppressed some of Napoleon's remarks on this event.

died in a similar manner. During the time of her labor, I was in an apartment close by, from whence I went to her room every now and then. After she had been some hours in labor, Dubois, the accoucheur, came to me while I was reclining on the sofa, with great alarm painted on his countenance, and said, 'that the empress was in a state of great danger, that there was a wrong presentation.' I asked him if he had ever seen anything of the kind before. Dubois replied, 'that he had, but very rarely, perhaps not one in a thousand, and that it was very afflicting to him that so extraordinary a case should happen with the empress.' Forget," said I, "that she is empress, and treat her as you would the wife of a little shopkeeper in the Rue St. Denis. This is the only favor I ask of you. Dubois then asked, 'if it were necessary that one should be sacrificed, which should he save, the mother or the child?' The mother, certainly," I replied, "it is her right. I then accompanied Dubois to the bed-side, encouraged and tranquillized the empress as much as possible, and held her while the forceps were applied. The child was apparently dead when born, but by frictions and other means he was restored to life. His birth produced a delirium of joy in the nation. On the discharge of the first gun that announced the interesting event, all the population of Paris, in the greatest suspense, ran into the streets, the public walks, and the parks, counting the number of guns. Twenty-one guns were to have been fired for the birth of a princess, and one hundred and one for a prince. At the discharge of the twenty-second gun, the Parisians rent the skies with acclamations and expressions of universal delight. Almost all the powers of Europe sent ambassadors extraordinary to compliment me on the happy event. The Emperor of Austria was represented as his god-father by his brother, the Duke of Wurtsburg, and the Emperor Alexander sent his minister for the home-department to Paris to express his satisfaction on the occasion."*

* Soon after the birth of young Napoleon, his father contemplated building a superb palace, nearly opposite to the *Pont d'Jeana*, which was to have been called *Le Palais du Roi de Rome*, (The King of Rome's palace.) The governr

"Had the poor Princess Charlotte," added he, "had some person about her, who would have acted with energy as I did, she would have been saved. Now, through the neglect of her relations, and the imbecility, or something worse, of those *misérables* of accoucheurs, it is impossible to say what calamities may befall the British empire."

"No sooner was it known," continued Napoleon, "that the interests of France had induced me to dissolve the ties of my marriage, than the greatest sovereigns of Europe intrigued for an alliance with me. As soon as the Emperor of Austria heard that a new marriage was in agitation, he sent for Narbonne, and expressed his surprise that his family had not been thought of. At this time a union with a princess of Russia or of Saxony was contemplated. The cabinet of Vienna sent instructions on the subject to Prince Schwartzenburg, who was ambassador at Paris. Despatches were also received from the ambassador in Russia,

ment consequently endeavored to purchase all the houses situated upon the ground where it was intended to be built. Upon the spot of ground, which, according to the plan that had been traced out, was to form the extreme right of the front of the palace, there was a small house belonging to a poor cooper named Bonvivant, which, including the ground upon which it stood, was not, at the highest estimation, worth more than a thousand francs. The owner demanded ten thousand francs. It was referred to the emperor, who ordered that it should be purchased at that price. When the proper persons waited upon the cooper to conclude the agreement, he said that upon reflection, he should not sell it for less than thirty thousand francs. It was referred again to Napoleon, who directed that it should be given to him. When they came to conclude the business, the cooper increased his demand to forty thousand. The architect was greatly embarrassed, and did not know how to act; or in what manner he could again venture to annoy the emperor on the subject; at the same time he knew that it was impossible to conceal any thing from him. He therefore addressed him again on the subject. " *Ce drôle la nous abuse*," said he, "*pourtant il n'y a pas d'autre moyen ; allons il faut payer*," (This fellow takes advantage ; however, there is no other means—we must pay it.) The architect returned to the cooper, who increased the price to fifty thousand francs. Napoleon, indignant when informed of it, said, " *Cet homme la est un misérable, et bien je n'achetterai point la maison, et elle restera comme un monument de mon respect pour les loix*," (That man is a knave. I will not purchase the house at any rate—and it shall remain as a monument of my respect for the laws.) The Bourbons returned, razed the foundation of the intended palace, and threw down what had been erected ; the cooper's hovel fell to ruins, and its master, M. Bonvivant, now lives at Passy, Rue Basse, No. 31, where he earns a miserable existence by his trade.

stating the willingness of the Emperor Alexander to offer his sister, the Grand Duchess Anne. Some difficulties, however, presented themselves relative to the demand that a chapel for the Greek ritual should be established in the Tuileries. A privy council was held upon the subject, and the votes of the majority were for an Austrian princess. I consequently authorized Prince Eugene to make the overture to Prince Schwartzenburg, and articles of marriage, similar to those between Louis the Sixteenth and Marie Antoinette, were signed. The Emperor Alexander was not pleased that his overtures were slighted, and thought that he had been deceived, and that two negotiations had been carried on at the same time, in which he was mistaken."

"It has been said," added Napoleon, "that the marriage of Marie Louise was one of the secret articles of the treaty of Vienna, which had taken place some months before; this is entirely false. There was no thought whatever of an alliance with Austria, previous to the despatch from Narbonne, relating the hints which had been made to him by the Emperor Francis and by Metternich. In fact, the marriage with the Empress Marie Louise was proposed in council, discussed, decided, and signed within twenty-four hours, which can be proved by many members of the council who are now in existence. Several were of opinion that I ought to have espoused a French woman; and the arguments in favor of this were so strong, as to incline me to balance for a moment. It was hinted, however, by the court of Austria, that declining to choose a princess out of one of the reigning houses of Europe, would be a tacit declaration of intentions to overturn them, whenever opportunities should present themselves."

10*th*.—No improvement has taken place in Napoleon's health Had some conversation with him relative to the marriage of the Princess Elizabeth with the Prince of Hesse Homburg. "The English royal family," said he, "*va* incanagliarsi* with little petty princes, to whom I would not have given a brevet of *sous lieutenant*. When I marched upon Ulm, in 1805, I passed through

* A word probably invented by Napoleon, and intended to convey a meaning of degradation in a very strong manner.

Stutgardt with my army, where I saw your princess royal the Queen of Wirtemberg,* with whom I had several conversations, and was much pleased with her. She soon lost whatever prejudices she might have originally entertained against me. I had the pleasure of interfering to her advantage, when her husband, who was a brute, though a man of talent, had ill treated her, for which she was very grateful to me. She afterwards contributed materially towards effecting the marriage between my brother Jerome and the Princess Catherine, daughter of the king by a former marriage."

16*th*.—While in James Town, I was asked by Mr. Barber, of the Cambridge, who had opened a shop in the town, " how did Bonaparte like the portraits ?" Being ignorant of his meaning, I asked for explanations. He said, that I surely must know what he alluded to, and after some more conversation informed me that he had brought out two engravings of young Napoleon, for sale, thinking that it would please the French, and induce them to give him some custom. That, on his arrival, he had mentioned the circumstance, and that both of the portraits had been taken by the governor and Sir Thomas Reade, Sir Hudson Lowe declaring that he was glad to have an opportunity of sending such articles to Bonaparte. Mr. Barber appeared much surprised and disappointed when he learned from me that they had not reached Longwood.†

17*th*.—Went to Plantation House. The governor, after having made some inquiries about the state of Napoleon's health, and that of General Gourgaud, and whether I had complied with the desire he had expressed on the 21st, that I should show to Captain Blakeney the letter in which Lord Liverpool's name was mentioned ? I replied, that as he had left it to my option, whether to

* I have been informed, from a source entitled to the highest credit, that the Queen of Wirtemberg wrote an account of this interview to her mother, Queen Charlotte, in which she expressed very favorable opinions of Napoleon, and, in describing his person, concluded in the following manner, "*and he had so bewitching a smile.*"

† On my departure from St. Helena, in August, 1818, neither of the engravings had been sent to the father.

show it or not, I had preferred the latter, seeing that the business had occurred a long time ago; that at the *time* I had offered to show it, which he had refused to accept, and also, because he had said he considered the offer to show it as an insult. That it was necessary for me to be very cautious, and as I did not know why I was now required to show the letter, I had declined doing so. His excellency was not pleased with this reply, and began to abuse me in his customary manner, saying, that "I constantly insulted him as governor." I replied, that it never had been my intention to insult him either in word or deed; that I was very sorry if constructions, so foreign from my intentions, should have been put upon them. Sir Hudson Lowe then got up, and looking at me, in a menacing manner, said, "Upon your word of honor, sir, I ask you if you have had any other conversation with Napoleon Bonaparte than upon medical subjects, for a month past?" I replied, "Perhaps there may have been on other subjects, not interesting!" "I do not allow *you*, sir, to be a judge of whether they were uninteresting or otherwise. You have no authority for holding any communications with Napoleon Bonaparte, unless upon medical subjects, and then only when sent to for that purpose. Have you had any communication with any other person of his family?" "Certainly, sir, I have had." Without waiting to know whether those communications were medical or otherwise, he burst out with, "You have no authority, sir, to hold any communication whatsoever with any of his family, who are subject to the same restrictions as himself, unless upon medical subjects, and then only when sent for, and when finished you are to leave them. You have no business to go amongst them, unless for medical purposes. Have you, sir, had any communication with any of them unless upon those subjects?" I replied, by referring his excellency to his own orders, that I should not hold any other communication than medical with them. "This reply, sir, as usual, is not a direct one. You make it a practice to go to town when ships arrive, which I do not approve of. You go to collect news for General Bonaparte." I answered, "that I was an English officer, and, as such, would not give up my rights; moreover, that I, as well as others, was desirous of purchasing the necessaries of life as soon as they were landed, and before any monopoly took place to increase the price. That, if he intended to prohibit me from going to town, I had to request orders to that effect in writing." This Sir Hudson refused, saying with a sneer, "the request is worthy of the place you come from, and the people with whom you associate. I do not think a person under a pledge to Napoleon Bonaparte ought to be received into company, and I do not approve of your going to town when ships arrive. You are suspected by me, sir." I replied, " that I was under no other pledge to Napoleon than one which was tacitly understood in every society of gentlemen." The governor said, " that it was presumption and insolence for me to dare to judge of the line of conduct his majesty's government had thought proper to pursue with respect to Napoleon Bonaparte." I replied, "that I did not attempt to judge of that, that I merely mentioned what was the custom of society." "You are a suspected man, sir, you are suspected by *me.*" "I cannot help that, sir. It is a consolation to me, however, under such circumstances, to have the *mens conscia recti.*" This, the governor said, was a fresh insult, which he followed up by a volley of abuse.

"You took an opportunity, sir, of staying in town the other day, when a ship arrived, instead of coming here to report, as you ought to have done," said his excellency, after he had a little recovered his breath. "It was in compliance with your own instructions, sir, on the 30th of January. You then told me in the presence of Major Gorrequer, that when I saw Mr. Baxter or Sir Thomas Reade in town, it might supersede the necessity of my coming to Plantation House on that day. Having, therefore, seen and explained to Mr. Baxter on that day what I had to say, I did not think it necessary to come up here." He endeavored to shuffle this off. I appealed to Major Gorrequer, if I had not repeated his excellency's own words? The governor said, in not the most moderate manner, that this appeal was an insult to him, and burst forth into a fresh paroxysm of invective, which lasted for a considerable time.

18th.—Napoleon more lively than he has been for a few days.

Had some further conversation with him upon the subject of the death of the Princess Charlotte, during which he observed, that had she been the wife of a poor mechanic, she would have been saved, and that one of *les dames de la halle de Paris* (the market-women of Paris) would have met with more care and attention from her relations and friends, than the heiress to the greatest throne in Europe had experienced from hers

He afterwards spoke of the plans which he had upon England.

"Had I succeeded in effecting a landing," said he, "I have very little doubt that I should have accomplished my views. Three thousand boats, each to carry twenty men and one horse, with a proportion of artillery, were ready. Your fleet having been decoyed away, as I before explained to you, would have left me master of the Channel. Without this, I would not have made the attempt. Four days would have brought me to London. In a country like England, abounding in plains, defence is very difficult. I have no doubt that your troops would have done their duty, but one battle lost, the capital would have been in my power. You could not have collected a force sufficiently strong to beat me in a pitched battle. Your ideas of burning and destroying the towns, and the capital itself, are very plausible in argument, but impracticable in their accomplishment. You would have fought a battle and lost it. 'Well, then,' you would say, ' we have been beaten, but we have not lost our honor. We shall now endeavor *de tirer la meilleure partie* (to make the best of) from our misfortune. We must make terms.' I would have offered you a constitution of your own choice, and have said, 'Assemble in London deputies from the people to fix upon a constitution.' I would have called upon Burdett and other popular leaders to organize one according to the wishes of the people. I would have declared the * * fallen from the * * *, abolished the nobility, proclaimed liberty, freedom, and equality. Think you, that in order to keep the house of * * * one the * * * your rich citizens, merchants, and others of London, would have consented to sacrifice their riches, their houses, their families, and all their dearest interests, especially when I had made them comprehend that I only came to * * * * * away, and to give them liberty? No, it is contrary to history and to human nature. You are too rich. Your principal people have too much to lose by resistance, and your *canaille* too much to gain by a change. If, indeed, they supposed that I wanted to render England a province of France, then indeed *l'esprit national* (national spirit) would do wonders. But I would have formed a republic according to your own wishes, required a moderate contribution, barely sufficient to have paid the troops, and perhaps not even that. Your *canaille** would have been for me, knowing *que je suis l'homme du peuple, que je sors de la canaille moi-même*, (that I am the man of the people, that I spring from the populace myself,) and that whenever a man had merit or talent, I elevated him without asking how many degrees of nobility he had; knowing, that by joining me, they would be relieved from the yoke of the aristocracy under which they labor. There is not a *canaille* in the world, not even the Prussian, worse treated. Excepting the obligation of serving as soldiers, the German *canaille* are better off than yours. You have no more regard for yours than if they were so many Helots, and you treat them precisely as if they were such. To my lords and my ladies, to the aristocracy and the *gentlemen*, (in English), oh, indeed, you pay every kind of attention and regard; nothing can be too good for them; no treatment kind enough; but for your *canaille*, bah! they are so many *chiens*, (dogs;) as your contractors said when furnishing provisions to the French prisoners, 'it is too good for those French dogs.' You yourself have got a great deal of *la morgue aristocratique* (aristocratical) in your head, and appear to look down upon your *canaille* as if they were a race of inferior beings. You talk of your freedom. Can anything be more horrible than your pressing of seamen? You send your boats on shore to seize upon every male

* Napoleon frequently used the word *canaille*, not in a degrading sense, but as the people, distinct from the nobles.

that can be found, who, if they have the misfortune to belong to the *canaille*, if they cannot prove themselves *gentlemen*, are hurried on board of your ships to serve as seamen in all quarters of the globe. And yet you have the impudence to talk of the conscription in France; it wounds your pride because it fell *upon all ranks*. Oh, how shocking, that a *gentleman's* son (in English) should be obliged to defend his country, just as if he were one of the *canaille!* And that he should be compelled to expose his body, or put himself on a level with a *vile plebeian!!* Yet God made all men alike. Who forms the nation? Not your lords, nor your fat prelates (*panciatti*) and churchmen, nor your *gentlemen*, nor your oligarchy. Oh! one day the people will avenge themselves, and terrible scenes will take place."

"That conscription," continued Napoleon, " which offended your *morgue aristocratique* so much, was conducted scrupulously according to the principles of equal rights. Every native of a country is bound to defend it. The conscription did not *écraser* (crush) a particular class like your press-gang, nor the *canaille*, because they were poor. It was the most just, because the most equal mode of raising troops. It rendered the French army the best composed in the world. The conscription would have become a national institution, instead of being regarded as a punishment or a servitude. It would have been a point of honor to have served the country, and the time would have come, that a girl would not have married a youth that had not paid the debt he owed to it. The love of glory is the inheritance of a Frenchman."

" Were you a nation," continued he, " of half savages, of poor wild mountaineers, or of ferocious shepherds, like the Scythians; then indeed you might destroy your capital, and desolate your country, in order to stop the progress of an invader. Even if you were as poor, as wild and as ignorant as the Spaniards, perhaps you might destroy some of your towns and habitations. But you are too rich and too selfish. Where is there one of you who would say, ' I will destroy my house, abandon my property to be pillaged, my wife and daughters to be violated, my sons to be massacred!! And for what? To keep * * * * * * on the * *, and Lord Bathurst and the Archbishop of Canterbury in their employments of twenty thousand a year. All this I will do against a man who offers terms, who proposes to give us a constitution according to the wish of the nation.' No, no. It is more than could be expected from *man*. Pitt himself was well aware of it, and one of the means which he took to form the coalition against me, was, by asserting, that a descent was possible; that if it were effected, England would be conquered before twelve months; that then all the continent would be at my mercy and my disposal; that England once fallen, all was lost. This the King of Prussia told me afterwards."

Napoleon now repeated what he had said once before relative to the inhabitants of Moscow not having assisted in setting fire to the city; but on the contrary, having done their utmost to extinguish it; and proceeded thus: "The English, after a battle, finding that we did not come to plunder and destroy them, that we did not injure or molest the inhabitants, that their wives and daughters remained unviolated; for I would not have allowed the smallest outrage to be committed. Instant death would have been inflicted on whoever attempted it. They would have seen that we did not come to rob, or to destroy them, but merely to * * * * * *. If, indeed, war were waged, as in ancient times, when the male prisoners were massacred or made slaves of, and the women became the concubines of the victors, then the conquest of the nation would have been impossible. But no: you would have seen us advancing, and molesting the population as little as your own soldiers. Everything would have been done to conciliate and to harmonize."

I now made some observations to Napoleon about his own government in France. "The system of government," said he, "must be adapted to *l'esprit de la nation*, (the spirit of the nation,) and to circumstances. In the first place, France required a strong government. While I was at the head of it, I may say that France was in the same state as Rome, when a dictator was declared necessary for the salvation of the republic. Successions of coalitions against her existence were formed by your gold amongst all the powerful nations of Europe. To resist successfully, it was necessary that all the energies of the country should be at the disposal of the chief. I never conquered unless in my own defence. Europe never ceased to make war upon France and her principles. *Il nous fallut abattre sous peine d'être abattus,* (they must either have destroyed us, or have been destroyed.) Between the parties that agitated France for a long time, I was like a rider seated on an unruly horse, who always wanted to swerve either to the right or to the left ; and to make him keep a straight course, I was obliged to let him feel the bridle occasionally. The government of a country just emerged from a revolution, menaced by foreign enemies, and agitated by the intrigues of domestic traitors, must necessarily be *dur* (rigid.) In quieter times my dictature would have finished, and I should have commenced my constitutional reign. Even as it was, with a coalition always existing against me, either secret or public, openly avowed, or denied, there was more equality in France than in any other country in Europe.

"One of my grand objects was to render education accessible to every body. I caused every institution to be formed upon a plan which offered instruction to the public, either gratis, or at a rate so moderate, as not to be beyond the means of the peasant. The museums were thrown open to the *canaille.* My *canaille* would have become the best educated in the world. All my exertions were directed to illuminate the mass of the nation instead of brutifying them by ignorance and superstition.

"Those English," added he, "who are lovers of liberty, will one day lament with tears having gained the battle of Waterloo. It was as fatal to the liberties of Europe in its effects as that of Philippi was to those of Rome ; and like it, has precipitated Europe into the hands of triumvirs, associated together for the oppression of mankind, the suppression of knowledge, and the restoration of superstition."

Recounted to the emperor the treatment I had experienced yes-

...erday at Plantation House. "I do not believe," said he, "that in all the armies of Europe a man of so ignoble a character could be found. It is the height of baseness for a superior to insult officially an inferior. This man's disposition makes him like a person afflicted with an inveterate itch; he has need of continually rubbing against something. But independent of his natural uneasiness, his intentions are, by bad language and bad treatment, to irritate you into a breach of respect to him as governor, which he will convert into an act of violence, and proceed against you for an *attentat* (outrage) upon him in his official capacity. You are in a very dangerous situation. He has a witness who is his creature, and who will sign everything that he dictates, and have no other conscience or will than his. You have only your own word to plead; and this man's conduct in endeavoring to make a spy of you, by ill treatment and abuse, is so extraordinary, that people unacquainted with him will with difficulty believe it. I see no other mode for you to act than to maintain an absolute silence. Hear what he has to say, and reply not, unless in answer to medical questions. To those he has a right to expect an answer; but to anything else say, 'I do not know,' or, 'it is no business of mine.'"

20*th.*—Underwent a few more interrogations from Sir Hudson Lowe, in which I had the good fortune to leave his house, without having been assailed with any outrageous language.

23*rd.*—Cipriani complained this day of inflammation of the bowels, which from the moment he made it known to me presented most formidable appearances. He was very largely bled, put into a warm bath, and recourse had to all the vigorous remedies usually administered in such cases. Only temporary relief, however, was obtained; and the unfavorable symptoms returned with increased aggravation. It was soon evident that his life was in the most imminent danger; and the advice and assistance of other professional men were called in. All, however, was useless, and the complaint was rapidly hurrying him on to dissolution. Cipriani himself, though conscious of his danger, preserved the greatest calmness and composure. Napoleon, who had an affection for him as his countryman, and a man wholly devoted to his service, was extremely anxious for his recovery, and frequent in his inquiries. On the 25th, Cipriani was in a state in which persons laboring under the same complaint are sometimes seen. He had experienced some relief from suffering: but it was doubtful whether it arose from the diminution of the violence of the complaint, or was that cessation of pain preceding dissolution, produced by mortification The last was my own opinion; but there was nothing certain. He was in a state of extreme weakness. Nourishment was administered to him at short intervals, which was retained on his stomach. While in this state of doubt, Napoleon, with whom I had been repeatedly during the day, to report the state of the patient, sent for me at 12 o'clock at night. I mentioned that Cipriani was lying in a kind of stupor. "I think," said he, "that my appearance before poor Cipriani would act as a stimulus to slumbering nature, (*la natura che dorme*) and will rouse her to make new efforts which may finally overcome the disease, and save the patient." He endeavored to illustrate this, by describing the electric effects which had been produced in many instances by his appearance on the field of battle at most critical moments and times. I replied, that Cipriani was still sensible; and that I knew the love and veneration he had for his master to be so great, that on his appearance before him, he would make an effort to rise in his bed, which exertion, in the weak state in which he was, would probably produce syncope, during which his soul, already *tra si e no*, to quit or to remain in its earthly tenement, would most probably take its departure.* After this and other explanations on the subject, Napoleon acquiesced in my opinion, that he should not try the experiment; observing, that in such cases, *les hommes de l'art* (professional men) were the best judges.

At ten o'clock the following morning, symptoms decidedly mortal made their appearance, and about four, poor Cipriani was numbered with the dead.

Cipriani was a man possessed of strong, but uncultivated talents

* It is well known to medical people, that in cases of great debility the raising of a patient's head from the pillow, has sometimes produced dissol

Though artful, he had the appearance of openness and candor. He had, however, many good qualities. He was generous and charitable. Like most of his countrymen, he was an ardent friend, and a bitter enemy, and had strong national spirit. He was a republican in principle, and manifested more attachment to Napoleon in his misfortunes, than he had ever shown for him in his grandeur. He was regarded by his master in a very confidential light. Had he enjoyed the benefit of an early education, he would probably have made a figure in the revolution. He had been unwell for several days before he complained, during which, in all probability, latent inflammation had been going on. His corpse was followed to the grave* by Counts Bertrand and Montholon, by myself, and by all the household who could attend. So much was he esteemed at St. Helena, that several of the most respectable of the inhabitants, and some of the officers of the 66th regiment, voluntarily joined the funeral procession. Had he been buried *within* the limits, Napoleon himself would have attended.

Immediately after his death, I reported the circumstance to Napoleon, who remarked, " Where is his soul? Gone to Rome, perhaps, to see his wife and child, before it undertakes the long final journey."

Some days before his demise, Cipriani told me, that not long after the governor had put into execution his rigorous measures towards the inmates of Longwood, Santini, who was of a merry disposition, had been observed to be much altered, and apparently thoughtful and melancholy. One day he came into Cipriani's room, and avowed his intention of shooting the governor the first time that the latter came to Longwood. Cipriani asked him if he was mad, and endeavored to dissuade him from the attempt, by using all the arguments in his power. Although Cipriani had much influence over him, Santini was unmoved, and accompanied his declaration with many oaths peculiar to the inferior order of Italians. He had his double-barrelled gun loaded with ball, with which he intended to dispatch the governor, and then to finish himself. Cipriani, finding his arguments fruitless, went to Napoleon, to whom

* See Count Bertrand's letter, Appendix, No. XIII.

ne communicated the affair. The emperor immediately sent for, and questioned Santini, who avowed his intentions. Napoleon then commanded him, as his emperor, to drop all thoughts of injuring Sir Hudson Lowe, and succeeded, though not without some reluctance on the part of Santini, in making him abandon his project. Santini was a most determined character, and brave as a lion. Besides being master of the small sword, he had a sure and deadly aim with fire-arms; and there is little doubt that, had it not been for this prohibition, he would have effected his intentions.

March 6th.—The progress of the disease in the emperor continues to advance a little, though slowly. Found him reading a volume of Corneille, upon whom he pronounced some warm eulogiums, observed, that to the sentiments which he inspired, France was indebted for some of her glorious deeds, and added, that if Corneille had lived in his time, he would have made him a prince.

He then conversed about himself: said, that he believed Nature had calculated him for great reverses—that he had a soul of marble. After which he made some comparisons of his own conduct with that adopted by his enemies towards him.

"If I had been actuated by the spirit which prevailed with the Bourbons," said he, "or even according to the laws of reciprocity, I should have caused the Duc D'Angoulême to be tried, in retaliation for the attempts he had made upon me, the proscription against my person by the Bourbons, and the declaration of the allied powers,* placing me out of the pale of the law, and inviting my assassination. By the laws of the national assembly, existing against any of the members of his family who should re-enter France, I could have had him shot within twenty-four hours. Instead of doing so, I ordered that every respect should be paid to him, and care taken of his person, and that he should be conducted to Cette for embarkation."

"Maitland," said Napoleon, "was not an accomplice in the snare that was laid for me by your ministers, when they gave him orders to receive me on board of his ship.† He

* See Appendix, No. XIV.   † See Appendix, No. XV.

is *un brave homme* (a brave man,) and incapable of participating in the infamous transaction that took place.' He was deceived as well as mysef, and probably in bringing me to England, thought that I should have been allowed to live there, subject to such restrictions as had been imposed upon my brother Lucien." He then observed, that he had formed too good an opinion of the English, and had believed the influence of the voice of the people upon the ministers, to have been much more powerful than it was in reality. "Previous to going on board the Bellerophon," added he, "some debates were held upon the propriety of the measure. Some naval officers, to whom it was mentioned, strongly urged that I should not venture on such a step. They said, the English are the most interested people on earth. Interest is their god, and they will calculate what may result from ill or well treating you. If they think that they shall gain anything by it, they will hurry you away, and bury you in one of their colonies, where you will be exposed to every species of bad treatment that hatred can suggest. They were right," added he; "some of them had been in the *pontons*, and knew what you were better than I did. I did not conceive it possible that a great nation could countenance the persecution of a man, who had fallen into their hands, after having been twenty-five years their enemy."

He then delivered, as follows, some explanation of the causes which had produced his fall: "Had it not been for that fatal suspension of arms, in 1813, to which I was induced to consent by Austria, I should have succeeded. The victories of Lutzen and Wurtzen had restored confidence to the French forces. The king of Saxony was triumphantly brought back to his capital; one of the corps of the French army was at the gates of Berlin, and the enemy had been driven from Hamburgh. The Russian and Prussian armies were preparing to pass the Vistula, when the cabinet of Austria, acting with its characteristic perfidy, advised the suspension of hostilities, at a time when it had already entered into engagements with Russia and Prussia; the armistice was only a delusion to gain time necessary to make preparations, it being intended to declare against France in May. The unexpected successes obliged it to act with more circumspection. It was necessary to gain more time, and negotiations went on at the congress of Prague. Metternich insisted that Austria should have the half of Italy, and made other exorbitant conditions, which were only demanded, in order to be refused. As soon as she had got her army ready, Austria declared against France. After the victory of Dresden, I was superior, and had formed the project to deceive the enemy, by marching towards Magdeburg, then to cross the Elbe, at Wittenberg, and march upon Berlin. Several divisions of the army were occupied in these manœuvres, when a letter was brought to me from the King of Wirtemberg, announcing that the Bavarian army had joined the Austrians, and to the amount of eighty thousand men, were marching towards the Rhine, under the command of Wrede; that he, being compelled by the presence of that army, was obliged to join his contingent to it, and that Mentz would soon be invested by a hundred thousand men.

"This unexpected defection entirely changed the plan of the campaign, and all the preparations made to fix the war between the Elbe and the Oder, became useless. At Leipsic, afterwards, I was victorious on the 16th, and should have succeeded on the 18th, had not the whole Saxon army, which occupied one of the most important positions in the line, deserted to the enemy, with a train of sixty pieces of cannon, which were immediately turned against the French. Notwithstanding this, the field of battle remained in possession of the French, and the allies made a retrograde movement on the same day. During the night I ordered the army to retire upon our supplies behind the Ister. The defection of some other German corps afterwards, and the premature blowing up of the bridge at Liepsic, caused the most disastrous effects. When the army had passed the Saale, it should have rested to recover from its fatigues, and receive ammunition and other supplies from Erfurth. Intelligence, however, arrived, that the Austro-Bavarian army under Wrede, had arrived on the Mein by forced marches, and it was necessary to march against it. Wrede was driven from his position at Hanaw, completely beaten, and himself wounded. Conferences afterwards took place at Francfort, and proposals for peace were offered on condition that I should renounce the protectorate of the confederation of the Rhine, Poland, and the departments of the Elbe; but that France should be preserved in her limits of the Alps and the Rhine. Those conditions were accepted as bases. This congress, however, like the others, turned out to be a delusion, as at the moment that those pacific proposals were made, the allies violated the neutrality of Switzerland, which they entered in large force. At Chatillon, afterwards, they presented their *ultimatum*, in which they demanded that France should be reduced to the limits she had previous to 1792, which I rejected. Had it not been for the subsequent treachery of Talleyrand, Marmont, and Augereau, the allies would not have succeeded in forcing upon the throne a detested family, against whom for twenty-five years the nation had combated; and France would not have been degraded by the spectacle of a king upon the throne, who had the baseness publicly to declare that he owed it to the Prince Regent of England.

28th.—Twenty-seven volumes of books were sent to Longwood by Sir Hudson Lowe on the 12th, and seven on this day, with some numbers of the *Lettres Normandes et Champenoises*. These formed the entire of the supply of books and pamphlets sent by his majesty's ministers,* (or through them,) since the arrival of the Phaeton in 1817. Napoleon observed, "*C'est une bassesse dont je ne croyais pas même que Lord Bathurst fut capable*," (it is a meanness that I did not believe even Lord Bathurst would be capable of.)

---

* Mr. Goulbourne promised Count Las Cases, on the return of the latter to Europe, that every interesting book and new publication should be sent to Longwood, with a copious and regular supply of newspapers, French and English, of different descriptions. Whether the worthy secretary performed his promise or not, I am not able to say. None, however, except some unconnected numbers of the Times and Courier, Observer, &c., with a few straggling French papers, of a very old date, reached Longwood during my residence there. In one instance, in March, 1817, I think, the governor permitted me to take the Morning Chronicle for some weeks, as a great favor, which was not again repeated.

It has been a rule* for some time, that all captains of merchant ships which arrive, are obliged to submit a list of their books, newspapers, &c., to Sir Hudson Lowe, and those of a political nature are specifically required to be sent to him, under a pretence of desiring to forward them to Longwood, where, however, none of the books have arrived ; and but very few newspapers. The Edinburgh Review is specially sought after by his excellency and staff."

April 4th.—Some days ago a circumstance occurred which threw some light upon the motives which had induced the governor to oblige me to visit Plantation House twice a week. One of the foreign persons residing in the island informed Count Montholon, that the commissioners had seen an account of the state of Napoleon's health in the bulletin of that day. Count Montholon knowing that no bulletins were issued by me, asked for explanations, which were given, and by which it appeared, that surreptitious bulletins were made by a person who never saw Napoleon, and who consequently could not be a judge of his complaint. Those fictitious reports were sent from Plantation House to the commissioners, and transmitted by them to their respective courts. I apprehend that every conscientious reader will be of opinion that those bulletins ought to have been shown to me, I being the only medical man who saw the patient, and consequently the only person capable of judging of their correctness.†

10th.—Sir Hudson Lowe having failed in the application that he made in London to procure my removal from St. Helena, had recourse to an expedient which insured him success. He caused a letter to be written to me this day by Sir Thomas Reade, in which he informed me that I was not to pass out of Longwood, without assigning any reasons for a measure by which it appeared

---

* See Appendix, No. XVI.

† Sir Hudson Lowe, when he could no longer refrain from giving some account of this transaction, endeavored to slur it over, by stating to Count Bertrand, that the fictitious bulletins were merely repetitions of my conversations with Mr. Baxter. If this were true, why conceal them from me?

that the governor had imposed upon me restrictions even more arbitrary and vexatious than those which he had inflicted upon the French; for by confining me to Longwood, within the precincts of which he allowed no persons to enter without a pass, he deprived me of English society; while at the same time he prohibited me from holding any other intercourse, even with the French, than that relating to my profession.* As soon as I received this letter, I went to the Briers, with the intention of laying the affair before Admiral Plampin, who sent word by his secretary that he would not see me. I then wrote a letter to Sir Hudson Lowe, tendering my resignation, and another to Count Bertrand, in which I explained the step that I had been compelled to take, and the motives which urged me to adopt it.

14*th.*—Napoleon sent for me to give me an audience prior to my departure. During which he declined receiving any more medical advice from me in the situation in which I was placed by Sir Hudson Lowe, and addressed me in the following words: "*Eh bien, Docteur, vous allez nous quitter. Le monde concevra-t-il qu'on a eu la lacheté d'attenter à mon médecin? Puisque vous êtes un simple lieutenant, soumis à tout l'arbitraire et à la discipline militaire, vous n'avez plus l'indépendance necessaire pour que vos scours puissent m'étre utiles; je vous remercie de vos soins. Quittez le plutôt possible ce séjour de ténèbres et de crimes; je mourrai sur ce grabat, rongé de maladie et sans secours; mais votre nation en sera dishonourée à jamais.*"† He then bade me adieu.

* It is almost unnecessary for me to explain to the reader, that I was neither able nor inclined to obey this arbitrary mandate

† " Well, Doctor, you are going to quit us. Will the world conceive that they have been base enough to make attempts upon my physician? Since you are no more than a simple lieutenant subjected to arbitrary power and to military discipline, you have no longer the independence necessary to render your services useful to me. I thank you for your care. Quit as soon as you can this abode of darkness and of crimes. I shall expire upon that pallet, consumed by disease, and without any assistance. But your country will be eternally dishonored by my death." It may be proper to inform the reader, that though Napoleon generally conversed in Italian with me, as I spoke the language with considerable fluency, from having resided several years in that classical country, whenever he became animated, he always broke out into French, and also whenever he was at a loss for a word.

May 9th.—Sir Hudson Lowe, finding that he could not succeed in his plan of establishing another surgeon with Napoleon and that the latter was determined not to receive him, and having been made to comprehend by the commissioners,* that if Napoleon died while he kept me in confinement, (without bringing me to a trial, or even preferring any charge against me), or under the hands of any surgeon forced upon him, strange surmises would arise in England and in Europe respecting his death, of which they themselves should be unable to render a satisfactory explanation, decided upon removing the restrictions he had imposed upon me. Accordingly he released me, after having kept me in confinement twenty-seven days; during which time I was successively assailed, in correspondence, by all his staff; and in order to ensnare me, frequently required to return by a dragoon who waited, answers to letters composed after several days' reflection, by the united wisdom of Sir Hudson Lowe and his staff. As this correspondence has been already before the public, I shall not now trouble the reader with it.

In the letter containing the order for my release, his excellency felt himself obliged to acknowledge me as Napoleon's private surgeon, a point which he had contested before.

A despatch sent by Sir Hudson Lowe to Longwood, containing some extracts from a correspondence of Lord Bathurst, stating, amongst other matters, that permission would be given, that a list of persons, not exceeding fifty in number, resident on the island, should be drawn up by Count Bertrand, and submitted to the governor for approval, and that such persons should be admitted to Longwood at seasonable hours, with no other pass than the invitation of General Bonaparte; it being under-

* I have been informed, that some very animated discussions took place at Plantation House on this subject, in one of which the governor, while debating with Baron Sturmer, burst forth into one of the paroxysms of anger he so frequently manifested towards me. The baron very coolly made his excellency stop opposite to a large looking-glass, in which he begged of him to contemplate his own features, adding, that he should not desire to afford his court a better representation of what was occurring at St. Helena, than the figure in the mirror before him.

stood that they were on such occasions to deliver in their invitations with their names, as vouchers, at the barrier; it being clearly understood, that the governor was to reserve a discretionary power, to erase from the list any individuals to whom he might consider it inexpedient to continue such facility of access.

10th.—Previous to allowing me to resume my medical functions at Longwood, Napoleon, in order to put a stop to the fabrication of any more bulletins, required that I should make out a report of the state of his health once a week, or oftener if necessary. A copy of which should be given to the governor if he required it. This I immediately communicated to Sir Hudson Lowe, who not only did not require it, but absolutely prohibited me from making him (Sir Hudson) any written report.

Napoleon's state of health had become worse since last month The pain was more constant and severe, &c.

Considerable indignation was excited in the island at the con duct which had been pursued towards Napoleon.

16th.—A proclamation issued by Sir Hudson Lowe, and placarded in the most conspicuous manner, interdicting all officers, inhabitants, and other persons whatsoever, from holding any correspondence or communication with the foreign persons under detention on it.*

18th.—Captain Blakeney ordered by Sir Hudson Lowe to assemble all the English servants at Longwood, and read to them the proclamation of the 16th. This was done without notice being given to their masters. Napoleon, when informed of this, ordered that the English servants employed at Longwood House, in place of Santini and the others sent away by Sir Hudson Lowe, should be discharged.

20th.—Had some conversation with the emperor upon the work published by Mr. Ellis on the embassy to China, and the conversation at Longwood which that gentleman had published. Napoleon observed, that having learned that Mr. Ellis had been secretary to a mission to Persia, a short time after General Gardanne had quitted Ispahan, he had questioned

* See Appendix, No. XVII.

him as to the progress that Russia had made on the Persian side. "I told him," added Napoleon, "that if Russia succeeded in attaching the brave Polish nation to her she would no longer have a rival, because she would restrain England by menacing the latter's possessions in India, and Austria, by the great moral superiority of her troops, and by the followers of the Greek Church, who are so numerous in Hungary and Gallicia; and that appearances rendered it probable that a Greek patriarch would one day officiate in Sancta Sophia. I also mentioned to him, that if England adopted the system of founding her power upon her land forces, and on maintaining armies on the continent, those armies would mask her real forces, and she would commit the same fault that Francis the First was guilty of at the battle of Pavia, by placing himself with the *élite* of his cavalry before a formidable battery, which would have assured him the victory, had he not prevented it from firing by masking it. I told him that your riots in England signified nothing, and that your constables were sufficient to re-establish order, if at the same time your ministers directed all their attention and care towards the amelioration of the administration, to the prosperity of your manufactures and your commerce. That above all, you must not be ashamed of being merchants; from that source your power springs; but that if the misery was real, as asserted by Lord Wellesley, and was caused by the too great efforts made by England during twenty years, in that case too violent measures employed upon the mass of the people would be topical applications likely to produce madness in them. I said that you have amongst you men too wise, not to open, at the same time that they applied these violent remedies, channels which would discharge the acrimonious humors, restore health and ease to the people, and cause misery to disappear.

"During all the conversations I had with Mr. Ellis," continued he, "which lasted about half an hour, not one word was said about St. Helena. Count Montholon had no conversation on the subject with Mr Ellis, or any other of the legation. Mr. Ellis made no inquiries on the spot, never visited the interior of the establishment, knew nothing, saw nothing, and heard nothing about it, at least from the French. And yet in his work he has the impudence to play the part of a judge, who had heard the complaining parties on the spot. But that passage has not been written by his hand. It is the invention of some *commis* to Lord Bathurst, who has imposed the insertion of it upon him. Such a prostitution of his name reflects but little credit upon that diplomatic character."*

He made some observations upon the contrast between the governor's proclamation and conduct and the despatches sent by Lord Bathurst: said, that the despatch was merely got up to have the appearance of doing something to benefit his situation, while in reality nothing was done.

In the course of the conversation, Napoleon observed, that but little reliance was to be placed on the writings of a man in forming a judgment of his private character or conduct, which he illustrated by informing me that Bernardin St. Pierre, whose writings were so sentimentally beautiful, and breathing principles of humanity and social happiness in every page, was one of the worst private characters in France.

June 7th.—The Mangles store-ship arrived.

11th.—With the exception of the painful inflammatory affection of the cheeks, the so frequent recurrence of which has been prevented by the extraction of two more teeth, Napoleon's state of health has become much worse. He accordingly consented on this day to adopt the practice recommended to him, which was consequently commenced on this day. He has been confined almost entirely to his apartments for nearly six weeks.

20th.—The officers of the 53d regiment had done me the honor to elect me an honorary member of their mess; and on the departure of that regiment from the island, the officers of the 66th regiment had conferred a similar honor upon me. Sir Hudson Lowe employed Sir Thomas Reade to fill the mind of Lieutenant-Colonel Lascelles (the commanding officer) with the most insidious calumnies against me, in consequence of which Lieutenant-

* Mr. Ellis has since been appointed to a lucrative situation at the Cape of Good Hope, which, I believe, is the gift of Lord Bathurst.

Colonel Lascelles called upon Lieutenant Reardon of the regiment (a friend of mine,) to whom he related, that it had been insinuated to him by Sir Thomas Reade that I had become displeasing to the sight of the governor, that the officers of the regiment ought to expel me from their mess, as a person who had submitted to insults from the governor, who had turned me out of his house, and consequently that I was unfit for their society; insinuating also, that my expulsion would be very agreeable to Sir Hudson Lowe, who, he observed, had said that he should consider any person who was seen to associate with me as his personal enemy. Lieutenant-Colonel Lascelles concluded with begging of Lieutenant Reardon to persuade me to withdraw privately from the mess, as my presence there was obnoxious to the governor; protesting, however, that personally he had a great esteem for me, and that he would be one of the first to invite me to dine there as a guest.

Reflecting, that if I slunk away secretly, opportunity would be furnished to my enemies to paint me in the blackest colors, and to represent that my conduct had been such as to compel the officers of the 66th to turn me out of the mess, and, being conscious of upright intentions, I immediately wrote to Lieutenant-Colonel Lascelles the letter in the Appendix marked No. XVIII. In the evening I met him coming to see me. He made many professions of friendship and esteem for me, but said that as the governor was displeased with me, he begged I would withdraw privately from the mess, that Sir Hudson Lowe desired it, and that he was afraid of his resentment being exercised upon himself, and upon the officers of the regiment, if I did not comply with his wishes. He concluded by stating, that Sir Thomas Reade had shown him part of my correspondence with the governor, and some secret documents which had never been communicated to me, and professing his esteem, in which sentiment, he said, he knew he was joined by every officer in the regiment I replied, that clandestine misrepresentations, from their being unknown to me, might remain unrefuted; that no person was secure from the breath of calumny: that, however, I was ready to submit the whole of the correspondence between the governor and myself to the judgment of the officers of the regiment, or to submit to any other scrutiny that he or they might desire, and to abide by their decision; but that I never would renounce the honor which the officers of the 66th had conferred upon me in granting me a seat at their table, unless (according to the custom of the army) by a vote of the mess, or by an order from the governor.

This reply was communicated to Sir Hudson Lowe, who, probably having his own reasons for not allowing the correspondence to be submitted to the judgment of a corps of officers, sent an order by the Brigadier-General Sir George Bingham (as I have been informed) to Lieutenant-Colonel Lascelles, to exclude me from the mess, which was communicated to me by the following letter, without assigning any reason for such act.

Deadwood, 23rd June.

DEAR SIR,—As commanding officer of the 66th regiment, I beg leave to inform you, that I feel it expedient on my part to say, that I cannot any longer allow you to be an honorary member of the 66th's mess.

I am, dear Sir,
Your obedient servant,
C. LASCELLES.

Barry O'Meara, Esq.

Being desirous of obtaining every authentic information to establish the fact, that this new outrage had been effected by the orders of Sir Hudson Lowe, I waited upon Sir George Bingham, by whom I was very politely received, and informed that he had been commanded to carry into execution the above order.

25th.—Sent the following letter to the Deadwood camp:

To the Officers of the 66th Regiment.

Gentlemen,—In consequence of the extraordinary mission which I accepted, having been detached from that branch of the service to which I belong, the officers of the 53rd regiment, taking into consideration the isolated situation in which I was placed, were pleased to do me the honor of electing me an honorary member of their mess, in which I continued as long as the regiment remained in the island. You, gentlemen, shortly after your arrival, condescended to confer upon me a similar honor, by which I have benefited for nearly a year. By a fatality, which at this moment persecutes me, *orders emanating from a superior power prohibit me from any longer enjoying in your society* the great, the only consolation it was possible for me to experience in this dreary abode. I cannot, however, return to my solitude without returning my most sincere thanks to you for the many marks of friendship and kindness with which you have honored me, and to assure you, that the esteem, respect, and gratitude, which I bear to you, individually and collectively, are indelibly engraven upon the heart of one, who, at his last moments, will exult in saying that he was deemed worthy a seat at your table.

    I have the honor to be,
     Gentlemen,
      With the greatest respect,
       Your most obliged Friend,
    (*Signed,*)   BARRY E. O'MEARA,
        Surgeon, Royal Navy

Longwood, 25*th June*, 1818.

26*th.*—The officers of the 66th regiment were pleased to return the following reply :—

            Deadwood, 26*th June*, 1818.

Dear Sir,—As president last night, I had the honor of communicating to the mess the contents of your letter of the 25th instant, and am directed by the *commanding officer and officers, composing it, to say it is with much regret they hear of your departure as an honorary member of the mess*, and to assure you, they always conceived your conduct while with them, to be perfectly consistent in every respect with that of a gentleman.

I am also directed to say, the mess feel much indebted for the very flattering expressions of esteem contained in your letter.
And have the honor to be,
Dear Sir,
Your very humble Servant,
(*Signed,*)   Chs. M'Carthy,
Lieut. 66th Regiment.
To *Barry O'Meara, Esq.,*
Surgeon R. N., Longwood.

27th.—Napoleon much affected by a severe catarrhal affection, caused by the extreme humidity of his rooms. Discontinued some of the remedies he was taking, and reported the state of his health to the governor.

July 15th.—Several cases of wine sent by the Princess Borghese through Lady Holland, arrived last month. A few were sent to Longwood, and the remainder deposited in the government stores by order of Sir Hudson Lowe. Napoleon expressed on this, as well as on many other occasions, sentiments of great affection towards the Princess Pauline, and declared his conviction that no sacrifice would be too great for her to make for his benefit; adding, that he had no doubt she would endeavor to obtain permission to come out to St. Helena.* He also spoke of the Princess Hortense in very high terms, whom he pronounced to be a lady possessed of very superior talents. Likewise of the Princess Eliza. He expressed in a very handsome manner his sense of the attention and kindness manifested for him in his misfortunes by Lady Holland, at a time when he was abandoned by many, from whose gratitude he had reason to expect some little notice. He observed that the members of the family of the great Fox abounded in liberal and generous sentiments.

20th.—Went to town, and tried to procure a copy of the observations on Lord Bathurst's speech, some of which I was informed had arrived on the island. Captain Bunn, of the Man-

---

* The princess subsequently demanded permission to proceed to the place of her brother's exile, as will be seen in the Appendix, No. XIX.

gles, to whom I applied for one, professed his surprise that such an application should be made from a person belonging to Longwood, for immediately after his arrival, Sir Hudson Lowe and Sir Thomas Reade had taken five copies of the pamphlet from him, assigning as a reason for taking so many, that they wanted to send two or three to Longwood. He added, that those two persons had been very particular in requiring him to render an account of the books that he had brought out, and had possessed themselves of all the modern publications on political subjects, making a demand for all the copies of the Edinburgh Review he might have brought with him.

25th.—After having paid a professional visit to Napoleon, whose malady was by no means altered for the better, and while entering my room at about half-past four o'clock, Captain Blakeney delivered me the following letter :*

Plantation House, July 25th, 1818.

Sir,—I am directed by Lieutenant-General Sir Hudson Lowe to inform you, that by an instruction received from Earl Bathurst, dated the 16th of May, 1818, he has been directed to withdraw you from your attendance upon General Bonaparte, and to *interdict you all further interviews with the inhabitants at Longwood.*

Rear-Admiral Plampin has received instructions from the Lords Commissioners of the Admiralty as to your destination when you quit this island.

You are in consequence to leave Longwood immediately after receiving this letter, without holding any further communication whatsoever with the persons residing there.

I have the honor, &c.,

EDWARD WINYARD,

Lieut. Col: Military Secretary.

Barry O'Meary, Esq., Longwood.

* A letter of a similar import was sent to Count Montholon by Sir Hudson Lowe, containing instructions from Lord Bathurst, that Mr. Baxter should be directed to attend in my place.

Humanity, the duties of my profession, and the actual state of Napoleon's health, alike forbade a compliance with this unfeeling command, especially as my situation was of a civil nature, similar to other naval officers in the employ of the excise or customs. My resolution was adopted in a moment. I determined to disobey it, whatever might be the consequences; Napoleon's health required that I should prescribe for him a regimen, and prepare the medicines which it would be necessary for him to take in the absence of a surgeon, an absence likely to be of long duration, as I was perfectly sure he would accept of none recommended by Sir Hudson Lowe. I accordingly went instantly to Napoleon's apartment. Having obtained admission, I communicated to him the order which I had received. "*Le crime se consommera plus vite*," (The crime will be the sooner consummated) said Napoleon; "I have lived too long for them. *Votre ministère est bien hardi*," (Your minister is very bold) added he: "when the Pope was in France, sooner would I have cut off my right arm than have signed an order for the removal of his surgeon."

After some more conversation had taken place, and I had given him such medical instructions as I could upon the sudden, Napoleon said, "When you arrive in Europe, you will either go yourself, or send to my brother Joseph. You will inform him, that I desire he shall give to you the parcel containing the private and confidential* letters of the Emperors Alexander and Francis,

* On my return to Europe, I used every exertion to obtain the important letters in question. Unfortunately however for posterity, my efforts have not been attended with success. Before the Count de Surveillers had left Rochefort for America, apprehensive that he might be seized by the allied powers, he judged it prudent to deposit his precious charge in the hands of a person upon whose integrity he thought he could rely; but who, it has appeared since, basely betrayed the count, as some months ago a person brought the original letters to London for sale, for which he demanded 30,000*l*. This was immediately communicated to some of his majesty's ministers, and to the foreign ambassadors, and I have been credibly informed, that the Russian ambassador paid 10,000*l*. to redeem those belonging to his master. Amongst other curious passages, which have been repeated to me by those who have been favored with their perusal, the following occurs in reference to Hanover. His majesty of Prussia stated, that "*he always entertained a paternal regard for that country;*" and it appeared that the sovereigns, in general, *made earnest supplications for territory.*

the King of Prussia, and the other sovereigns of Europe with me, which I delivered to his care at Rochefort. You will publish them, to *couvrir de honte* (to cover with shame) those sovereigns, and manifest to the world the abject homage which those vassals paid to me, when asking favors or supplicating for their thrones. When I was strong, and in power, *ils briguèrent ma protection et l'honneur de mon alliance*, (they courted my protection and the honor of my alliance,) and licked the dust from under my feet. Now, in my old age, they basely oppress, and take my wife and child from me. I require of you to do this, and if you see any calumnies published of me during the time that you have been with me, and that you can say, 'I have seen with my own eyes that this is not true" contradict them."

He soon after dictated to Count Bertrand the letter, an extract of which is given in another part of this work, which he signed, adding a postscript in his own handwriting, and assuring me, that those few words would say more to the empress for me, than if he had written pages in quarto; he then presented me with a superb snuff-box, and a statue of himself; desired me, on my arrival in Europe, to make inquiries about his family, and communicate to the members of it, that he did not wish that any of them should come to St. Helena, to witness the miseries and humiliations under which he labored. "You will express the sentiments which I preserve for them," added he. "You will bear my affections to my good Louise, to my excellent mother and to Pauline. If you see my son, embrace him for me; may he never forget that he was born a French prince! Testify to Lady Holland the sense I entertain of her kindness, and the esteem which I bear to her. Finally, endeavor to send me authentic intelligence of the manner in which my son is educated." The emperor then shook me by the hand and embraced me, saying, "*Adieu, O'Meara, nous ne nous reverrons jamais encore. Soyez heureux.*" (Adieu, O'Meara, we shall never see each other again. May you be happy.)

For the authenticity of the foregoing conversations and details I pledge myself. I think it right also to mention, that I am in possession of other conversations and documents of great importance, delivered by Napoleon himself, which it might be imprudent to make known at present. Their publication will be a matter for future consideration.

APPENDIX

PLAN OF LONGWOOD.

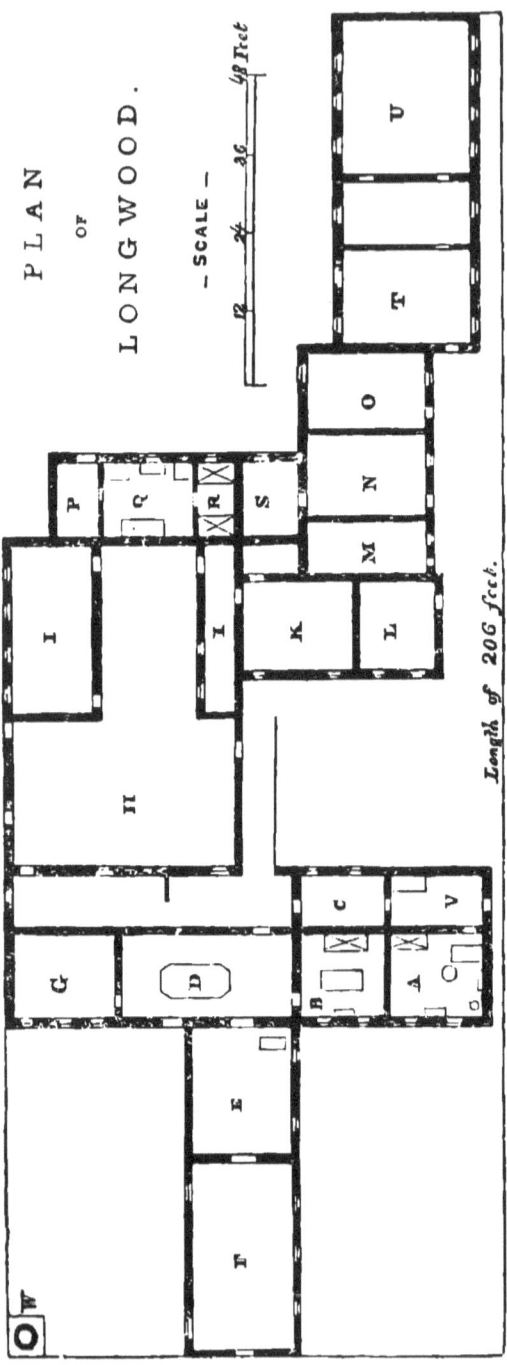

A The Emperor's bed-chamber.
B His study.
C Passage where the servant waited.
D Dining-room.
E The saloon.
F Antechamber for the reception of **strangers**.
G Library.
H The courtyard.
I The servants' halls.
K The kitchen.
L Apartment first occupied by Count Las Cases.
M Apartment of the officer attached to the establishment.
N and S Apartments of General Gourgaud.
O Dr. O'Meara's apartment.
P Count Las Cases' servants' apartment.
Q "   "   "   study.
R "   "   "   bedchamber.
T and U Count Montholon's family.
V The Emperor's bathing-room.
W Tent where the Emperor often breakfasted in fine weather, and dictated during the day.

APPENDIX.

The island of St. Helena is situated in latitude 15° 55′ S., and longitude 5° 46′ W., in the southeast trade wind. It is about ten miles and a half in length, six and three quarters in breadth, and twenty-eight in circumference. The highest part of it is Diana's Peak. It is distant from the nearest land (Ascension) about six hundred miles, and twelve hundred from the nearest continent—the Cape of Good Hope. Its appearance is the most desolate and unpromising that can be imagined. Its exterior presents an immense mass of brown rock, formed of different sorts of lava, rising from the ocean in irregular, rugged, and perpendicular precipices, of a burnt and scorified appearance, totally void of vegetation, from three to fifteen hundred feet high, diversified with hideous, deep, and narrow ravines, descending to the sea, and in some places forming landing-places. The island is composed of lava, cooled in different states of fusion, which, with the total absence of any primitive substance, its conical hills, the *puzzolana*, and other volcanic productions found in it, clearly show that it has undergone the action of fire. James Town, the only one in the island, is situated in the bottom of a deep wedge-like ravine, flanked on each side by barren and tremendous overhanging precipices, on whose sides and summits huge loose rocks continually menace the inhabitants with destruction. The one on the left from the sea is called Rupert's Hill, and that on the right Ladder Hill. There is a steep and narrow road, called the side path, cut along the former, and a good zig-zag road leads along the latter to the country-seat of the governor. The first view of the town is pleasing, especially to those who have been long at sea, and resembles that of a scene at the theatre. Opposite to the town is James' Bay, the principal anchorage, where the largest ships lie perfectly secure, as the wind never varies more than two or three points, and is always off the land, and favorable for sailing. The town consists of a small street along the beach, called the Marino, and the main street, commencing from this, and extending in a right line to a distance of about three hundred yards, where it branches off into two lesser ones. There are about one hundred and sixty houses, chiefly built of stone, cemented with mud, lime being scarce on the island. The principal houses, however, are plastered with this article, generally white-washed, and roofed with shingles. The others are covered with boards and earth. There is a church, a botanical garden, a hospital, a tavern, and barracks. On the left from the beach is situated the castle, the town residence of the governor. There are some breweries, in which beer is brewed of a quality equal to our best table beer.

The houses are in general neat on the exterior, though deficient in many of the conveniences and comforts of England. They chiefly consist of shops, and boarding or lodging-houses. East India and English goods are to be had, but the latter at an enormous price. Tea is the only commodity to be purchased cheap. We found on our arrival that provisions were very scarce; indeed, the necessaries of life were to be procured with great difficulty, and at an exorbitant rate. Such was the scarcity of cattle, that killing a bullock was an affair of state, and a regulation existed prohibiting the inhabitants from slaughtering even their own cattle, without having first obtained official permission from the governor and council.* The sheep are very small, weighing from twenty to thirty pounds each. Mutton, when to be had, sells from about one shilling and sixpence per pound, to two shillings. Fowls are very dear, from six to ten shillings each. Ducks, ten shillings; geese, fifteen; and a turkey, from one pound five to two pounds sterling. Veal very difficult to be had, and about two shillings per pound. Pork, one shilling and threepence. Cabbages, from tenpence to half-a-crown each. Carrots, a shilling per dozen. Potatoes, six to eight shillings per bushel. Eggs, per dozen, five to six shillings. Peas sometimes to be had, but exorbitantly dear.

* The difficulty of obtaining permission to slaughter cattle induced some of the inhabitants to have recourse to the expedient of precipitating a bullock down the steep sides of the ravines, in order to break some of its bones, and thus have a pretext to kill him.

The principal supply of fish is mackerel, which is caught in abundance. There are albicore, boneta, bulls' eyes, cavally, and many other kinds, and at times, but very rarely, turtle. There is also a sort of cray-fish called long legs, and some species of crabs.

There are a few wild peacocks, some partridges and pheasants, which constitute the only game on the island. These last are roya' game, and are solely reserved for the governor, there being a heavy penalty liable to be levied upon any person killing one who does not immediately send it to the governor. No hares are to be found, and but few rabbits. Lodging is excessively dear—five shillings a night being the price for residents, and ten for passengers. Board and lodging is thirty shillings a day for a grown person, fifteen for a child, and ten for a servant, for which there is a middling table, and a modicum of wine. English porter, and all wines, except Cape, are dear. The sale of every description of spirits is prohibited. The goats, which were once so numerous, and so destructive to the young trees, are nearly extirpated. The houses are overrun with rats and mice, which abound in numbers scarcely credible to those who have not been at St. Helena, and the ravages they commit are incalculable. There are also swarms of musquitoes of two kinds, one called the day, and the other the night musquito, whose bites are tormenting; numbers of cock-roaches, some scorpions and centipedes, and a sort of fly extremely annoying to the cattle and horses. Caterpillars and grubs are astonishingly numerous, and the ravages they commit upon the young green plants are almost incredible; whole plantations of vegetables are said to have been sometimes destroyed by the former in a night. Fuel is extremely scarce and dear; coals are obliged to be sent from England. The resources of the island are very few, and I may with truth venture to assert, that on board of the Northumberland alone there was a greater number of artificers and mechanics than it contains. Labor is excessively dear—the common wages of a working man being a dollar a day, and those of a mechanic from seven to ten shillings.

James Town is defended by a line of works along the beach (to the left of which, from the sea, is the landing-place), and by strong seaworks on Ladder Hill, Rupert's Hill, by Munden's and Banks' batteries. Across the sea-line there is a drawbridge, and a gate leading into the main stree', which is closed at night. The approach to the town is round a conical hill called Sugar Loaf Point, where ships are obliged to send a boat to declare their names, country, &c., before they are permitted to anchor. There are besides this landing-place five or six others, not, however, easily practicable, excepting to a sailor.

A stream of water runs through and supplies the town and shipping in the bay, which, with water-cresses, a few vegetables, and beer, are the principal refreshments to be had by those passengers or others whose pockets are not well supplied.

The population of the island (exclusive of the military) is reckoned at about two thousand nine hundred souls, of whom about seven hundred and eighty are whites, thirteen hundred blacks, and the rest Lascars, Chinese, &c. The whites are either of British descent or natives of Great Britain. The islanders are, however, very jealous of these last, and look upon them as intruders, who, in return, have nicknamed the natives *Yam Stocks.* The English language is spoken with a barbarous pronunciation. The religion of the established church prevails. Their customs are a mixture of English and tropical. Their chief food consists of salt meat, rice, and fish, the first of which they obtain in allotted quantities from the East India Company's stores at a reduced price Fresh meat is a luxury rarely indulged in, except by the upper classes, and is with difficulty to be had even by them. Their vegetables are generally sold or bartered to the ships and troops. A very few years ago there was not a plough upon the island. Latterly, however, owing to the exertions of the late governor, Major-General Beatson, there are several. The majority of the inhabitants are shop-keepers, and live in the town, resorting to the country for amusement or health. Generally speaking, their minds are but little improved by education, and the few who have been brought up in Europe, on their return soon acquire a sovereign contempt for their relatives and neighbors.

The enormous price of provisions and other necessaries of life, necessarily prevents much hospitality from being manifested by the inhabitants. With the exception of Mr. Balcombe's family, in general strangers could only hope to meet attention from the proprietors of the boarding-house where they live, some of whom are the principal persons on the island, and a few years ago included amongst their number the second member of council. Evening parties are, how-over, occasionally given; and the young ladies of the island—some of whom are very pretty, and very uneducated—do not require a long courtship, or much persuasion, to induce them to quit the rock where they had their birth.

The interior of the island is composed of alternate ridges of mountains and ravines, the former of which vary in height from six hundred to two thousand six hundred feet. Diana's Peak, the highest in the island, is two thousand six hundred and ninety-seven feet above the level of the sea. The face of the country presents a most striking contrast, being composed of a great variety of mountains and valleys, of barrenness and verdure. Some parts consisting of immense stupendous and sterile rocks, separated by deep and frightful dingy-colored chasms, several hundred feet perpendicular, with huge detached masses of naked rock sticking up here and there, with an occasional patch of green, others of verdant pasturages and gardens, ornamented with trees, and houses erected in the valley or on the declivities, which, with a few cattle, some sheep, and occasionally a horse grazing along the steep sides of the hills, give an agreeable relief to the eye, fatigued with the view of the tremendous precipices and gaping red ravines in the neighborhood. This contrast induces the beholder to consider the cultivated portion picturesque and romantic. The view from Sandy Bay Ridge, and from the summit of Diana's Peak, is sublime. The greatest part of the island, however, is barren, and inexpressibly desolate and repulsive in its appearance, and even a large portion of that which is susceptible of culture is now overrun with the blackberry,* which was introduced a few years ago as a curiosity. The roads are in general bridle paths, twining round the brows of the hills, or creeping up the steep sides, and over the sharp ridges of the mountains, and sinking into the profundities of the ravines. There were only two carriages on the island, which belonged to the governor, and were dragged along by bullocks.

Amongst the prettiest and most desirable spots on the island, may be mentioned—first, Plantation House, next Colonel Smith's, Rosemary Hall, Mr. Doveton's, at Sandy Bay, the Briers, and Miss Mason's. All of these have the advantage of good gardens, shady walks, verdure, and brooks of water, and, comparatively, are pleasant

---

* **Rubus Pinnatus.**

abodes. Plantation House and grounds, in particular, would, in any part of Europe, be esteemed a handsome and romantic residence.

That the reader may not be led to imagine that I am inclined to enhance its beauties, I shall extract the description given of it in the last work published upon St. Helena. "Proceeding about three quarters of a mile is the entrance to Plantation House, the official country establishment for the governor; it is a mansion of considerable elegance, pleasantly situated, with extensive gardens, and cultivated lands, laid out in good style, and kept in excellent order; adorned with a variety of fine trees and shrubs, collected from Europe, Asia, Africa, and America, brought from the most remote parts of the world, and from climates the most opposite, yet all thriving in great luxuriance—all flourishing alike."

It is sheltered by the immense ridges of mountains* forming Diana's Peak, and Halley's Mount, intersecting the island, and trending to the south, from the south-east wind, which, in exposed situations, is so destructive to vegetation.

When it was understood that Longwood had been fixed upon for the abode of Napoleon, it at first excited some surprise in the minds of the islanders, as the situation was so bleak and exposed, that it had never been inhabited by any family for more than a few months in the year; but this surprise soon subsided, as it was supposed that a suitable winter residence would be provided for him, when the new governor arrived.

Longwood is a large plain, situated on the summit of a mountain on the *windward* side of the island, nearly two thousand feet above the level of the sea, and containing a number of gum-wood trees, (*conyza gumifera,*) which being nearly all of the same size and inclination, in consequence of the trade wind continually blowing from the south-east, presents a monotonous and melancholy appearance. The

---

* In the journeys which I was obliged to take twice a week to Plantation House, I frequently left Longwood amidst fog and drizzling rain, and found fine weather at Plantation House estate; and indeed the change generally began after having passed the mountains above Hut's Gate. This may be accounted for by the clouds having been attracted by the high mountains, called the Backbone of the island. Fine weather in the town, and very bad in the mountains, at one and the same time, was an every-day occurrence. It is singular that thunder and lightning are unknown in St. Helena. This arises, probably, from the electric fluid being attracted by Diana's Peak and the other conical hills, and conducted into the sea.

APPENDIX. 257

leaves of the gum-wood are small, narrow, and chiefly confined to the ends of the branchlets, consequently do not afford that thick foliage necessary to intercept the rays of the sun. There is no water, except what is brought from the distance of nearly three miles. No continuous shade. Exposed to a south-east wind constantly charged with humidity, its elevated situation causes it to be enveloped in fog, or drenched with rain for the greatest part of the year. The soil is a tenacious argillaceous clay, which in wet weather collects and adheres to the shoes of the pedestrian, forming so ponderous a mass as materially to impede his progress. For a month or six weeks during the year there is fine weather; for two or three a powerful vertical sun prevails; and for seven or eight, the weather is wet and most disagreeable. Though Longwood is generally covered with fog and wet, the sky occasi. ally clears up, and the rays of the sun beam forth in transitory splendor. Soon after, the hemisphere becomes again obscured, thick fogs cover the plain, and rain, impetuously forced along by the eternal south-east trade wind, drenches whoever has been induced to hazard a walk by the delusive appearance of sunshine. These changes of temperature often occur several times in the course of the day, and are one cause of the unhealtniness of St. Helena. In consequence of the tenacious nature of the clay, the rain penetrates very little into the surface, and runs off to the ravines in the neighborhood. The violence of the wind is destructive to vegetation, and, together with the ravages of the grub, and the want of water, for two or three months, renders abortive almost every attempt towards cultivating the garden. The plant which thrives best at Longwood is the spurge, a most offensive weed.

That some readers may not be led to suppose that I have exaggerated any of the inconveniences of Longwood, I shall take the liberty of making two extracts from the history of St. Helena, written by Mr. Brooke, an inhabitant of the island for about forty years; senior member of council, and now acting governor, possessing a large property in the island, and much more inclined to enhance it merits, than to point out its defects. "But it is only in the most sheltered spot of the island that the oak attains perfection; in exposed situations, the trade wind, blowing continually in the same direction, produces very baneful effects upon this as upon most other trees not indigenous to the soil."—page 288. And again, page 255: "Governor Dunbar was unwearied in his exertions to watch over the resources and fertility of the island. Experiments in the cultivation of oats, barley, and wheat, at *Longwood*, gave rise to such hopes of success, that a *barn* was erected there; but on a failure of subsequent crops, it was converted into a residence for the lieutenant-governor. This disappointment is supposed to have arisen either from drought, or some peculiarity of the climate or soil, and not, as has sometimes been asserted, from the depredations of rats."

A stronger proof that Longwood is the worst and the most unpleasant part of the island,* cannot be afforded, than by the fact of its not having been inhabited before Napoleon came to the island, except by the lieutenant-governor as a country residence for three or four months annually, and by the occasional presence of the company's farmers in a small hovel. None of the inhabitants of the island *ever made it a permanent abode*, well knowing its inconveniences. This incontrovertible *fact* " speaks volumes."

Upon the climate of St. Helena, I hope the following remarks, founded upon actual observation and experience, will not be deemed superfluous on the present occasion; and to render them more intelligible to the unprofessional reader, I beg leave to offer a few preliminary observations.

To sudden diurnal vicissitudes of temperature, especially when accompanied with rain or humidity, may be ascribed the greatest part of the diseases which affect the human constitution. Rapid transitions from heat to cold render the extreme vessels on the surface of the body torpid, impelling at the same time a quantity of blood upon some of the internal organs. Sudden atmospherical changes injure by the consent of parts between the exterior and the interior, producing in some climates, such as that of England, affections of the lungs; in tropical ones, where the biliary system is so liable to derangement, affections of the liver. The great sympathy existing between the skin, liver, and intestines, has never been more strongly exemplified

---

* In the sketch which I have given of the customs of St. Helena, I have omitted to mention one which perhaps may not be considered favorable to morality. Should pregnancy take place in the instance of any unmarried female of a respectable family, the seducer, if in either the civil or military employ of the Hon. the East India Company (who constitute about four-fifths of of the inhabitants of respectability,) is compelled to marry her under pain of losing his situation. I am not able to state whether this be a *custom* or a by-law of the company.

than by the number of violent and fatal affections of the two latter organs, which have occurred, and are daily occurring, in St. Helena, where the atmospherical vicissitudes are so frequent and so rapid, and where such humidity prevails.

The interior of St. Helena, as has been already mentioned, is chiefly formed of successions of high, steep, and unequal ridges of hills, the most elevated of which are two thousand six hundred feet above the level of the ocean, divided by deep, narrow, and long ravines, some of which at the bottom are not more than a few feet above the level of the sea. Whoever, therefore, would ride a few miles, must calculate on passing through different climates every half hour; one moment becalmed in the bottom of the ravines he experiences the heat of the tropics, in a latitude of 15° 55' south; a moment afterwards, passing the aperture of some chasm, perspiring from every pore, the temporary lull is succeeded by a sudden and bleak blast from the mountains, the effects of which, combined with the humidity accompanying it, are to produce a rapid evaporation and abstraction of animal heat from the surface of the body, driving thereby the blood to the interior. Emerging from the valley, covered with perspiration, a similar cutting blast, producing the same effects, strikes you on reaching the summit of the mountains.

Reckoning one degree of reduced temperature for every two hundred feet of elevation, there will be found a difference of ten degrees of temperature between Longwood, which is about two thousand feet above the level of the sea and the town; to which may be added two or three degrees more, arising from the sharp south-east wind, loaded with humidity, generally prevailing in the high regions, producing a difference of evaporation between the mountains and the valleys, which, combined with the increase of elevation, reduces the temperature of Longwood twelve or thirteen degrees. Add to the foregoing, the frequent vicissitudes of temperature; at one moment assailed by a shower of rain and enveloped in fog, to the force of which the wind communicates such an impetus, as to cause it to penetrate the best great-coat in a few minutes; shortly afterwards, the sky brightening, the weather clearing up, and the scorching rays of a tropical sun beaming forth. This continues for a short time, and is suddenly followed by a repetition of fog, rain, and mist.* This alternate drench-

* " Hence it appears that St. Helena, during these last three years, had its full share of

ing and scorching is, of itself, sufficient (as every medical man will allow) to produce the most violent inflammatory affections of the viscera, particularly in those of the abdomen.

It would thus appear that St. Helena, in addition to the general causes of insalubrity to Europeans, which are inseparable from a tropical climate, has also local and peculiar causes for being particularly unhealthy, as the great mortality, to be hereafter described, amply proves. The most trifling cold or irregularity is frequently succeeded by a violent attack of dysentery, inflammation of the bowels or fever, proving fatal in a few days, if the most active and efficacious practice is not instantly adopted. A surfeit in a child, which in Europe would require nothing more than a little warm water to produce evacuation, there becomes a formidable disease, requiring the most powerful remedies; and if neglected only for a few hours, terminates fatally. To Europeans the climate is peculiarly unfriendly; and indeed, it is unfavorable to longevity in all subjects, even to the natives; as, on examination of the parish registers, it will be seen, that very few persons pass their forty-fifth year.* The most prevalent complaints are, dysenteries, inflammations of the bowels, liver affections, and fevers, all of them generally of a violent form. Dysenteries especially, and liver affections, (which are indeed frequently combined,) appear with the most concentrated and fatal symptoms, baffling the prompt exhibition of the most active and powerful remedies, and in spite of the acknowledged skill and experience of several able practitioners, these terminate fatally, in a proportion rarely witnessed in any British colony. During the first twelve or thirteen months after its arrival at St. Helena, the second battalion of the 66th regiment lost, by these diseases, FIFTY-SIX men, out of a strength of six hundred and thirty, being one in eleven; and still more recently, the Conqueror, which ship arrived in July, 1817, has

---

rain, and in much greater quantity than usually falls in London, which by an average of eleven years is no more than 21.25 inches, whereas the average of four years at St. Helena was 33.38 inches."—*Major-General Beatson's Introductory Chapter, relative to the island of St. Helena, page* xxxvi.

* "The only endemic disorders to which the natives are subject, are of the catarrhal kind; these, as they belong to the inflammatory class, may in some measure account, notwithstanding their general robust health, for the *few instances among the islanders of longevity* according to the information of a professional friend, who has assisted this to count with his opinion and judgment."—*Vide Brooke's History of St. Helena, page* 34.

lost, in eighteen months, almost entirely by the same complaints, ONE HUNDRED AND TEN MEN, out of a complement of six hundred, besides ONE HUNDRED AND SEVEN INVALIDED, and sent to England, being more than a third of her complement.

The number of deaths in the two battalions of the 66th regiment, I cannot positively state, but believe it to have exceeded one hundred and twenty men. A reference to the official returns will, however, sufficiently elucidate this point. In the West Indies, the proportion of deaths to the strength was, in the year 1814, as one to twenty-five, and of deaths to diseases, as one to thirty-six and two-thirds. Yet how trifling does the mortality there appear, when compared with that of St. Helena. At the latter place it was so great, that the governor and admiral, apprehensive of the effects which might be produced by a longer residence in the island, and doubtless, desirous of alleviating their miseries as far as they could, sent upwards of seventy of the sick in one month to England and the Cape. Above half of those sent to the last-named place (who were the worst cases) have been long ere now laid in their "quiet graves."

The Conqueror was also ordered to cruize to windward of the island for six weeks, without, however, much benefit having accrued from the measure. It is worthy of observation, that the Racoon ship's company had suffered severely from dysentery and hepatitis while stationed at St. Helena, but when sent to the Cape they recovered, and became very healthy, which state of health continued as long as the vessel remained *there*, but on her return to St. Helena, *dysentery* and *hepatitis* again appeared, and a heavy sick list followed.*

The loss of life among the crews of the following small ships whilst they were on the St. Helena station, is also very great—viz., *twenty-four in the Musquito*, complement one hundred men; sixteen in the Racoon, one hundred men; eleven in the Leveret, seventy-five men;

* Another strong instance of the insalubrity of the climate is to be found in the instance of the female convict-ship Friendship, which vessel arrived at St. Helena from England in the month of November, 1817. She had not remained more than eight or ten days to water before the dysentery made its appearance, and in the course of a few weeks above one hundred cases occurred. Previous to her arrival at St. Helena, not one instance of the complaint had occurred.

From the 20th November, 1815, to the 20th of the same month, 1816, there were admitted into the regimental hospital four hundred and thirty-eight patients, one hundred and seventy-nine of whom were afflicted with bowel complaints. The regiment was between five and six hundred strong.

fifteen in the Griffon, eighty-five men; besides numbers invalided, and sent to England on account of the same complaints. It is well known to naval officers, that, unless in *very sickly stations*, small vessels are generally very healthy, frequently not losing a man in a year. I was myself surgeon of a sloop of war in the West Indies, in which ship not a single death occurred during twelve months, though exposed for a considerable portion of that time to the influence of the noxious climate of Surinam.

The undeserved reputation for salubrity which St. Helena has hitherto enjoyed, has probably arisen from its being so little known, except to seamen and others, who, arriving after long voyages, were enchanted, like Dampier's sailors, to find themselves on shore anywhere, and who, during the few days they remained, found themselves relieved from scorbutic complaints by the use of the watercresses with which it abounds, and from its population being small, and chiefly composed of natives, who, of course, do not suffer so much as strangers from the effects of the climate in which they were born. Until the arrival of the state prisoner, very few Europeans resided for a continuance upon the island; and I can assert, from personal observation, that the greatest number of those now there, even of the officers, have suffered attacks, more or less severe, either of dysentery or hepatitis, in which number, I regret to say, I was myself included, and that the opinion of the medical officers, who had the best opportunity of forming a correct opinion, from actual experience on the island, is, *that the climate is extremely unhealthy*, and especially 'hat hepatitis and dysentery prevail to an extent and with a severity seldom to be paralleled. In order to convince the public that I am neither singular in my opinions nor inclined to exaggerate, I beg leave to refer the reader to a medical inaugural Dissertation* upon Dysentery and Hepatitis in St. Helena, composed by the candidate

---

* " Est nullus morbus perniciosior dysenteria exercitibus in omnibus partibus orbis terrarum degentibus; sed in tropicis regionibus grassatur vi maxima inter milites et alios ex Europa: et videtur intimus nexus interhanc et hepatitidem existere, nam sæpe conjunguntur, et raro accidit unum sine altero "—Dissertatio Medica, p. 15.

In an official letter from Dr. Baildon, dated Nov. 24, 1808, he expresses himself as follows:—" It will hardly be credited that soldiers and others are frequently brought to the hospital as far advanced in real scurvy as if they had just landed after a long voyage, and many who are brought for other complaints are considerably tainted with this disease.'
" On my arrival, I was much surprised with the great number of patients attacked with liver complaints."

for the degree of doctor in medicine in Trinity College, Dublin. The essay in question was written by Dr. Leigh, formerly surgeon to the second battalion of the 66th regiment, stationed at St. Helena.

No. I.
Letter from the Author to Admiral Lord Keith.

HIS MAJESTY'S SHIP BELLEROPHON,
Torbay, 7th August, 1815.

MY LORD: Application having been made to me yesterday by Count Bertrand to accompany General Napoleon Bonaparte to St. Helena, in quality of surgeon (as the surgeon who embarked with him in France is unwilling to proceed further), I beg to inform your lordship that I am willing to accept that situation (provided it meets with your lordship's approbation), and also on the following conditions—viz., that it should be permitted me to resign the above situation, should I find it not consonant to my wishes, on giving due notice of my intention thereof. That such time as I shall serve in that situation shall be allowed to count as so much time served on full pay in his majesty's navy, or that I shall be indemnified in some way for such loss of time, as surgeon on full pay, as it may occasion to me. That I am not to be considered in any wise depending upon, or to be subservient to, or *paid* by the aforesaid Napoleon Bonaparte, but as a *British officer*, employed by the British government; and, lastly, that I may be informed, as soon as circumstances will admit, of what salary I am to have, and in what manner, and from whom, I am to receive it. I have the honor to remain,

My Lord,
With the greatest respect,
Your Lordship's most obedient humble servant,
BARRY E. O'MEARA,
Surgeon H. M. S. Bellerophon.

To the Right Honorable Viscount KEITH,
Admiral of the Red, G. C. B., Commander-in-Chief.

_{Both of those diseases Dr. Baildon attributes to the "excessive use of spirituous liquors" Now, as in 1810, the government of St. Helena adopted measures to prevent any spirits from being landed, which had completely the desired effect; and as all houses for retailing spirits were abolished on the 15th of May, 1809, and wholesome beer substituted in lieu, it is clear that the prevalence of liver complaints in St. Helena since that period must be ascribed to other causes than to the excessive use of spirituous liquors.}

No. II.

Translation of the communication made by Sir Hudson Lowe to the persons composing the suite of the Emperor Napoleon.

DOWNING STREET, 10th January, 1816.

I have at present to let you know that it is the pleasure of his royal highness the Prince Regent, that on your arrival at St. Helena, you should communicate to all the persons forming the suite of Napoleon Bonaparte, including the domestics, that they are at liberty to quit the island immediately to return to Europe, adding that none will be permitted to remain at St. Helena, unless those who shall give a written declaration, which shall be deposited in your hands, that it is their desire to remain in the island, and to participate in the restrictions which it is necessary to impose upon Napoleon Bonaparte personally.

(Signed)   BATHURST.

Those amongst them who shall determine to return to Europe, must be sent by the first favorable occasion to the Cape of Good Hope. The governor of that colony will be charged to provide those persons with the means of passage to Europe.

(Signed)   BATHURST.

No. III.

Translation of the Paper signed by the French in Napoleon's suite.

We, the undersigned, desiring to remain in the service of the Emperor Napoleon, consent, *however frightful the abode in St. Helena may be,* to remain there, submitting ourselves to the restrictions, *however unjust and arbitrary,* which are imposed upon his majesty and the persons in his service.

(Here followed the signatures.)

No. IV.

Letter from the Governor, Sir Hudson Lowe, to Count Montholon.

PLANTATION HOUSE, August 17, 1816.

SIR: In pursuance of the conversations I have already had with you on the subject of the expenses of the establishment at Longwood, I do myself the honor to acquaint you, that having used all efforts to effect a reduction in them, without diminishing in any very sensible manner from the convenience or comforts of General Bonaparte, or any of the families or individuals that form his suite (*in which operation I am happy to acknowledge the spirit of concert with which you have assisted*), I am now enabled to transmit to you, for General Bonaparte's information, two statements, furnishing sufficiently precise data whereon to found a calculation of the probable and annual expense, should matters continue on the same footing as at present established.

The statement No. I. has been furnished me by Mr. Ibbetson, head of the commissariat department in this island. The latter has been framed by my military secretary.

The instructions I have received from the British government, direct me to limit the expenditure of General Bonaparte's establishment to £8,000 per annum. *They give me liberty at the same time to admit of any further expense being incurred* which he may require, *as to table and so forth*, beyond what this sum would cover, *provided he furnishes the funds whereby the surplus charges may be defrayed.*

I am now, therefore, under the necessity of requesting you would make known to him the impossibility I am under of bringing the expenses of his household on its present establishment, in point of numbers, within the limits prescribed, unless I make such a reduction under several heads as might naturally abridge from the conveniences which the persons around him now enjoy; and having been already *very frankly informed by him, as well as by yourself,* that he has at his disposal, in various parts of Europe, means whereby the extra, or even the whole, expense may be defrayed,[*] I beg leave to request being informed, previous to attempting any further considerable reduction, and which might prove inconvenient to him or the persons of his suite, if he is content such an attempt should be made, or *if he is willing to place at my command* sufficient funds to meet the extra charges which must otherwise be unavoidably incurred.

I have the honor to be, sir,
Your most obedient humble servant,
(Signed)   H. LOWE, Lieut.-General.

[*] *Explanatory Note.*—It was answered by the postscript of the letter of the 23d August to this part of Sir Hudson Lowe's letter, and he had been told that if there were a free correspondence, and if the wants here experienced were known in Europe, there was no doubt that millions would be offered from the different countries of Europe.

STATEMENT

SHOWING THE PROBABLE ANNUAL EXPENDITURE ON ACCOUNT OF GENERAL BONAPARTE AND SUITE ON THE ISLAND OF ST. HELENA.

			£	s.	d.	Total amount per ann. £ s. d.
Supplied.	By Commissariat Department.	Forage for thirteen horses daily,	720	4	7	
		Transport forage for one mule conveying the same,	46	10	2	794 2 3
		Pay of soldier in charge of the mule,	27	7	6	
Expense.	Of English servants attached to General Bonaparte's establishment,					675 0 0
Ditto.	Of public transport conveying the supplies furnished by the Purveyor at Longwood.	Forage for eight mules daily,	372	1	4	
		Pay for two muleteers in charge of the same,	109	10	0	577 7 7
		Rations of ditto,	68	8	9	
		Pay of two soldiers ditto ditto,	27	7	6	
Ditto.	Of public mechanics employed at Longwood House, whose services are likely to be wanted for a considerable time.	Two overseers, six carpenters, four sawyers, nine masons, three plasterers, and one painter,				939 17 6
Supplied.	By Mr. Defountain, in charge of the stores belonging to the East India Company.	Table stores and other necessaries for the house,				2,020 5 3
Ditto.	From government stores sent from England.	Wines: Claret, Grave, Champagne, Madeira,				2,445 10 0
	Do. by Mr. Balcomb, purveyor.	House and table expenses,				11,700 0 0

APPENDIX. 267

Proposed. Allowance to be granted to Mr. Balcomb, purveyor, at five per cent. on the account of the supplies, &c., furnished by hire, on the sum as above mentioned. } To be added, ...

Proposed. Salary to Surgeon O'Meara, attached to General Bonaparte and suite, not yet defined. } To be added, ...

$$\overline{19{,}152 \quad 2 \quad 7}$$

(Signed) D. IBBETSON,
A. Com. General.

Nota Bene.—In the sum of £11,700 is comprised a fixed expense of £672 for the table of the English officers on guard at Longwood. The Statement No. 2 is in every respect similar to this, with the single difference, that it enters less into detail, and is made, in round numbers, to £19,450, including the emoluments attached as a memorandum to the present statement.

No. V.

Supplies allowed by Government to the establishment at Longwood, consisting of forty-five persons, from October, 1816, to June, 1817.

DAILY.

Meat, Beef and Mutton included (lbs.)	82
Fowls (No.)	6
Bread (lbs.)	66
Butter (lbs.)	
Lard (lbs.)	2
Salad Oil (pints)	3 1-4
Sugar-candy (lbs.)	4
Coffee (lbs.)	2
Tea, green (lbs.)	1-2
Tea, black (lbs.)	1-2
Candles, wax (lbs.)	8
Eggs (No.)	30
Common sugar (lbs.)	5
Cheese (lbs.)	1
Vinegar (quarts)	1
Flour (lbs.)	5
Salt meat (lbs.)	6
Fire wood (cwt.)	3
Porter or ale (bottles)	3
Vegetables (in value)	£1
Fruit (in value)	10s.
Confectionery (in value)	8s.

PER FORTNIGHT.

Ducks (No.)	8
Turkeys (No.)	2
Geese (No.)	2
Loaf Sugar (loaves)	2
Fine Rice (bag)	1-2
Hams (not to exceed 14 lbs. each)	2
Coals (bushels)	45
Fish (in value)	80s

APPENDIX. 269

Milk (in value) . . . . . 98s.
Fresh Butter, Salt, Mustard, Pepper, Capers, Lamp Oil, Peas,
(not to exceed in value) . . . . . . 7l.

WINE DAILY.

Champagne, or Vin de Grave (bottles) . . 1
Madeira (bottles) 1
Constantia (bottles) 1
Claret* (bottles) 6

N. B. After the departure of the Count de Las Cases and Piontkowski, the meat was reduced to 72lbs. daily, and the number of fowls to *five*.

DAILY EXTRA EXPENDITURE, PAID BY THE FRENCH.

	£	s.	d.
One dozen of Eggs	0	5	0
Eight pounds of Butter, at 3s. per pound	1	4	0
Two pounds of Wax Candles, at 3s. 6d.	0	7	0
Three Fowls, at 6s. each	0	18	0
Four pounds of Sugar-candy	0	8	0
Two pounds of Loaf Sugar	0	6	0
One pound of Cheese	0	3	0
Vegetables	0	10	0
Two pounds of Salt Pork	0	2	6
One pound of Lard	0	1	0
One bottle of Oil	0	8	0
One pound of Rice, and one of Flour	0	1	0
Five pounds of common Sugar	0	1	6
One bottle of Vinegar	0	1	0
Paper for Kitchen, and Packthread	0	1	0
Four loaves of Bread, at 1s. 6d each	0	6	0
	£5	3	0

* Cape and Teneriffe wine for the servants, at the rate of a bottle a day, was also given by government, not included in the Schedule; being one pint more than the quantity daily allowed to the soldiers and sailors stationed at St. Helena.

WEEKLY EXTRA, DITTO.

	£	s.	d.
Two Turkeys	3	0	0
One Ham	3	0	0
One Roasting Pig	0	11	0
One bottle of Pickles	0	12	0
Three bottles of Olives	1	4	0
	£8	7	0

The above expenditure does not contain the quantity of meat bought by the French, amounting to from three to five sheep weekly and two calves monthly.

NO. VI.

Restrictions made by Sir Hudson Lowe, and communicated at Longwood, on the 9th of October, 1816; but which he had already put in execution by different orders, ever since the month of August preceding, and which he never communicated to the English officers of the service, ashamed, no doubt, of their contents.

Heads of some proposed alterations in the Regulations hitherto established for the persons under charge at Longwood.

I. LONGWOOD, with the road along the ridge, by Hut's Gate, to the signal-gun near the alarm-house, will be established as the limits.

II. Sentries will designate the external boundary, as well as that beyond which no person can approach Longwood House and garden, without the governor's permission.

III. The road to the left of Hut's Gate, and returning by Woodyridge to Longwood, never having been frequented by General Bonaparte, since the governor's arrival, the posts which observed it will for the greater part be withdrawn. Should he however wish at any time to ride in that direction, by giving the orderly officer timely notice of it, he will meet with no impediment.

IV. If he is desirous to extend his ride in any other direction, an officer of the governor's personal staff will always (on being informed in sufficient time) be prepared to attend him; and, should time not admit, the orderly officer at Longwood.

The officer who attends him, will be instructed not to approach towards him, unless so requested, nor to interfere in any respect with him during his ride, except so far as duty may require, on observing any departure from the established rules, when he will ride up and respectfully inform him of it.

V. The regulations already in force, for preventing communication with any persons without the governor's permission, will be required to be strictly adhered to : it is *requested !* therefore, *General Bonaparte will abstain from entering any houses, or engaging in conversation with the persons he may meet,* (except so far as the *ordinary salutations of politeness,* with which every one will be instructed to treat him, may appear to require,) *unless in the presence* of a British officer.

VI. Persons who, with General Bonaparte's acquiescence, may at any time receive passes from the governor to visit him, *cannot use such passes* to communicate with the *other persons* of his family, unless it is so *specifically expressed* in them.

VII. At sun-set, the garden enclosure round Longwood House will be regarded as the limits. Sentries will be placed round it at that hour, but will be posted in such a manner as not to incommode General Bonaparte with their personal observation of him, should he continue his walks in the garden after that time. They will be drawn round the house, as heretofore, during the night, and the limits will remain closed until the sentries are withdrawn entirely from the house and garden in the morning.

VIII. All letters for Longwood will be put up by the governor under a sealed envelope, and the packet sent to the orderly officer, to oe delivered sealed to any officer in attendance upon General Bonaparte, who will thus be assured the contents will have been made known to no other person than the governor.

In the same manner, all letters from persons at Longwood must be delivered to the orderly officer, put up under an outer envelope sealed, to the address of the governor, which will ensure that no other person than himself will be acquainted with their contents.

IX. No letters are to be received or sent, *nor written communication of any kind pass or be made known*, except in the above manner : nor can any correspondence be permitted *within the island,* except such communications as may be indispensable to make to the purveyor; the notes containing which must be delivered open, to the rderly officer, who will be charged to forward them.*

The above alterations will take place from the 10th instant

(Signed)   H. LOWE.

ST. HELENA, 9th Oct. 1816.

No. VII.

Translation of the proposal made by the Emperor, to assume the incognito.

IT occurs to me, that in the conversation which has taken place between General Lowe and several of those gentlemen, things have been stated relative to my position, which are not conformable to my ideas.

I abdicated into the hands of the representatives of the nation and for the profit of my son. I went with confidence to England, with intentions to live there, or in America, in the most profound retreat; and under the name of a colonel, killed at my side, resolved to remain a stranger to every political occurrence, of whatever nature it might be.

Arrived on board of the Northumberland, I was informed that I was a prisoner of war; that I was to be transported beyond the line; and that I was named General Bonaparte. In opposition to that of General Bonaparte, which it was wished to impose upon me, I was obliged to bear, ostensibly, my title of emperor.

Seven or eight months ago, Count Montholon proposed to remedy those little difficulties which were produced every moment, by adopting an ordinary name. The admiral thought it to be his duty to write on the subject to London; there the matter at present rests.

A name is now given to me, which has the advantage of not prejudging the past, but which is not in the forms of society. I am always disposed to take a name which enters into ordinary usage, and I reiterate, that when it shall be judged proper to discontinue this cruel abode, I am willing to remain a stranger to politics, whatever event may occur in the world. This is my opinion; whatever else may have been said on this subject is incorrect.

---

* Nothing can surpass the *elegance* of this composition, excepting its *grammatical correctness!* or, indeed, the *humanity* of the regulations themselves!

APPENDIX. 273

No. VIII.

Translation of the Remarks made by Napoleon on the slip of paper, containing the Governor's reply.

1. THE conduct which has been pursued here for six months, cannot be justified by some detached phrases of a correspondence with the minister. A long and voluminous ministerial correspondence is an arsenal provided with arms of every description.

2. The last regulations would be considered as injurious and oppressive at Botany Bay; whatever may be said upon it, they must be contrary to the will of the English government, which approved the regulations which were in force until the month of August last.

3 All the observations which Counts Bertrand and Montholon have made, have been useless. A free discussion has been interdicted by menaces.

No. IX.

Letter from Count Bertrand to Sir Hudson Lowe, relative to the presents sent by Mr. Elphinstone.

LONGWOOD, 9th of July, 18—.

GOVERNOR,—I have received the five cases which you took the trouble of sending to me, containing a chess-board and men, a box of counters, and two work-baskets in ivory, sent from Canton by Mr. Elphinstone. The emperor was surprised to perceive by your letter, that you think your duty required that those objects should not be sent. "*If I acted,*" you say, "*in entire conformity to the established regulations, I ought to have delayed sending them up.*" In this case, M. Governor, it would have been pleasing to us had you retained them.

But to what does this refer? Is it because those articles have not passed through the channel of the ministers? In the restrictions of the ministers, it is said, that *letters* must come through this channel, but not articles of clothing, busts, furniture, &c. We have constantly received from the Cape of Good Hope, many articles which have been sent to us. Besides, Lord Bathurst, in his speech, and you, yourself, in one of your letters, have denied, with indignation, that letters sent by the post, or by other opportunities, have been sent to London to be returned to this place. This cannot, nor has not, authorized you

VOL. II. 12*

to retain such objects as busts, furniture, books, or any other goods, which have no connection with security or detention.

Can it be because there is a crown upon the counters? No regulation can exist without being made known to us. Now, it never has been signified to us, that we cannot possess objects upon which there is a crown. It would be necessary, in that case, to make a new pack of cards for us, because on those which we possess, there is a crown. The linen, and the *small quantity* of plate which remains to us, are often sent to town, and are marked with a crown.

But, from whom has this regulation, of which you speak, emanated? From your government, which alone, according to the bill, has the right to make any? Your minister declared before parliament, that no restrictions whatever had been made since those which had been printed and communicated to Europe, and which your predecessor possessed, and which had been sent to you. He added, that you have not made any restrictions, but solely adopted measures of execution. Effectively you have not the right to make any.

The emperor does not desire favors from any body, and wishes nothing from the caprice of any person whatever; but he has the right to be informed of the restrictions which are imposed upon him. Your government, the parliament, and all nations have the same right. I therefore beg of you, sir, to communicate to us those new restrictions, and if such exist, they would be in contradiction to the assertion of Lord Bathurst, that they should have no other object than the security of detention. The emperor charges me to protest against the existence of any restrictions or regulations which shall not be legally notified to him, prior to being put in execution.

I have the honor, &c.,

(Signed)   COUNT BERTRAND.

No. X.

Letter from Count Bertrand to the Gunner.

LONGWOOD, 16th of July, 1817.

I HAVE received, sir, the marble bust of young Napoleon. I have given it to his father. It has imparted to him the most sensible pleasure. I regret that you have not been able to come and see us, and give us some details, which are always interesting to a father in the actual situation of affairs. It results from the letters which you have sent, that the artist esteems the value of his work to be one hundred guineas. The emperor has ordered me to send you a draft for *three hundred pounds sterling*.* The surplus is to indemnify you for the losses which he knows you have sustained in the sale of your little venture, as you were not permitted to land; and the chicaneries you have experienced by that event, which was in itself very simple, and would have procured you marks of esteem from every man of feeling.

Be so good as to communicate the emperor's thanks to the persons who have paid him this amiable attention.

I beg that you will acknowledge the receipt of this letter.

I have the honor to be, &c.,
    (Signed)   COUNT BERTRAND.
To M. RADOWICH, Master Gunner
on board the ship Baring.

No. XI.

The Governor's Reply to Count Bertrand's Letter relative to the Presents.

CASTLE, JAMESTOWN, July 25th, 1817.

SIR,—I have received your letter of the 10th instant. The frequent use in it of the imperial title, and the tone in which you convey your sentiments to me when you employ it, would perfectly warrant me in declining to acknowledge it, as being addressed to me in an admissible form, and in referring you to mine of the 30th August, 1816, to Count Montholon. I shall not, however, avail myself of these arguments for not replying to its contents.

The only object I had in view in addressing you on the 8th instant, was to avoid its being conceived I tacitly participated in, or approved the acknowledgment given to the imperial rank, in the crown placed everywhere over the initial of Napoleon on presents sent by a British subject particularly, and coming from a British factory.

Had I suffered them to proceed without any remark, the inference would have been obvious, I saw no impropriety in it; and I am too well aware how far this precedent might have been alleged, and what

* By means of some unworthy tricks, the poor man did not receive the money for nearly two years.

complaints would have sprung upon any future deviation from it, had I not explicitly made known the grounds upon which in this instance I had suffered them to reach you.

The donor's sentiments are his own, but I have a free right to the exercise also of my opinion, in not making myself the medium of them; and in suffering the presents to proceed, with no other qualification than what my note expressed, I went to the extreme boundary of what any attention to General Bonaparte's desires or expectations could demand of me.

You ask me, sir, "*est-ce à ce que ces objets ne sont pas arrivés par le canal du ministre?*" &c. (is it because these objects were not sent through the minister?)

I should have considered myself fully warranted in keeping them back upon the general principle of my instructions, without reference to the decoration upon them, until there was an express authority obtained from my government for their delivery, unless I assumed upon my own discretion to examine them and satisfy myself they covered no means of communication or assistance by which a clandestine intercourse was attempted.

That the latter was the principle upon which I was always ready to act, instead of waiting the delay of returns from England, was sufficiently apparent by my sending you the letter before the articles were even landed.

You observe, sir, I rejected with indignation the accusation, that letters brought by the post on private occasions should have been sent back to London to return to this country. I rejected, sir, with indignation, this accusation, and the reflections built upon it, because there was no foundation of truth or justice in them: because I revolted at that feeling which extracted injury and reproach from acts of attention, (for in sending their family letters I had exercised a discretion in favor of the persons who addressed me, not warranted by my instructions), but I did not admit that I had not the right, and was not fully justified in sending letters back to England, if I thought proper so to do, when they came by irregular channels. Presents may be as obnoxious to the security of detention as a letter, and *might require to be examined with a minuteness that would baffle any purpose of ornament or utility to be derived from them. A letter may be concealed under the squares of a chess-board, or the folds of a book cover,* as well as in the lining of a waistcoat; and I am not necessarily called upon to place my trust in any person by whom they are sent. If articles have been permitted to reach you, it has been because I have felt satisfied they were not of an objectionable nature; and you certainly have no reason to complain, sir, of the mode I have used my discretion in permitting generally every article that has arrived to be delivered, and in suffering many to proceed that had come addressed to myself, the transmission of which, from the delicacy of the persons who sent them, had been left entirely to my option.

You observe, sir, "*seroit ce parceque sur les jettons il y a une couronne?*" &c., &c., &c., (is it because there is a crown upon the pieces?) and ask if any regulation exists, which prevents your possessing an article with a crown upon it.

There is certainly, sir, no specific written regulation, prohibiting any article with a *crown* on it reaching Longwood, nor to prevent your possessing an object with such a decoration upon it; but it was in this case the imperial crown over the initial of Napoleon, carved, gilt, or engraved, on almost every article. His own abdication—the convention of Paris—and the acts of the British parliament, supersede the necessity of any regulation upon that head.

The articles now at Longwood, with the imperial crown on them, were thus marked before the abdication. I have never disputed their possession, nor any gratification they might afford.

The quotation from the debates in Parliament, I must beg leave to observe, is inexact, as taken from any newspaper I have seen. The papers themselves differ; for one speaks of regulations, another of instructions, not restrictions, being the same, (without any substantive alteration,) as those at first prescribed.

You say, sir, "*Vous n'avez pas le droit d'en faire,*" (you have not the right to do it.)

The act of parliament, the warrant, and instructions I possess, are, sir, my surest guides on this point; whilst I may at the same time, however, be allowed to observe, that the original instructions you wish to refer to as my only rule, have received a more ample interpretation than what their strict letter would imply in the degree of freedom from personal restriction General Bonaparte at present enjoys.

You add, "*L'Empereur ne veut de grace,*" &c., &c., (the emperor wishes no favor.)

I have not the pretension to bestow a favor on General Bonaparte, and still less the arrogance of subjecting him to any act of my caprice. He is under no restriction which my government does not know, and which all the world may not know.

It is not irrelevant on this occasion to observe, that at two interviews with General Bonaparte, he personally observed to me, that I was a general officer to act upon instructions, and not execute my duty as a "*consigne:*" (sentinel); at present it is as a *consigne*, it appears I am required to perform it. On another occasion he objected to "*aucune inspection directe ou publique*, (any inspection direct or public.) How do these suggestions accord with the narrow limit to which it is at present sought to restrict the exercise of my duties? The views you have now presented, coincide most with my own, (seeing that every exercise of my discretion even in points where I seek to act most favorably, only entails fresh discussion,) but where such opposing sentiments are conveyed to me, you must, sir, admit the difficulty of reconciling them.

You say, sir, "*L'Empereur me charge de protester contre l'existence de tout restriction,*" &c., &c., &c., (the Emperor directs me to protest against the existence of every restriction.)

Any communication made to me in the proper name of the person whom you thus designate, it is my bounden duty to consider, whereever circumstances will permit it. The notification of a regulation arising from a sudden case cannot, however, be made previous to the occurrence which calls it forth. The matter of which you now speak was not of a nature to require previous communication; but it was here, at all events, not carried into execution before communicated.

I have the honor to be, sir,
Your most obedient and most humble servant,
(Signed)   H. LOWE, Lieut.-General.*
Count BERTRAND.

No. XII.
Letter from Count Bertrand to the Governor, containing the grievances of Longwood.

LONGWOOD, 30th Sept., 1817.

GOVERNOR: I have made known to the Emperor that you did me

---

* For the *deep obscurity* and *rambling construction* of some passages in this state paper, it is hoped the reader will hold only its author responsible.

the honor to come to me the day before yesterday (Sunday); that you told me some anxieties had been excited in you respecting his ill health, and that as this was attributed to want of exercise, why did he not ride out on horseback?

I replied to you what had been said in various circumstances, and I have the honor to repeat to you now that the existence of the Emperor, particularly for the last six weeks, has been extremely painful; that the swelling of his legs increases every day; that the symptoms of scurvy which had been remarked in his gums are already such as to occasion him almost constantly acute pains; that the medical men attribute this to want of exercise; that ever since the month of May, 1816, that is to say, for seventeen or eighteen months, the Emperor has not been on horseback, has scarcely ever been out of his apartment, except sometimes, and very rarely, when he came about forty toises to visit my wife; that you know perfectly well what has prevented, and does prevent, the Emperor from going out, namely, the restrictions of the 9th October, 1816, which began to be put into execution six weeks after your arrival; that those restrictions contain, among others, a *prohibition from speaking or listening to any person we may meet, and from going into any house.* This makes him think that your intention was to compromise him with the sentries, and to outrage his character.

You have observed to me *that you have suppressed that part* of the restrictions, and such is the case. Admiral Malcolm, on his return from the Cape, made some observations to you on the subject, and you decided on suspending them, which you did by your letter of the 26th of December, 1816, *three months afterwards.* But you have several times insinuated *that you believe yourself authorized to re-establish them at any moment*, as well as *others equally unreasonable.* The restrictions of the 9th October, 1816, contain other articles of the same extravagant nature, which are not suspended. Fresh restrictions which you made on the 14th March, 1817, prescribe *that we are not to quit the extent of a road twelve feet wide.* It would thence result, that if the emperor were to quit that road, or enter into any house, *the sentries might fire upon him.* The emperor ought not to recognize such ignoble treatment. Several Englishmen of distinction at present in the island, on that passage being read to them (not being acquainted with the restrictions of the 9th October, 1816, and **of the**

11th March, 1817), reproached the emperor for sacrificing his health by not going out; but as soon as those restrictions were made known to them, their opinions changed, and they declared that no man of honor could act differently, and that, without pretending to compare themselves with him, they would in such a case have done as he did.

I added that if you wished to consult the officers who are in this colony, there is not one among them who does not regard the restrictions of the 9th October, 1816, and those of the 14th March, 1817, as unjust, useless and oppressive, and that all in the emperor's place would act as he did, holding such conditional leave to go out as an absolute prohibition.

I had also the honor to tell you, that according to the terms of the bill in parliament of the 11th April, 1816, you have not a right to make restrictions; that the bill grants that right only to the government, which cannot delegate it even to one of its ministers, and still less to an individual officer; that Lord Bathurst in his speech, in the month of March, in the house of peers, declared that you had made no new restriction, that all his correspondence had been in favor of the detained persons, and that you had the same instructions as your predecessor; that your predecessor had adapted the restrictions of government to local circumstances in a manner, if not convenient, at least tolerable; that things remained in this state for nine months, during which time the emperor used to go out, received even some English officers at his table, and sometimes had in his society the officers and inhabitants of the island; that this order of things *was not changed by an act of your government;* that during those nine months no inconvenience took place, and that nothing can have authorized you to substitute for an order of things so reasonable that which you have established; that the emperor would go out, ride on horseback, and resume the same way of life, if you would restore things to the state they were in at the time of your arrival; that in default of this, you would be responsible for the results of the restrictions of the 9th of October, 1816, and the 14th of March, 1817, which *you have no right to make,* and which, to the emperor, *are equivalent to an absolute prohibition to quit his apartments.*

You told me, sir, that the emperor's room was too small, that Longwood House was altogether bad, as you had declared it to be to your government; that the emperor having had a tent erected last year because there was no alley where he could walk in the shade, you proposed to establish a soldier's wooden barrack near the house, where the emperor might take his walks. I undertook to make known to him your proposition. He *considered this offer as a mockery* (those were his words), and analogous to the conduct pursued for these two years. If the house where he is be inconvenient, why has he been left there for these two years, and why do they not give him one of those in the island, situated in the midst of gardens, trees, shade and water? Why leave him upon this uncultivated point, exposed to the winds, and having nothing that can contribute to the preservation of life?

Let me be allowed, sir, to point out to your observation, that if you do not suppress the restrictions of the 9th of October, 1816, and of the 14th of March, 1817, and if you do not re-establish things as they were in the time of the admiral, the emperor cannot go out. *He considers, and will consider, that determination as a desire on your part to occasion his death.* He is entirely at your disposal. You can make him die of sickness; you can make him die of hunger; it would be a favor to make him die by a musket shot.

If you assemble the military and naval officers of this place, and the principal officers of health, *there is not one of them but will tell you that your restrictions are disgraceful*, and that a man of honor would sooner lie than acknowledge them; that they are of no avail to the security of the detention; that they are illegal. The text of the bill, and the speech of your minister, cannot leave any kind of doubt on this point. The medical officers will tell you that there is no more time to be lost; that in three or four weeks perhaps it will be too late; and although this great prince be abandoned by fortune, and there is an open field for calumnies and libels in Europe, yet a cry of indignation will be raised amongst all people; for there are here several hundreds of persons, French, English and foreigners, *who will bear witness to all that has been done to put an end to the life of this great man.*

I have, sir, always spoken to you to this effect, more or less forcibly. I shall speak to you of it no more, for denials, subtilties, and arguments, are very useless.

The question lies in two words; *do you or do you not wish to kill the emperor?* If you persist in your conduct *you will yourself have answered in the affirmative;* and unhappily, the object will probably be obtained after some months of agony.

Permit me, in concluding, to answer, on behalf of the officers who are with the emperor, and also on my own, to your letters of the 29th and 26th July last. Sir, you misunderstand our character: menaces have no power over us. For twenty years we have braved every danger in his service. By remaining voluntarily at St. Helena, in the *horrible situation* in which we are, and exposed to the strangest proceedings, we sacrifice to him more than our own lives and those of our families. Insensible to your menacing and your insinuations, we shall continue to fulfil our duty; and if there were any subjects of complaint against us before your government, we do not doubt that the Prince Regent, Lord Liverpool, and so many estimable men who form it, would know very well how to appreciate them. They know the respect due to the holy ministration which we fulfil; and even had we to apprehend persecution, we should adhere to our maxim, " Do your duty, come what may."*

  I have the honor to be, Governor,
    Your very humble and obedient servant,
     (Signed)   COUNT BERTRAND.

No. XIII.

Letter from Count Bertrand to his eminence Cardinal Fesch, announcing the death of Cipriani.

LONGWOOD, 22nd March, 1818.

MY LORD,—M. Cipriani, the emperor's maître d'hôtel, died at Longwood on the 27th February last, at four o'clock in the afternoon. He was buried in the Protestant churchyard of this place, and the ministers of that church have paid the same duties to him as they would have done to a person of their own sect. Care has been taken to insert in the *extrait mortuaire* which I shall send you, (but for which an extract from my letter may now serve,) that he died in the bosom of the Apostolical and Roman church. The minister of this place would willingly have assisted the deceased, and this last would have desired a Catholic priest; but as we have none here, he appeared not

---

* Fais ce que tu dois; advienne que pourra.

to wish a minister of another religion. I should be happy if you would make us acquainted with the rites of the Catholic church upon this subject, and if it be permitted that an English minister should administer to a dying Catholic. We cannot praise too much the good spirit and the zeal which the ministers of religion of this place have manifested on this occasion. Cipriani died of an inflammation of the bowels. He expired on Friday, and on the preceding Sunday he had attended without any foreboding of it. A child belonging to one of Count Montholon's servants died a few days before at Longwood. A *femme de chambre* died a few days ago of the same complaint. It is the effect of the bad climate of this place, where very few men grow old. Liver complaints, dysenteries, and inflammations of the bowels, carry off many victims amongst the natives, but especially amongst Europeans. We felt in this circumstance, and feel daily, the want of a minister of our religion. You are our bishop, we wish that you would send us a French or Italian priest. Be so good as to select a man of information under the age of forty, and who is not prejudiced by anti-Gallican principles.

M. Pieron has undertaken the office of maître d'hôtel; but he has been extremely ill, and although now convalescent, is still in a bad state. The cook is in a similar situation. It would be necessary that either you, or Prince Eugene, or the empress, should send a maître d'hôtel, and a French or Italian cook out of those who have served in the emperor's household, or in those of his family.

Your eminence will find added to this, 1st. Papers A. and B., which were found in M. Cipriani's portefeuille. 2nd. A pin which he was in the habit of wearing, and which I have thought proper to send for his wife. 3rd. The account of what is owing to him, amounting to the sum of 8,287 francs, or 345*l*. 5*s*. 10*d*., with a bill of exchange to be paid to his heirs. Knowing that you take care of his son, and that his daughter is with Madame, the emperor defers securing an independence to his two children, until he is made acquainted with the amount of the property left by Cipriani, who, it appeared, had large funds in Genoa.

I shall not afflict you by speaking of the emperor's health, which is very unsatisfactory. It has not, however, become worse since the hot season. I think that these details should be concealed from Madame. Do not give any credit to the false accounts that may be prevalent in Europe. Keep in mind as a rule and as the sole truth, that for twenty-two months the emperor has not left his apartments, except rarely, to visit my wife. He has seen nobody, but the two or three French who are here, and the English ambassador to China

I beg that your eminence will present my respects to Madame, and to the persons of the family, and accept the sentiments with which I have the honor to be, &c.

    (Signed)   COUNT BERTRAND.

No. XVI.

Extract of the Declaration signed by the Ministers of the Allied Powers at Vienna, March 13th, 1815.

THE powers who signed the treaty of Paris having reunited in congress at Vienna, and informed of the escape of Napoleon Bonaparte, and his forcible entry into France, owe to their own dignity and to social order, a declaration of the sentiments which this event has made them experience.

In thus breaking the convention which had established him at the island of Elba, Bonaparte has destroyed the only legal title to which his existence was attached. In appearing again in France, with projects of trouble and subversion, he has deprived himself of the protection of the laws, and has manifested in the face of the world that there can be neither peace nor truce with him.

The powers declare in consequence, that *Napoleon Bonaparte is placed out of the pale of civil and social relations ;* and that as an enemy and a disturber of the world, he is delivered up to *public vengeance !*

Then follow the signatures :

Austria.	Le Prince de Metternich.
	Le Baron de Wessemberg.
Spain.	P. Gomez Labrador.
France.	Le Prince de Talleyrand.
	Le Duc d'Alberg.
	Latour Dupin.
	Le Comte Alexis de Noailles.
Russia.	Le Comte de Rasoumouski.
	Le Comte de Stakelberg
	Le Comte de Nesselrode.

APPENDIX.

Great Britain.	Wellington ! ! ! Clancarty. Cathcart. Stewart.
Portugal.	Le Comte Palmela. Saldanha. Lobo.
Prussia.	Le Prince d'Hardenberg. Le Baron de Humboldt.
Sweden.	Lowenhielm.

No. XV.

Protest of the Emperor Napoleon.

I HEREBY solemnly protest in the face of God and of men, against the violation of my most sacred rights, in forcibly disposing of my person and my liberty. I came voluntarily on board of the Bellerophon. I am not the prisoner, but the guest of England.

As soon as I was seated on board of the Bellerophon, I was upon the hearths of the British people. If the government, in giving orders to the captain of the Bellerophon to receive me as well as my suite, only intended to lay a snare for me, it has forfeited its honor, and disgraced its flag.

If this act be consummated, the English will in vain boast to Europe of their integrity, their laws, and their liberty. British good faith will be lost in the hospitality of the Bellerophon.

I appeal to history; it will say that an enemy, who for twenty years waged war against the English people, came voluntarily in his misfortunes to seek an asylum under their laws. What more brilliart proof could he give of his esteem and his confidence? But what return did England make for so much magnanimity? *A hospitable hand was pretended to be held out to that enemy; and when he confided to it in good faith, he was immolated!*

(Signed)   NAPOLEON.

August 4th, 1815.

No. XVI.
Island of St. Helena Port Regulations.

I. THE commanders of the Hon. East India Company's ships, and the masters or commanders of all merchants' vessels permitted to touch at this island, are not to land themselves, or suffer any person whatever belonging to their ships or vessels to come ashore, until the following regulations have been made known to all persons on board— a list of passengers, and a roll of the ships company sent to the governor, and his permission obtained for such as are to land.

II. The commander of every ship or vessel is required most explicitly to declare in the first instance, whether any disorder whatever prevails, or has prevailed, on board, without regard to its being considered by him, or his surgeon, to be *contagious* or *otherwise*, and report any deaths that may have taken place, and the causes of the same, during the course of his voyage.

III. All letters and packets, for whatever person addressed, residing on shore (except such as come by regular mails, which are to be sent to the post-office,) are to be delivered to the officer by whom these regulations are communicated, who will leave the same at the office of the secretary of government, where those to whom they are addressed will receive them.

IV. Should the commander, or any of his passengers, or any person whatever on board his ship, have under his or her charge any letters, packages or parcels, to the address of, or destined for any of the foreign persons under detention on this island—it is desired they will make it known forthwith to the governor himself, putting the letter or parcel, if of small bulk, under a sealed envelope, to his address, and waiting his directions respecting any package of a larger species.

V. The commander of the vessel only, after these regulations have been read and published on board, is at liberty to land, when he will immediately wait on the governor, if in town, as well as the naval commander in chief; and if the governor should not be in town, will call to report his arrival at the quarters of the deputy adjutant-general.

VI. The commanders, officers, and all passengers who are afterwards permitted to land, will call at the town-major's office to read and sign the island regulations, before they proceed to their lodgings, or visit any house or person whatever.

VII. No passenger or other person landing from ships touching there, is to leave James' Valley without permission, for which they are to apply to the deputy adjutant-general.

VIII. No person whatsoever, having permission to land, is to visit Longwood, or the premises belonging thereto, nor to hold communication of any sort, by writing or otherwise, with any of the foreign personages detained on this island, without communicating directly his intentions and wishes thereupon to the governor, and obtaining his permission for the same. And should any letter or other communication, from any of the foreign personages above alluded to, be received by any person whatsoever, it is to be brought without loss of time to the governor, previous to answering or taking any further notice whatever thereof. The same rule to apply to all packages which may be received, or attempted to be delivered.

IX. The commanders of East India ships, and the masters of all descriptions of merchant vessels permitted to touch at this island, are not to allow any persons whatsoever, on board of, or belonging to their ships or vessels, to come on shore *on leave*, without the governor's authority, nor is any person to sleep on shore without his permission.

X. No boat belonging to the ships of the East India Company, or to merchant vessels of any description, is to land between sun-set and sun-rise, nor at any time during the day, without a proper officer being in charge of her, and if she is ordered to remain on shore for any purpose, he must take care to keep her laying at a distance from the wharf to admit of other boats landing without interruption. Boats loading or unloading, are to use every expedition to get out of the way of others.

XI. All boats belonging to the company's ships, or merchant vessels of every description, are to quit the shore by sun-set, and are immediately afterwards to be hoisted in on board their respective ships, under such circumstances as the admiral may direct.

XII. No boat belonging to a company's ship, or a merchant vessel of any description, shall board or send a boat alongside any vessel coming in. No boat will be permitted to land at any other place than at the wharf.

XIII. No company's ship or merchant vessel of any description, is to anchor at this island between sun-set and sun-rise, nor sail after sun-set, nor before ten o'clock in the morning—nor are they to make sail at any time until the permission flag is hoisted to each ship or vessel.

XIV. If the permission flag should be hoisted to any vessel a short time before sun-set, and she not already hove her anchor up and under weigh, she is not to attempt to move until the signal may be repeated the morning following.

XV. The commander of all ships or vessels are strictly prohibited from permitting any fishing-boat belonging to the island to go alongside, without a permit signed by the governor, or suffering any boat belonging to their ship to board, or otherwise communicate with a numbered fishing-boat of the island.

XVI. Should a fishing-boat attempt to communicate with any vessel, either approaching the island, or at anchor off it, or with any boats belonging to such vessel, the commander of her, or his officers, are required to give immediate notice thereof to the flag-ship, and to the deputy adjutant-general, taking the No. of the boat, or detaining her, as circumstances may direct.

XVII. The commanders of ships *possessing newspapers which may contain late or interesting intelligence, are requested to deliver them to the person by whom these regulations are communicated, for the information of the governor*, who will cause them to be carefully returned.

XVIII. No gunpowder is to be landed without previous notice being given to the commissary of stores, and the master attendant, in order that proper precautions may be adopted to prevent accidents.

XIX. No horse, mare, or gelding can be landed without a permit from the secretary to government.

XX. No wines of any sort whatsoever shall be landed without a permit, signed by the secretary to government.

XXI. The honorable court of directors having prohibited the importation of India spirits, it is regulated that whoever shall violate this order shall incur a fine of £100 sterling; nor is brandy, gin, West India rum, cordials, and the like to be landed, except in small quantities, upon obtaining a permit for the same, and upon paying a duty at the rate of 12s. per gallon; but the landing of any spirits, in whatever quantity, without a permit, will subject the offender to the penalty as above.

XXII. The whaling vessels are not to throw their *try-works* overboard whilst at this anchorage, under the penalty of £50, half of which sum will be paid to the informer.

XXIII. The commanders or masters of all ships or vessels are to give forty-eight hours notice previous to their departure, provided they intend to remain for so long a period. This notice is to be left in writing at the office of the secretary to government, and the master attendant, between the hours of ten in the forenoon and two in the afternoon. The foretop-sail is likewise to be kept loose forty-eight hours previous to the ship or vessel's departure.

XXIV. The commander or master of any ship or vessel is not, on any pretence whatever, to leave any person upon the island, or take any person from it, of whatever description, without written permission from the governor.

XXV. No commander, passenger, or any other person whatever, on board the honorable company's ships or any other that may anchor at this island, is to take charge of any letters or packets for conveyance to Europe, the Cape of Good Hope, South America, or elsewhere, unless such as are made up in a regular mail at the post-office, or have been received from the secretary to government, or the deputy adjutant-general.

The commander of the ship or vessel will fill up the report, of which the form is annexed, for the governor's information, and transmit the same by the officer who communicates these regulations.

No. XVII.

Proclamation issued by Sir Hudson Lowe, a few days after having sent Lord Bathurst's letters, making an offer of allowing fifty persons, selected by Napoleon, to enter Longwood.

WHEREAS it has been ascertained that a present had been delivered to an inhabitant of this island, in the name or on the part of one of the foreign persons under detention at Longwood, which present was soon afterwards returned, in consequence of the person to whom it had been delivered becoming sensible that his acceptance of it, unless with the governor's knowledge and authority, would have been a breach of the proclamations in force. The governor, however, deems it expedient, in enforcement of the above said proclamation (with reference also to the general injunction contained in the warrant, dated

16th April, 1816,) to give public notice, and public notice is hereby given *to all officers, inhabitants, and other persons whatsoever, residing on or resorting to this island, that they are not only interdicted (as by the proclamation of October* 15, 1815,) *from holding any correspondence or communication with the foreign persons under detention on it,* except only such as may be regularly authorized by him; and as farther (by public notice of the 11th May, and proclamation of the 28th June, 1816,) from receiving, delivering, or rendering themselves *the channel for the conveyances of any communication whatsoever* from or to the said persons, without his express authorization; but where any unauthorized communication shall have been or may be conveyed, or attempted to be conveyed, it behoves all those who are acquainted with it to give the governor immediate information of the same (or the nearest civil or military authority, should the case so require,) in order that the necessary steps may be taken thereupon, under pain of otherwise being considered as privy to the same, and held answerable accordingly.

Given at the Castle, James Town, this 16th day of May, 1818.

HUDSON LOWE,

Lieut.-General, Governor, and Com.-in-Chief.

(Signed)   By his Excellency's command.

G. GORREQUER,

Act. Mil. Sec.

By order of the Governor, in council.

T. H. BROOKE,

Secretary to Government.

No. XVIII.

Longwood, 20th June, 1818.

Sir: Having been informed by Lieut. Reardon, of your regiment, that you had charged him to intimate to me "that you had been informed by Lieut.-Colonel Sir Thomas Reade, that his excellency the governor was very angry at my being an honorary member of the 66th mess, and that I was not fit society for them; that you had seen part of a correspondence between the governor and myself, which had been sent home, and that you thought I had used the governor ill; that you had intended to call a meeting of the officers, in order to signify to me that until the business between the governor and myself was cleared up, I should not have the honor of dining with them, but that you thought it would be better to intimate it to me privately by Lieut. Reardon, in order that I might withdraw quietly."

The assertion which has been conveyed to you that I have committed any action of a nature to render me unfit for the society of the officers of the 66th regiment, I declare *to be a base and insidious calumny.* I have demanded frequently, and am now ready to appear before any competent court of justice, to repel anything which may be brought against me, whether in the form of suspicions, conjectures, reports of spies, semi-proofs, or direct charges. If there is any basis whereon to ground such aspersions, why not bring me to—wha. every Englishman is entitled to by the laws of his country—a trial? But his excellency himself, in a letter written from his dictation, has disclaimed "*bringing any accusations whatever against any part of my conduct.*" It is by a fair and open investigation that the disreputable source from whence the clandestine denunciation against me has sprung will be clearly shown, and which will manifest that a refusal to comply with verbal insinuations contrary to my conscience has been the cause of the wrath and oppression with which I have been visited.

Let those who are conscious of guilt have recourse to indirect and secret measures. Publicity, and not concealment, is my desire; and in order to clear up the business between the governor and myself, I shall be extremely happy to submit the *whole of the correspondence* alluded to for the perusal and consideration of the officers of the 66th regiment, by whose decision thereupon I am content to abide, and any other scrutiny which may be thought proper, either by yourself or the officers, I am also perfectly ready to submit to.

I have too much confidence in the justice, honor, and liberality of so enlightened a corps of officers as the 66th, to suppose for a moment, that they will condemn unheard to dishonor, (a punishment worse than death,) an officer whom they have considered worthy of a diurnal place at their table; and therefore beg, sir, that in case of their meeting for the purpose of taking into their consideration the calumnies which have been so insidiously instilled into your mind against me, they will not refuse me what is not denied to the vilest of culprits; but vouchsafe me an audience in my defence, prior to coming to any decision, unless indeed his excellency the governor gives an *order* for exclusion; in which case, I beg to have a copy of the same in writing, to show that such a measure was the arbitrary act of an individual, and not the result of the opinion of a most respectable corps of officers.

I remain, sir, with much respect,
Your most obedient humble servant,
(Signed)   BARRY E. O'MEARA,
Surgeon.

Lieut.-Colonel LASCELLES,
Commanding 66th Regiment.

No. XIX.

Translation of the Letter from the Princess Pauline Borghese to Lord Liverpool.

ROME, 11th July, 1821.

MY LORD,—The Abbé Buonavita, who has just arrived at Rome from St. Helena, which he left on the 17th of last March, has brought us the most alarming news of the emperor's health. I enclose you copies of letters, which will give you the details of his physical sufferings. The malady by which he is attacked is mortal in St. Helena, and in the name of all the members of the family, I claim a change of climate from the English government. If so just a demand be refused, it will be sentence of death passed upon him, and in this case, I demand permission to depart for St. Helena, to rejoin the emperor and to receive his parting breath.

I beg of you, my lord, to have the goodness, without delay, to solicit this authorization from your government, that I may be able to depart as soon as possible. As my state of health does not allow me to travel by land, my intentions would be to embark at Civita Vecchia to proceed to England, and to avail myself there of the first vessel which may sail for St. Helena; but I should wish that I may be permitted to go to London, in order to provide myself with whatever may be necessary for so long a voyage.

If your government persists in suffering the emperor to perish upon ne rock of St. Helena, I entreat that your lordship, in order to remove all difficulties which might retard my departure, may extend your care to prevent the court of Rome from opposing obstacles. I know that the moments of the emperor's life are counted, and I should eternally reproach myself if I did not employ all the means in my power to soften his last hours, and to prove my entire devotion to his august person. If there should be any English vessels in Leghorn harbor at the moment of my departure, I would ask as a favor tha' one might be permitted to take me at Civita Vecchia and bring m. to England.

I beg, my lord, that you will communicate my letter and the encolsed copies to Lady Holland, who has always given proofs of the greatest interest for the emperor, and assure her of my sentiments of friendship, and receive for yourself those of my consideration.

(Signed)   PRINCESS PAULINE BORGHESE.

TRANSLATIONS OF THE LETTERS ENCLOSED.

From Dr. Antommarchi to Sig. Simeon Colonna.

ST. HELENA, 17th March, 1821.

MY DEAREST FRIEND,—In my preceding letter of the 18th of July, last year, I informed you of the disease (*chronic hepatitis*) endemic in this climate, with which the Emperor Napoleon was afflicted, and of the ameliorations which had been obtained by a long and rational treatment, together with the successive considerable changes for the worse, by which the ameliorations were alternated to that epoch. Continuing now to give you an account of the same, I shall tell you, that from the above-mentioned time, his majesty has become worse daily, so that in six months, the disease of the biliary viscus has made so great a progress, that the hepatic functions are entirely disordered, and consequently the digestive functions are almost annihilated.

His majesty is now reduced to such a state as not to be able to take any nourishment except liquids, which quickly pass almost unchanged by the mouths of the absorbent vessels of the lymphatic system. It is not certain that this nourishment of liquids is well adapted to his majesty's stomach, as frequently a few moments after taking, or in the act of swallowing, they are rejected by vomiting. To this effect, and to relieve my own special responsibility, I declare openly to the imperial family, and to all Europe, that the progress of the disease which affects his majesty in this climate, (which is a proximate cause of such complaints,) and the symptoms which accompany it, are most serious.

Dear friend, the medical art can do nothing against the influence of climate; and if *the English government does not hasten to remove him from this destructive atmosphere, his majesty will soon, with anguish 1 say it, pay the last tribute to the earth.*

Such a crime certainly cannot be attributed to the medical art, but solely to the *unhappy and desolate situation* in which his majesty is placed.

Continue your attachment to me, pay my respectful compliments to our common friends, and believe me to be always with much esteem, Your affectionate friend,
(Signed) F. ANTOMMARCHI.

P.S.—I offer the *undoubted facts* stated above, in opposition to the gratuitous assertions in the English newspapers relative to the good health which his majesty is stated to enjoy here.

From the Count de Montholon to her Highness the Princess Pauline Borghese.

LONGWOOD, ST. HELENA, 17th March, 1821.

MADAM,—The emperor charges me to render to your highness an account of the deplorable state of his health; the liver complaint with which he has been attacked for several years, and which is endemic and mortal in St. Helena, has made a frightful progress in the last six months. The benefit which he had experienced from the care of Dr. Antommarchi, has not lasted: several relapses have taken place since the middle of last year, and every day his decay becomes more sensible; his weakness is extreme; he can scarcely bear the fatigue of a ride in the carriage for half an hour with the horses at a walk, and cannot walk in his room without support. To the liver complaint another disease is joined, equally endemic in this island. The intestines are seriously affected; the functions of digestion are no longer performed, and the stomach rejects everything it receives. For a long time the emperor cannot eat either meat, bread, or vegetables; he is supported only by soups and jellies. *Count Bertrand wrote to Lord*

Liverpool in last September, to demand that the emperor should be removed to another climate, and to let him know the absolute need which he had of mineral waters. I have entrusted M. Buonavita with a copy of the letter. *The governor, Sir Hudson Lowe, refused to allow it to be sent to his government,* under the vain pretext that the title of emperor had been given to his majesty. M. Buonavita departs this day for Rome. He has experienced the cruel effects of the climate of St. Helena, a twelve months abode here will cost him ten years of his life. The letters which Dr. Antommarchi has given to him for his eminence Cardinal Fesch, will give your highness fresh details upon the emperor's disease. The *London newspapers* continually publish fabricated letters dated from St. Helena,* the intention of which evidently is to impose upon Europe. The emperor reckons upon your highness to make his real situation known to some English of influence. *He dies without succor upon this frightful rock; his agonies are frightful!*

      Deign to receive,
        Madam,
    (Signed)   COUNT DE MONTHOLON.

From Count Bertrand to Lord Liverpool, alluded to by Count Montholon in the preceding letter.

          LONGWOOD, 2d Sept., 1820.

MY LORD,—I had the honor of writing to you on the 25th of June, 1819, to let you know the state of the health of the Emperor Napoleon, attacked as it has been by chronic hepatitis, since the month of October, 1817.

Doctor Antommarchi arrived at the end of last September, from whose treatment he at first found some relief, but since then, the doctor has declared, as will be seen in his journal and reports, that the state of the patient has become such, that the remedies can no longer struggle against the malignity of the climate; that he has need of mineral waters; that all the time he can remain in this abode will

---

* At the time Napoleon was in this deplorable state, letters were published in some of the *ministerial newspapers*, purporting to have come from St. Helena, and representing him to be in *perfect health ;* others describing him to be *in the habit of going about the island shooting wild cats.* Whether those letters were concocted in St. Helena or forged in London, I shall not attempt to decide.

only be a state of painful agony; that a return to Europe is the only means by which he can experience any relief, his strength being exhausted by a stay of five years in this frightful climate, a prey to the worst treatment.

The Emperor Napoleon charges me to demand of you, that he shall be transferred to a European climate, as the only mode of lessening the evils to which he is a prey.

(Signed) COUNT BERTRAND.

P.S.—I had the honor to send this letter to Sir Hudson Lowe under *un cachet volant*, which he returned to me with the addition of the enclosed letter. This induces me to send it direct to you. I suppose that he has taken a copy of it, which he will send you along with his own observations, and that this circumstance shall not have caused any delay. (Signed) COUNT BERTRAND.

Longwood, 3rd Sept., 1820.

Letter sent by order of Sir Hudson Lowe to Count Bertrand, in reply to the preceding one.

PLANTATION HOUSE, 2d Sept., 1820.

SIR,—The governor's instructions not admitting him to receive any letter from the persons residing with Napoleon Bonaparte, where the title of emperor is given to him, I am directed in consequence to return you the enclosed.

The governor at the same time desires me to observe, that no letter* was ever received by him from you, to the address of Lord Liverpool, of the date of 25th of June, 1819. I have the honor to be, &c.

(Signed) S. GORREQUER, Military Secretary.

Proclamation, in which the authority of Parliament is assumed by the Governor of St. Helena.

(*Referred to in Vol. II. p.* 146.)

PROCLAMATION, by Lieut.-General Sir Hudson Lowe, K.C.B., Governor and Commander in Chief for the Honorable East India Company, of the Island of St. Helena, and commanding his Majesty's forces on the said island.

BY virtue of the powers and authority vested in me by a warrant

---

* As Sir Hudson Lowe refused to receive or to forward letters in which Napoleon was not styled as he thought proper to name him, the letter alluded to was sent to England by a private hand.

APPENDIX. 297

in the king's majesty's name, bearing date the 12th day of April, in the present year, and in the fifty-sixth year of his majesty's reign, authorizing and commanding me to detain in custody Napoleon Bonaparte, and him to deal with and treat as a prisoner of war, under such restrictions, and in such manner as shall have been, or shall be from time to time signified to me under the hand of one of his majesty's principal secretaries of state, and to prevent the rescue or escape of the said Napoleon Bonaparte; in the due execution whereof, all his majesty's officers, civil, naval, and military, and all his loving subjects, whom it may concern, are required to be aiding and assisting as occasion there may be; public notice is hereby given, that two acts have been passed in the present session of the British parliament, the one for detaining in custody the said Napoleon Bonaparte, and adjudging capital punishments on those who may be assisting in his escape; and the other for regulating the intercourse of shipping with the island of St. Helena, during the time Napoleon Bonaparte shall be detained in custody.

Copies of these two acts are hereunto annexed.

In furtherance of the objects for which these acts have been passed, it is hereby publicly made known, that the various regulations hitherto issued on this island, in regard to the safe custody of the said Napoleon Bonaparte, and of the prevention of any undue correspondence or communication with him, his followers and attendants, are to remain in full force.

It is farther made known, that if, after this notice, any person or persons whatever shall infringe the regulations established for his custody, or *shall hold correspondence or communication with him, his followers, or attendants,* who are, by their own acquiescence, placed under the same restrictions as himself, or shall receive from, or deliver any letters or communications to him, or them, *without the express authorization of the governor,* or the officer commanding on the island for the time being, *signified to them in writing under his hand; such person or persons will be considered as having acted against the provisions and express objects of the said act of parliament, and be proceeded against accordingly. And should, from any infraction of the rules established for his custody, or from any correspondence or communication with either him, his followers, or attendants, the escape or rescue of the said Napo-*

leon *Bonaparte be effected, such person or persons will, after this notice, be considered as having been knowingly instrumental to and assisting in the same, and be prosecuted with all the rigor which the law enacts.*

It is farther declared, that if any person or persons shall have any information of any attempted rescue or means of escape, and shall not make an immediate communication of the same to the governor, or officer commanding for the time being, or shall not do his or their utmost to prevent the same taking effect, they will be regarded as having connived at, and assisted in, the said rescue or escape, and his or their offence be judged by the laws.

Any person or persons who may receive letters or *communications for the said Napoleon Bonaparte, his followers or attendants,* and shall not immediately deliver or make known the same to the governor, or officer commanding for the time being, or who shall furnish the said Napoleon Bonaparte, his followers or attendants, with money, or any other means whatever, whereby his escape might be furthered, *will be considered in like manner to have been assisting in the same, and will be proceeded against accordingly.*

All letters or communications for or from the said Napoleon, any of his followers or attendants, whether sealed or open, are to be forwarded to the governor without loss of time, in the same state in which they may have been received.

And whereas it is not the object of the regulation hereby promulgated to induce any unusual or unnecessary rigor, but to enforce the due execution of the rules heretofore established, and to prevent the ill effects which might result from ignorance and inconsiderateness, as well as design, it is in consequence made known to all those persons whose duty calls upon them to attend near the place where the said Napoleon Bonaparte, his followers or attendants, reside, or who have business which has any relation to them, that they will be furnished, upon due application, with regular licenses and authorities from the governor of the island, signed with his hand. And nothing is to be construed from the acts of parliament, or these regulations, as warranting any violent or improper demeanor against him or them, so long as he or they observe the restrictions under which **the laws and** the instructions of his majesty's government *has* placed them.

APPENDIX. 299

Given under my hand in James' Town, in the island of St. Helena, the 28th day of June, 1816.
    (Signed)   HUDSON LOWE,
                 Governor and Com.-in-Chief.
By command of the governor.
    (Signed)   G. GORREQUER,
                 Act. Mil. Sec.

ADDITIONAL DOCUMENTS

NOT NOMINATIVELY REFERRED TO, BUT WHICH ARE OF IMPORTANCE TO ILLUSTRATE THE WORK.

Terms of the Capitulation of El-Arish, for the violation of which part of the garrison of Jaffa were shot.

The commandant of the Fort of El-Arish, and the other three commandants of the troops, to the general-in-chief.

WE have received the capitulation which you have addressed to us. We consent to deliver the fort of El-Arish into your hands. We will return to Bagdat by the desert. We send you the list of the agas of the fort, who promise upon oath, for themselves and their troops, not to serve in Djezzar's army, and not to return to Syria for the space of one year, reckoning from this day. We will receive a pass and colors from you. We will leave in the castle all the supplies which are found there. The whole of the agas in the fort solemnly swear by our Lord, Moses, Abraham, and by the PROPHET, to whom may God be propitious, and by the Koran, to execute faithfully all these articles, and above all not to serve Djezzar. The MOST HIGH and HIS PROPHET are witnesses of our good faith.

    (Signed)   IBRAHIM NIRAN, Commandant of the Fort of El-Arish.
                    EL. H. HADJEZ MOHAMMED, Colonel of the Maugrebins.
                    EL. H. HADJY ZADYR, Aga of the Arnauts.
                    MOHAMMED AGA, Chief of the Commissaries.

Lettre de L'Empereur Napoléon, addressée au Comte de Las-Cases, après son enlèvement de Longwood.

Mon cher Comte Las Cases:—Mon cœur sent vivement ce que vous éprouvez; arraché, il y a quatorze ou quinze jours d'auprès de moi, vous êtes enfermé au secret, sans que j'aie pu recevoir ni vous donner aucune nouvelle, sans que vous ayez communiqué avec qui que ce soit, Français ou Anglais; privé même d'un domestique de votre choix.

Votre conduite à Sainte-Hélène a été, comme votre vie, honorable et sans reproche; j'aime à vous le dire.

Votre lettre à votre amie de Londres n'avait rien de répréhensible; vous y épanchiez votre cœur dans le sein de l'amitié. Cette lettre est comme les huit ou dix autres que vous avez ecrites à la même personne, et que vous avez envoyées ouvertes. Le commandant de cette île ayant eu l'indélicatesse de scruter les expressions que vous confiez à l'amitié, vous les a reprochées. Dernièrement il vous a menacé de vous renvoyer de l'île, si vos lettres contenant encore quelques plaintes. En agissant ainsi, il a violé le premier devoir de sa place, le premier article de ses restrictions, et le premier sentiment de l'honneur. Il vous a ainsi autorisé à chercher les moyens de répandre, par effusion, vos sentimens dans le sein de vos amis, et de leur faire connaître la conduite coupable de ce commandant; mais vous êtes sans artifices; il a été bien facile de surprendre votre confiance!

On cherchait un prétexte de saisir vos papiers. Une lettre à votre amie de Londres ne pouvait autoriser une visite de la police chez vous; car elle ne contient aucun complot, aucun mystère: elle n'est que l'expression des sentimens d'un cœur noble et franc. La conduite illégale et précipitée que l'on a tenue en cette occasion porte le caractère d'une haine basse et personnelle.

Dans les contrées les moins civilisées, les exilés, les prisonniers, et même les criminels, sont sous la protection des lois et des magistrats. Les personnes nommées pour les garder ont des chefs, soit dans l'administration, soit dans l'ordre judiciaire pour les surveille, r. Mais sur ce roc, le même homme qui fait les réglemens les plus absurdes, les exécute avec violence; il transgresse toutes les lois, et il n'est personne pour restreindre les excès de son caprice.

On enveloppe Longwood d'un voile que l'on voudrait rendre impénétrable, pour cacher une conduite criminelle. Ce soin fait suspecter les intentiones les plus odieuses.

Par des bruites artificieusement semés, on a essayé de tromper les officiers, les étrangers, les habitans de cette île, et même les agens étrangers qui, à ce que l'on dit, sont entretenus ici par l'Autriche et la Russie. Certainement le gouvernement anglais est trompé de la même manière par des rapports artificieux et mensongers.

Vos papiers, parmi lesquels on savait qu'il y en avait qui m'appartenaient, ont été saisis sans aucune formalité, près de mon appartement, *avec des exaltations d'une joie féroce.* J'en fus instruit quelques momens après ; je regardai par la fenêtre, et je vis qu'on vous enlevait. Un nombreux état-major caracolait autour de vous ; je crus voir les sauvages des îles de la mer du Sud, dansant autour des prisonniers qu'ils vont dévorer.

Votre société m'était nécessaire ; seul vous lisez, vous parlez et entendez l'anglais. Combien vous avez passé de nuits pendant mes maladies! cependant je vous engage et, au besoin, je vous ordonne de requérir le commandant de cette île de vous renvoyer sur le continent ; il ne peut point s'y refuser, puisqu'il n'a action sur vous que par l'acte volontaire que vous avez signé. Ce sera pour moi une grande consolation que de vous savoir en chemin pour de plus fortunés pays.

Arrivé en Europe, soit que vous alliez en Angleterre, ou que vous retourniez dans la patrie, perdez le souvenir des maux qu'on vous a fait souffrir. Vantez-vous de la fidélité que vous m'avez montrée, et de toute l'affection que je vous porte.

Si vous voyez un jour ma femme et mon fils, embrassez-les ; depuis deux ans je n'en ai aucune nouvelle, ni directe, ni indirecte. Il y a dans ce pays, depuis six mois, un botaniste allemand, qui les a vus dans le jardin de Schœnbrunn, quelques mois avant son départ. Les barbares ont empêché qu'il vînt me donner de leurs nouvelles.

Toutefois, consolez-vous, et consolez mes amis : mon corps se trouve, il est vrai, au pouvoir de la haine de mes ennemis ; ils n'oublient rien de ce qui peut assouvir leur vengeance. Ils me tuent à coups d'épingles ; mais la Providence est trop juste pour permettre que cela se prolonge long-temps encore. L'insalubrité de ce climat dévorant, le manque de tout ce qui entretient la vie, mettront je le sens, un terme prompt à cette existence, *dont les derniers momens seront l'opprobre du caractère anglais.* L'Europe signalera un jour avec horreur cet homme hypocrite et méchant, que les vrais Anglais désavoueront pour Breton.

Comme toute porte à penser qu'on ne vous permettra **pas de venir** me voir avant votre départ, recevez mes embrassemens, l'assurance de mon estime et de mon amitié. Soyez heureux.

Votre affectionné,
(Signé) NAPOLEON.

Longwood, 11 Décembre, 1816.

Translation of the Declaration of the Emperor Napoleon.

On the 11th, 12th, 13th, 14th, and 16th August, 1819, attempts were made for the first time to violate the pavilion inhabited by the Emperor Napoleon, which to this epoch had been constantly respected. He resisted against this violence by shutting and locking the doors. *In this situation, he reiterates the protestation which he has made, and caused to be made several times, that the right of his door shall not be violated unless by walking over his corpse.* He has given up everything, and for three years has lived concentrated in the interior of six small rooms, in order to escape from insults and outrages. If baseness is carried to the degree of envying him this refuge, it has been determined to leave him no other than the tomb. Laboring for two years under a chronic hepatitis, a disease endemic in this place, and *for a year deprived of the assistance of his physicians by the forcible removal of Doctor O'Meara in July,* 1818, *and of Doctor Stokoe in January,* 1819, he has experienced several crises, during which he has been obliged to keep his bed sometimes for fifteen or twenty successive days. At the present moment, in the midst of one of the most violent of the crises that he has yet experienced, confined to his bed for nine days, having only patience, diet, and the bath, to oppose to the disease; *for six days his tranquillity has been disturbed by threats of an attack, and of outrages which the Prince Regent, Lord Liverpool, and all Europe well know he will never submit to.* As the wish *to debase and to insult him is daily manifested,* he reiterates the declaration he has already made, that he has not taken, nor will he take any notice, nor has he ordered, nor will he order any answer to be given to any despatches or packets, the wording of which shall be done in a manner injurious to him, and contrary to the forms which have been established for four years, to correspond with him through the intermediation of his officers; that he has thrown, and will throw into the fire, or out of the windows, those insulting packets, not wishing to innovate anything upon the state of affairs that has existed for some years.

      (Signed)   NAPOLEON.
LONGWOOD, 16th August, 1819.

This declaration I have been informed was called forth by the following circumstance: while Count Moutholon was sick, Sir Hudson Lowe, ingenious in inventing new vexations, refused to correspond with Count Bertrand, and wanted to insist upon having a direct correspondence with the emperor, *either by the visit of one of his officers twice a day to him, or by letter*. To attain this, he sent Sir Thomas Reade or Major Harrison to Longwood several days, who entered the house, proceeded to the outer door of Napoleon's apartments, against which they continued to knock for some time, exclaiming, "*Come out, Napoleon Bonaparte!*"—"*We want Napoleon Bonaparte!*" &c.; concluding this scene of uncalled for outrage by leaving behind them packets of letters addressed to "Napoleon Buonaparte," written in the usual Plantation House style.

INDEX

ABSTINENCE, Napoleon's, ii. 149.
Accouchement of the Countess Bertrand, i. 208.
——————— of Marie Louise, ii. 216.
Adamant, arrival of, i. 196.
Admiralty, English, i. 297.
Albuera, battle of, ii. 110.
Alexander, Emperor of Russia, his character, i. 141, 153. His views on Turkey, 234 Asks Napoleon's advice respecting the conduct of his ambassador in China, 317 His attention to military trifles, ii. 18. Proposes that Napoleon should marry his sister, 88.
Alexandria, i. 230.
Algerines, i. 106, 189, 308.
Allies, their declaration at Vienna, ii. 284.
Ambassadors, not the representatives of sovereigns, ii. 98.
Ambassadors, Persian, anecdote of, ii. 171.
Amherst, lord, his embassy to China, i. 288. Ought to have gone through th Ko-tou, i. 291, ii. 31. Arrives at St. Helena, and visits Napoleon, 58. The emperor's opinion of his embassy, 97.
Amiens, the treaty of, first violated by the English, i. 326.
Anecdotes, i. 22, 35, 65, 77, 111, 198, 263, 299, 314, 316, 317 ; ii. 8, 9, 28, 61, 4½, 90, 96, 103, 125, 126, 157, 171, 175, 205, 208, 217.
Anglesea, marquis of, wounded at Waterloo, ii. 89.
Angouleme, duc d', ii. 231.
Antommarchi, Dr., his letter to Signor S. Collonna, ii. 343.
Archambaud, i. 102.
Arcola, i. 314, ii. 130.
Aristocracy, English, condemned by Napoleon, i. 294, ii. 146, 224.
Army, Napoleon's confidence in, ii. 157.
Artois, count d', his conduct at Lyons, i. 64. His escape, ii. 157.
Assassination, defended by Talleyrand, ii. 108.
Assassination, Napoleon's few precautions against, ii. 130.
Assassination, fears of at Longwood, ii. 159.
Assassination, of General Duphot, ii. 208.
Assassination (intended), of Napoleon, 209, 210, 211, 212, 213, 214, 218, 276, 281.
Assassination (intended), of Joseph Bonaparte, ii. 182.

Assassination (intended), of Saliceti, ii. 183.
Assassination (intended), of Sir. H. Lowe, ii. 230
Atheism, denied by Napoleon, i. 273.
Austerlitz, battle of, i. 140.
Austria, the emperor of, his private understanding with Napoleon after the return from Elba, i. 127. His character, 318. Forbids the murder of Napoleon, ii. 14. Implores pardon of Napoleon, 14. His ideas of high birth, 173.

BAGGAGE, excess of, in the English armies, ii. 19.
Baildon, Dr., ii. 262.
Balcombe, Mr., i. 262, ii. 52.
Balcombe, Mrs., i. 237, 255.
Balcombe, Misses, i. 237, 255.
Balmaine, count, i. 103, 292, 314, 321 ; ii. 173.
Balston, captain, ii. 43.
Bankruptcy, national, ii. 107.
Barber, Mr. ii. 220.
Baring, gunner of the, ii. 49, 55, 59, 274.
Baring, Mr., letter of his firm to Bertrand, ii. 101.
Barras, character of, i. 116, ii. 95, 130. Made general-in-chief by the convention, 212
Barrere, ii. 96.
Bathurst, lord, i. 19, ii. 34, 77, 237, 274.
Bavarians, defection of, ii. 233.
Baxter, Mr., i. 172, 175, 176.
Beauharnois, Eugene, his first interview with Napoleon, i. 111.
Bed-room, Napoleon's, described, i. 25.
Beet-root, sugar from, i. 260.
Belgians, attached to Napoleon, i. 261.
Belgium, ii. 23.
Bergen-op-Zoom, siege of, ii. 110.
Berri, duke de, i. 256.
Bernadotte, ii. 14, 214.
Bernstorf, his despatches opened, ii. 169.
Bertrand, count, accompanies Napoleon to St. Helena, i. 1. Takes up his abode at Hut's Gate, 11. Receives a visit from Sir H. Lowe respecting the necessity of Napoleon being daily seen by some British officer, 24. Condemned to death by the French government, 51. Removes to Longwood, 104. His brother no longer an exile, 261. Bill drawn by him for Sir H. Lowe's approval, 262. Receives a letter from Messrs. Baring & Co., ii. 101. Wishes for a certificate of life for the countess, 104. Letter to Sir H. Lowe, respecting Mr. Elphinstone's presents, 273. To the gunner of the Baring, 274. To Sir H. Lowe respecting the grievances at Longwood, 278. To Cardinal Feson, 282. To Lord Liverpool, 295.
Bertrand, countess, i. 11. Her accouchment, 208.
Bessiere, Madame la Marechal, i. 279.
Bingham, Sir George, i. 151.
Bingham, Lady, i. 267.
Blacas, i. 138, 298, 299.
Blakeney, captain, ii. 120.
Blucher, character of, i. 123. His contempt for the French, 264. Saved by his Cossacs, 264

Bonaparte, Buonaventura, ii. 174.
Bonaparte, Joseph, i. 143, 221. ii. 182.
Bonaparte, Lucien, ii. 170, 171.
Bonaparte. Napoleon, leaves the Bellerophon for the Northumberland, i. 1. His habits during the voyage to St. Helena, 4. Arrival at St. Helena, 5. Residence at the Briars, 6. Removes to Longwood, 10. Begins to write his memoirs, 11. Generosity to an old Malay, 12. Space allotted to his walks, 12. Precautions against his escape, 13 His opinion of Marat, 15. Of Miss Williams' "Present State of France," 15. His hours of rising, 15. Habits at Longwood, 16. Refuses to see Sir Hudson Lowe, 17 Subsequent interview with Sir Hudson, 18. Opinion of Sir G. Cockburn, 18, 21. Disapproves of, and alters the paper sent for the signature of his friends, 20. His aversion to St. Helena, 20. Interview with Captain Hamilton, 21. With Colonel and Miss Wilks, 21. Anecdote of Corvisart, 22. Reproaches the English government for sending out ships without chronometers, 22. Questions O'Meara as to his precise situation, relative to himself, 26. His opinion of Sir H. Lowe, i. 27, 57, 79, 101, 105, 130, 141, 146, 151, 152, 173, 175, 184, 186, 220, 230, 232. ii. 76, 104, 152, 203. Apprehensions of the gout, i. 28. Affected with catarrhal symptoms, 30. Character of Sir J. Moore, 34. Of Kleber, 34. Account of Villeneuve and of his death, 35. Character of Barre, 36. Anecdotes in proof, of the poverty of St. Helena, 37. His practice in case of malady, 38. His opinion respecting marriage, 37. Conversation respecting Warden, 38 His idea of necessary improvements in London, 38. His opinion of Sir P. Malcolm, 40 Of Lord Holland, 41. Receives Mr. Baxter, 42. His toilette, 51. Complains of a pair in his right side, 52. Receives Colonel Keating, 52. Rides out for the first time for eight weeks, 55. His birth-day, 55. His conversation with Sir H. Lowe, 57. His opinion of Sarazin, 60. Writes a letter to the English government, complaining of Sir H. Lowe, 62. Complains of being deprived of the newspapers, 63. Character of the king of Prussia, 64. Of the Bourbons, 64. Anecdote of an old woman, 65. Character of Soult, 65. Wishes to send sealed letters to bankers in Paris or London, 68. Orders his plate to be broken up for sale, 74. His intended mode of living in England, 76. Praise of Prince Leopold, 85. Number of his establishment reduced, 89. His declaration, 97. His reasons for retaining the title of emperor, 100. Characters of Savary and Fouche, 101. His idea of national titles, 101. One of his cheeks tumefied, 105. Of the Algerines, 106. Of the Neapolitans, 106. Of the English national debt, 107. Of the English as soldiers, 107. Of the battle of Waterloo, 108. Of Wellington, 108. Of Pitt's politics, 109. Of the English seamen, 110. Of the French seamen, 110. Of the American, 110. Seriously indisposed, 111. Recovers, 111. Of the Empress Josephine, 111. Of Eugene Beauharnois, 111. Indisposed, 112. Refuses medicine, 112. His reason for encouraging the Jews, 113. Of the free-masons, 114. Of Carnot, 115. Of Barras, 116. Of the Poles, 118. His intention for crowning Poniatowsky, 118. His march to Moscow, 118. Abode there, 119. Of the conflagration, 120 Of religion, 121. Of man, 122. Confesses himself a predestinarian, 123. Of Blucher 123. Of the English soldiers, 124. Of the Italians, 125. Of the Prussians, Russians, and Germans, 125. Of Prince Charles, 126. Of Schwartzenburg, 126. Of General O'Hara, 126. Of the siege of Toulon, 126. Of the Neapolitans, 127. His private understanding with the Emperor of Austria after the return from Elba, 127. Always willing to make peace with England, 128. His character of Sir Sydney Smith, 129. Challenged by Sir S. Smith, 130. Of his intentions with regard to Spain, 130. Opinion of Talleyrand, 132. Account of Duroc, 135. Anxiety for Las Cases, 139. Of the distresses in England, 139. Of the king of Saxony, 141. Of the king of Bavaria, 141.

Of Alexander, 141. Fears for his memoirs, 141. Opinion of his brother Joseph, 143 His concern for O'Meara, 144. Wishes Las Cases to leave St. Helena, 145. Opinion of Desaix, Kleber, Soult, Moreau, 146. Of Lasnes, 147. Of Massena, 148. Of Pichegru, 148. Recounts his early life, 154. Denies having offered his services to England, 154. Of General Paoli, 155. Of the English expedition to Copenhagen, 155. Of the English smugglers, 155. Of the expedition to Walcheren, 157. Of Robespierre, 160. Of the situation of England, 161. Of the probability of a revolution in France, 168. Of Georges' conspiracy, 169. Of Moreau's death, 169. Of St. Priest's death, 170. Narrow escape on the island of Lobau, 170. Attack of nervous fever, 171. Wishes his body to be burnt, 171. Character of Pozzi di Borgo, 179. Desires to have an interview with Las Cases before his departure, 180. Protests against Sir H. Lowe's conduct, 183. Presents O'Meara with a snuff-box, 187. Of the attack on Algiers, 189. Of Nelson, 190. Of the treatment of the French prisoners, 199. Of the detainment of the English travellers, 201. Of Miot, 202. Reply to the charge of poisoning his sick, and causing four thousand Turks to be shot at Jaffa, 202. Visits Countess Bertrand, 208. Account of Ceracchi's conspiracy, 209. Of the infernal machine, 210. Of the attempt to assassinate him at Schoenbrunn, 212. Of a similar attempt against him, in his own chapel, 214. Intended to invade England, 215. Opinion of the canaille, 216. Would abolish flogging in the navy, 216. More national spirit in England than in France, 217. Proposed a commercial treaty with England, 218. Had not aimed at universal dominion, 218. His mode of paying off the English national debt, 218. Of Catholic emancipation, 219. Anger towards Sir H. Lowe for having excepted Admiral Malcolm's intermediation, and then not moving in the business, 220. Message to Sir H. Lowe, 220. Disputes with Sir H. Lowe respecting his restrictions, 220, 225, 228. Complains of the English, 227. Disputes respecting the restrictions, 230. His belief in fatality, 230. The English should have retained possession of Alexandria, 231. Letter to the Emperor Paul, 232. Of his assassination, 233. Agreement with him to invade India, 234. Danger to India from the Russians, 235. Anxiety for Count Montholon, 236. Of Grouchy, 237. Of Soult, 237. Of Ney, 238. Of Mouton Duvernet, 238. Was the sovereign of the people, 239. The English guided by interest, 239. Remarks upon Longwood, 240. The means of extricating England from her difficulties, 243. Of Sir H. Lowe's cruelty, 244. Of Carnot, 246. Of Clarke, 246. His intentions towards England, 247. Denies having expressed any abhorrence of the English uniform, 247. Asks O'Meara his opinion of himself, 248. Denies having ever committed any crimes, 248. His mode of acting, 248. Of Warden's book, 255. Expresses his errors, 256. Of the prisoners at Jaffa, 256. Of Wright, 256. Of Lord Castlereagh, 259. Of Talleyrand 259. Of the means of relieving the commercial distresses of England, 260. France would have been independent of colonial produce, 260. The Belgians attached to him, 261. Nearly taken prisoner by the Uhlans, 263. People more anxious to learn the *sottises* than the qualities of a great man, 264. The answers sent up by Sir H. Lowe full of imbecility, 267. Of Talleyrand, 267. Of the report of his having turned Mahometan, 268. His contest with the Imans, 268. His plans for making canals in Egypt, 270. Of Menou, 270. Of the 13th Vendemiaire, 270. Of the French bulletins, 271. Of the English ministry, 271. Of Talleyrand's mission to Warsaw, 274. Of Ney, 275. Of Lavalette, 275. Of Pichegru's conspiracy, 276. Of Madame Montholon, 280. Complains of swellings in his legs, 280. Of Pichon, Chateaubriand, &c. 280. Of Fox, 281. Of his treatment at Elba, 282. Of Ferdinand of Spain, 283. Of Josephine, 284. Of Waterloo, 284. Of Wellington, 284. His contempt for libels, 286. Of Goldsmith, Pichon, and the Quarterly Review, 286. Of his marriages, 287. Intentions with respect to England, 288. Of

INDEX.

Lord Amherst's embassy, 288. Refuses to see Lord Amherst, if presented by Sir. H Lowe, 290. Of the plague, 290. Of the English manufactures, 291. His encouragement to French trade, 291. Of Lord Amherst's embassy, 291. Of his departure from Egypt, 292. Conversation with Capt. Cooke and Mr. Mackenzie, 293 Liked by the English sailors. 293. Of Waterloo and Wellington, 294. Of the English national spirit, 295. Of Good Friday, 295. His oath at his corronation, 296. Of Hoche, 296. Of the English Admiralty, 297. Of French and English liberty, 297. Of Lord Castlereagh, 298. Of Blacas's forgery, 298. Of Louis, 299. Of Mademoiselle Raucour, 299. Made the burial grounds independent of the friars, 300. Would not consent to the peace of Chatillon, 301. Of Davoust, Suchet, Massena, Clausel, Gerard, and Soult, 302. Of Cornwallis, 304. Asylum in England offered to him by Lord Castlereagh, 305. Of Baron Stein, 308. His power to destroy Prussia and Austria, 306. Of Metternich, 307 Lord Whitworth's interview with him, 307. The machiavelism of the English ministry, 308. His dislike to the pirates of Algiers and Tunis, 308. Of Lord Exmouth, 309. Assisted in the passage of the Meuse by the English seamen, 310. His guard formed by them at Elba, 310. Delighted with the races, 311. The English ought to have submitted to the Chinese etiquette, 313. His advice to the Emperor of Russia on the same subject, 313. Refuses his consent to Talleyrand's proposal of procuring the assassination of the Bourbons, 313. Employed in writing an account of the seven years' war of the Great Frederick, 313. His opinion of medicine, 314. Anecdote of the Marseillois, 318. Prohibited the making of eunuchs under pain of death, 317. His habits of business, 318. Opinion of the Emperor of Austria, 318. Of the Corsicans, 321. Continues to write his observations on the works of Frederick the Great, 322. Of the Corsicans, 323. Of Sir H. Lowe, 324. Of the French prisoners in England, 325. Of the attack by the English on Copenhagen, 326. Of the seizure of the Spanish frigates, 326. The peace of Amiens violated by the English, 326. The English offer to assist in making him King of France, on condition of his surrendering to them Malta, 326. Of Captain Wright, 328. Of the French and English prisoners, ii. 3. Of the Princess of Wales, 8. Of Prince Leopold, 8. Of the plots against his life, 8. Of the Venetians, 10 Of Count D'Entraigues, 10. Of Moreau, 12. Of Pichegru's plot, 13. Of the Emperor of Austria, 14. Of Bernadotte, 14. Of Bruyas, 15. Of the French and English Sailors, 17. Of the Emperor Alexander and the King of Prussia 18. Of the English armies, 18. Of the English cavalry, 19. Of Russia, 21. Of the Emperor Paul, 21. His own final intentions in regard to Europe, 23. Of the Duke d'Enghien, 24. Of Pichegru, 24. Of Cromwell, 25. Of Madame de Stael, 28. Of the embassy to China, 30. Of the proper policy of England, 30, 36. Of the French prisoners, 41. Of Santini, 46. Anxiety to possess his son's bust, 50. Character of his mother, 50. Of Josephine, 51. Of Murat, 52. Of Neapolitans, 54. Possibility of his remaining in France, after the battle of Waterloo, 54. His title to the crown of France, 59. Visit from Lord Amherst, 61. His general policy, 63. Of Wurmser, 65. His precautions against the plague, at Jaffa, 68. Letter to Sir H. Lowe, 69. Message to Sir H. Lowe, 70. Thinks that he is harshly treated, that he may be driven to suicide, 76. Reply to Lord Bathurst's speech, 77. Of Poussilguere, 79. Of the Mamelukes, 79. His birthday, 79. Anecdote of two English sailors, 80. Of the Prince of Orange, 81. Of the Queen of Prussia, 82. Malta the fittest place for his abode, 82. His wish to visit England incognito, 85. His plan to attack the allies in Paris, 86. Alexander's wish that he should marry his sister, 88. Of Narbonne, 88. Nearly taken prisoner at Waterloo, 89. Of the concordat with the Pope, 91. Of Spain, 92. His History of Corsica, 93. His prize-essay at Lyons, 94. Of Robespierre, 94. Of Marat, 94. Of Herbert, Chaumette, Collot d'Herbois, 95. Of Marie

INDEX.

Antoinette, 96. Anecdote of Sieyes, 96. Of the embassy to China, 97. Of Captain Wright, 102. Of Sir S. Smith, 102. Of Lord Wellington, 103. Of the means of relieving the distress of England, 107. Of English manners, 109. Of Marshal Jourdan and the battle of Albuera, 110. Of Wellington's mode of carrying on sieges, 110. Conversation with Admiral Plampin respecting naval affairs, 112. His intended invasion of India, 112 Of Surinam, 114. Of the pontons, 115. Of the Manuscript venu de St. Helene, 116. O' Sir Hudson Lowe's offer to build him a new house, 119. Of Mr. Boys, 121. Of the English Catholics, 121. Much pleased with the races, 122. Of Miss G * *, 126. Persists in staying at home to avoid insults, 128. Of the Edinburgh Review, 129. Takes no precautions against assassination, 130. Nearly drowned when a boy, 131. His property seized by * *, 132. Of the talents requisite for a good general, 132. Of earthquakes, 132. Of the proper policy of the English in regard to India, 134. Seriously indisposed, 136. Of patron saints, 143. Anecdote of an Italian priest, 143. Of medical men, 144. Anecdote of Sieyes, 145. Of Larrey, 146. His dislike to medicine, 149. His abstinence, 149. Communicates his wishes to Sir H. Lowe through Bertrand, 153. Of his reception by the French on his return from Italy, 155. His confidence in the French army, 157. Refuses to be styled General Bonaparte, 160. Refuses the advice of O'Meara, 163. His grief at his son's being disinherited from the succession to the Duchies of Parma, &c., 167. His feelings when in private, 167. Of the London post-office, 168. Of Lord Cochrane, 170. Anecdote of a Persian ambassador in Paris, 171. Of Lucien, 171. Of his foster-brother, 172. Of Talma, 173· His wishes respecting his body after death, 199. Disapprobation of the English custom of shutting up shops on Sunday, 202. Refuses to see Mr. Baxter, 203. Anecdote of Richelieu, 205. Of his having been generally acknowledged emperor, 207. Of the treaty of Tolentino, 208. Of the Venetians, 209. The convention saved by him, 212. His humanity to his soldiers, 212. His conduct to Col. Pepin, 213. Of Marie Louise, 216. His respect for the laws, 218. Of his marriage, 218. His plans against England, 223. His government in France, 226. His admiration of Corneille, 231. His opinion of Maitland, 231. Causes of his downfall, 232. Of the campaign of 1813, 232. Letters to the empress in favor of O'Meara, 247. Presents to O'Meara, 247. His proposal to assume the incognito, 272. His protest, 285. Letter addressed au Comte de Las Cases, 282. His declaration, 285.
Bonvivant, n. 218.
Bourbons, i. 115, 239, 242, 251, 296, 299. ii. 25, 63, 91.
Bouvet de Lozier, i. 277.
Boys, Mr., censured by Napoleon, ii. 121.
Briars, (the,) account of, i. 6
Brienne, battle of, i. 263.
Brooke, Mr., ii. 104.
Brooke's History of St. Helena, extracts from, ii. 267
Bruyes, admiral, ii. 15.
Bulletins, i. 271. ii. 235.
Burdett, Sir Francis, ii. 40.
Bust of young Napoleon, ii. 49, 50, 51, 52, 50.

CAMBRIDGE store-ship, ii. 16.
Cambronne, ii. 157.
Campan, Madame, ii. 96.
Campaign of 1813, ii. 32.
Campbell, colonel, i. 314.

INDEX.   311

Campbell, captain, i. 314.
Canaille, i. 216, 263.
Canals, intended by Napoleon in Egypt, i. 269.
Cannes, ii. 157.
Canosa, Prince of, ii. 179.
Capri, commanded by Sir H. Lowe, ii. 170. Surrendered by him to the French, 193.
Carnot, sketch of his life, i. 115. Clarke's conduct towards him, 115. His character ii. 96.
Caroline, queen, ii. 74.
Cassetti, ii. 177.
Castlereagh, lord, i. 161, 243, 247, 25., 282, 288, 298, 305. ii. 87, 91, 127, 297.
Catholics, emancipation of, i. 219. ii. 121, 129.
Cavalry, English, inferior to the French, ii. 19.
Caulaincourt, i. 263. ii. 127.
Ceracchi, his attempt against the life of Napoleon, i. 209.
Cesar, Napoleon's coachman, i. 211
Charles, a mulatto, i. 103.
Charles, prince, his character, i. 126.
Charlotte, princess, ii. 81. Her death, 216.
Chateaubriand, i. 281, 323.
Chatham, lord, i. 327.
Chatillon, peace of, i. 301. ii. 86.
China, i. 291, 288. ii. 31, 99.
China, emperor of, his edict, i. 288.
Churchill, Mr., i. 292.
Churchill, Misses, i. 292.
Ciphers, easily read, ii. 168.
Cipriani, dangerously ill, ii. 228. His death, 229.
Clarke, his conduct to Carnot, i. 246. His character, 246.
Clausel, i. 302.
Cochrane, lord, ii. 170.
Cockburn, Sir George, sails with Napoleon, i. 1. Evening parties, 9. Repairs Longwood, 9. Stations two cruizers of St. Helena, 14. Calls on Gourgaud's mother in Paris, 254. His opinion of Napoleon, 265. His own character by the emperor, i 76, 138.
Codicil to Napoleon's Will, ii. 200.
Coffee grows in the south of France, i. 261.
Cole, Mr., ii. 105.
Colonies, English, France independent of their produce, i. 261.
Commerce, distress of the English, i. 243, 260.
Commerce, treaty of, proposed by Napoleon to England, i. 217.
Commissioners of France, Russia, and Austria, their arrival at St. Helena, i. 39.
    Sir H. Lowe's aversion to them, ii. 158.
Concordat of the Bourbons with the Pope, ii. 91.
Condorcet, ii. 83.
Congress of Vienna, their determination to send Napoleon from Elba to St. Helena, i. 61
Conscription, ii. 225.
Conspiracies against Napoleon—
        by Ceracchi, i. 209.

Conspiracies by St. Regent Imolan, &c., i. 210, 212.
 by a young man at Schoenbrunn, i. 212
 by a Saxon, i. 214.
 by Pichegru, i. 276.
 by the Allies, i. 282.
Conspiracy, Napoleon's disregard of, ii. 130.
Convention, in danger, ii. 212. Offer the chief command to Napoleon, 212. Saved by Napoleon, 212.
Cook, captain, i. 293.
Cooper, (French,) anecdote of, ii. 218.
Copenhagen, the expedition to, i. 155, 326.
Corneille, ii. 231.
Cornwallis, marquis of, i. 304.
Corsica, history of, by Napoleon, ii. 93.
Corsicans, their character, ii. 321, 323.
Corvisart, his character, i. 22. Refuses to attend Louis, 299.
Coster, i. 276.
Cossacs, i. 263, 264.
Courier newspaper, ii. 102.
Crime, Napoleon denies having committed any, i. 246, 257.
Crescentini, ii. 317.
Cromwell, ii. 25.
Curate of St. Rioque, i. 300.

D'Angouleme, duc, ii. 231.
D'Angouleme, duchess, i. 299.
D'Artois, count, i. 64. ii. 157.
Daru, count, ii. 10.
David transport, arrival of, i. 241.
Davie, captain, ii. 58.
Davoust, i. 266, 302.
Deadwood, camp at, i. 12, 163, 311. Races at, ii. 122.
Debt, (the national) of England, i. 107, 218, 243.
Declaration of the Allies, ii. 284, 285.
Deciphering, (private office for,) in Paris, ii. 169.
Defection of the Bavarians, ii. 233.
Dejeune de trois Amis, ii. 130.
D'Enghien, duke, i. 206, 257, 278, 287. ii. 24.
Denon, i. 267.
D'Entraigues, count, his arrest by Bernadotte, ii. 11. Betrays the Bourbons, 11. Escapes to Switzerland, 11. Calumniates Napoleon, 11.
Desaix, i. 146, 191. ii. 12.
Desgenettes, his conduct at Jaffa, i. 204.
Desnouttes Lefebvre, i. 157.
Destiny, Napoleon's belief in, i. 123, 230, 315, 317. ii. 130, 149, 153.
Directory, French, their conduct towards Napoleon, ii. 156. Corrupted by the Venetians, 209.
Disturbances in England, i. 262.
Dominion, (universal,) not aimed at by Napoleon, i. 218, 281.

INDEX. 313

Dorset, duchess of, ii. 65.
Douglass, major, i. 129.
Downfall, (Napoleon's,) its causes, ii. 232.
Drake, i. 174.
Dubois, ii. 217.
Duphot, general, ii. 208.
Duroc, i. 135. ii. 20.

EDINGBURGH REVIEW, ii. 117, 129.
Education, ii. 227.
Egypt, Napoleon's plans for making canals there, i. 269. Reasons for leaving it, 292.
El-Arish, capitulation, ii. 351.
Elba, Napoleon's reasons for quitting it, i. 282.
Ellis, embassy to China, ii. 238.
Elphinstone, Mr., his presents to Napoleon, ii. 61, 273.
Emancipation, Catholic, i. 219. ii. 129.
Embassy, Lord Amherst's to China, i. 288, 291, 312. ii. 30, 98.
Emperor, disputes with Napoleon concerning that title, 96, 99.
Enghien, duc d', i. 206, 257, 278, 287. ii. 24.
England, i. 139, 161, 215, 252, 259, 262, 282, 288, 291, 305. ii. 36, 84, 109.
English, Napoleon's opinion of them, i. 151, 239, 325. Their dislike of the French, 21 Their detention in France, ii. 23. Their preference of the bottle to women, ii. 109.
English commerce, remedy suggested by Napoleon for its relief, i. 243, 259.
English manufactures, i. 201.
English national debt, i. 218. ii. 30.
English travellers, their detainment in France, i. 201. Will change the English feeling towards Napoleon, 238.
Entraigues, count d', ii. 10, 12.
Escapes, Napoleon's at Arcola, ii. 130. At Toulon, 130. From drowning, 131.
Esling, battle of, ii. 93.
Eunuchs, the making of, prohibited by Napoleon, ii. 317.
Exmouth, lord, his expedition against Algiers, i. 309.
Expenditure, table of that established at Longwood, ii. 266.
Experiment, her arrival at St. Helena, ii. 34.

FAGAN, colonel, ii. 56.
Fatalism, Napoleon's belief in, i 123, 230, 315. Anecdote in confirmation of it, 316 Napoleon's belief in it, 317, ii. 130, 149, 152.
Fehrzen, major, ii. 20.
Ferdinand, king of Spain, i. 249, 283. ii. 62, 92.
Fere, (regiment de la,) ii. 131.
Festing, captain, i. 284.
Fetes, given to Napoleon on his return from Italy, i. 156.
Firing, (insufficiency of,) at Longwood, ii. 7. Furniture broken up to supply the want of it, 108. Fresh complaints of its deficiency, 111. Sir H. Lowe regulates it by the consumption at Plantation House, 114.
Flogging in the navy, i. 216.
Fontainbleau, (treaty of,) violated by the Allies, i. 282.
Fouche, his character, i. 101. Worse than Robespierre, ii. 95. Never in the confidence of Napoleon, 97.

Fox, i. 281. ii. 63, 65.
Franceschi, Cipriani, ii. 176.
Frederick the Great, his seven years' war, i. 313, 322. His character as a general ii. 132.
Freemantle, admiral, ii. 193.
Freemasons, i. 114.
French heiress, ii. 127.
French prisoners, i. 200.

GENERALS, talents requisite to, ii. 132
Gentilini, i. 103.
Georges, i. 156, 187, 276.
Gerard, i. 302.
Goldsmith, i. 286.
Good-Friday, i. 295.
Gor, captain, i. 314.
Gorrequer, major, i. 68, 69, 75, 80, 137, 174.
Government, (Napoleon's) defended, ii. 226.
Gourgaud, ii. 140.
Graham, general, ii. 110.
Grassini, i. 317.
Grouchy, i. 237, 296.
Gunner, (of the Baring,) his present of a bust of young Napoleon to the emperor, ii. 49, 51, 55, 59. Count Bertrand's letter to him, 274.
Gustavus, anecdote of, ii. 28.

HALL, William, dismissed from Longwood, ii. 34.
Hamilton, captain, his interview with Napoleon, i. 21.
Harrison, major, his conduct to Napoleon, ii. 303.
Haugwitz, i. 140.
Hebert, ii. 95.
Heiresses, French, ii. 127.
Hepatitis, (first appearance of,) in Napoleon, ii. 149.
Hobhouse, Mr., sends his "*Last Reign of the Emperor Napoleon*," to Bonaparte, i. 53 Kept back by Sir H. Lowe, ii. 205.
Hoche, general, i. 296.
Hodson, major, i. 266.
Holland, lord, his protest against the second reading of Bonaparte's detention bill i. 41

JAFFA, i. 202, 256. ii. 67.
Jews, encouraged by Napoleon, i. 113.
Imans, Napoleon's religious contest with them, i. 368.
Imolan, one of the contrivers of the infernal machine, i. 210
Impuissance of Gustavus, ii. 28.
Impuissance, supposed, of Napoleon, ii. 28.
Incognito, proposals made by the emperor to assume it, ii. 272
India, i. 231, 234. ii. 112, 134.
Innes, captain, i. 314.
Invasion of England, i. 215. ii. 223

INDEX.

Intrigue, anecdotes of, by Napoleon, ii. 125, 127.
Joseph Bonaparte, his character, i. 143. Sovereignty of Spanish South America proposed to him, 221. His affection for Napoleon, 222. ii. 182.
Josephine, the empress, i. 111, 284, 287. ii. 51.
Jourdan, marshal, his character, ii. 110.
Journal, Las Cases', seized by Sir H. Lowe, i. 143.
Ireland, i. 288, 296.
Italians, their fidelity to Napoleon, i. 125.
Julia, arrival of, i. 221.

KEATING, colonel, presented to Napoleon, i. 52.
Kleber, his character, i. 34, 147, 269.
Koller, baron, ii. 87.
Kolli, baron, ii. 62.
Ko-tou, i. 288, 289, 313. ii. 30, 67, 98.

LABEDOYERE, at the battle of Waterloo, ii. 90. At Grenoble, 157. His character, 215
La Haye, i. 276.
Lama, the Grand, ii. 43, 44, 45, 46.
Larry, his opinion that it would be an act of humanity to comply with the wishes of the sick at Jaffa, i. 204. His character, ii. 146.
Lasnes, his character, i. 147.
Lavalette, i. 275.
Las Cases, count, i. 133. Taken into custody, 137. Napoleon wishes him to leave St. Helena, 145. Alters his opinion of Sir H. Lowe, 149. His motives for following Napoleon, 166, 172. Leaves St. Helena, 184. Sends provisions to Napoleon, 202. The cause of Napoleon's irritation against Sir H. Lowe, 274, 279.
Las Cases, jun. his letter to Mr. O'Meara, i. 242.
Lauderdale, lord, ii. 207.
Leipsic, battle of, ii. 233.
Le Musa, i. 308.
Lentils, ii. 120.
Leopold, Prince, ii. 8.
Leslie, his pneumatic machines for making ice, i. 56.
Letters, regulation of, as applied to Napoleon and his suite, i. 13. All that pass through the London post-office, opened, ii. 167.
Libels, Napoleon's contempt for, i. 265, 280, 286. ii. 28, 199.
Liberty, French and English compared, i. 297.
Liberty, declared by Lord Castlereagh to be merely a usage, ii. 87. The battle of Waterloo fatal to it, 227.
Liver-complaint, its prevalence at St. Helena, ii. 260.
Liverpool, Lord, packet addressed to him from Longwood, ii. 51.
Lobau, island of, i. 170.
Lodi, i. 314.
London post-office, ii. 168.
London, Napoleon's wish to visit it incognito, ii. 85.
Longwood, description of, i. 6. Improvement of, 9. Napoleon there, 9. The drawing-room on fire, 50. Scarcity and bad quality of the water, 228. Incredible number of rats, 303. Scarcity of fuel, ii. 7. Overrun with spurge, 77. Scarcity of fuel, ii. 108 Idem, 111. State of Count Montholon's apartments, 120. Earthquake, 132.

Lorri, Ignatio, ii. 172.
Lowe, (Sir Hudson,) his arrival at St. Helena, i. 17. His instaliation, 17. Visit to Long wood, 17. First interview with Napoleon, 18. Sends a declaration to Longwood for the signature of Napoleon's suite, 19. His charges relative to the treatment of the French, 23. Orders the shopkeepers to give them no credit, 23. Forbids all communication with them, 23. Places sentinels to keep all visitors from Longwood, 23. Grows more suspicious, 24. Pays several visits to Longwood, and at last obtains an interview with Napoleon, 24. Alarm at a tree that overhangs the ditches, 24. Orders it to be grubbed up, 24. Visits Count Bertrand, 25. Informs him that Napoleon must be seen daily by some British officer, 25. Wishes Napoleon to dismiss O'Meara, 29. Issues a proclamation forbidding any person to bear letters to or from Napoleon, or any of his suite, 30. Wishes to reduce Bonaparte's establishment, 56. Sends a letter to Longwood, demanding £12,000 per annum for the maintenance of Napoleon and suite, 57. Threatening language respecting Napoleon, 61. Complains of Napoleon's letters, 77. Expects an apology from Napoleon, 83. Imposes fresh obligations on the French, 80. Letter to Napoleon in answer to his declaration, 98. Regulations respecting sentinels, 116. Objects to let the produce of Napoleon's plate be at the disposal of the French, 130. Makes a fresh reduction in the allowance of meat and wine, 136. Threatens to send Las Cases off the island, 171. Allows Las Cases to return to Longwood, 172. Letter to Napoleon, 180. Refuses permission to Las Cases to see Napoleon previous to his departure, 184. Sends up some coffee for the use of Napoleon,199. Mistakes the meaning of the phrase "nous ecrivons," in a letter of Bertrand's, 225. Interference in the kitchen, 226. Selects the newspapers for Napoleon's perusal, 240. Desires O'Meara to repeat Napoleon's conversations, 241. Has recommended Lord Bathurst to raise O'Meara's salary to £500 per annum, 242. His economy, 261. Surprise at the French expenditure, 262. Anger against Las Cases for sending provisions to Napoleon, 262. Allows more liberty to Napoleon, 266. Inspects the ditches, 272. Declares his wish to accommodate, 279. Expects Captain Poppleton to be a spy on the followers of Napoleon, 318. Changes the livery of Napoleon's servants, ii. 46. Reproaches O'Meara with not having vindicated him to Napoleon, 68. Hi. minute examination of the bills, 105. His anger against Mr. O'Meara for having borrowed Napoleon's horse for Miss Eliza Balcombe, 121. For having lent books to Napoleon, 123. His dislike to the commissioners, 158. Disputes with Bertrand respecting the conveyance of letters, 158. Refuses to allow Napoleon the title of emperor, 161. Anecdote of his being duped when commanding the island of Capri, 176. His letter to Count Montholon, 264. His reply to Count Bertrand, 275.
Louis, his letter to Napoleon, i. 357. His qualities, 229. His timidity, 300. Forced upon the French, ii. 24.
L'Ouverture, Toussaint, ii. 113.
Lucien Bonaparte, ii. 170, 171.
Luxembourg, ii. 132.

MACARTNEY, lord, his embassy to China, ii. 97, 98, 99, 100.
Machiavelism, more practised by the English ministry than any other, i. 808.
Machine, infernal, i. 210, 218, 266. ii. 8.
Machines, too numerous, i. 291.
Macirone, colonel, ii. 47.
Mackenzie, Mr., i. 293.
M'Lean, Dr., i. 143.
Mahometanism, i. 288.

Maitland, captain, ii. 231.
Mahratta, princess, ii. 135.
Malady, Napoleon's remedy for, i. 37.
Malcolm (Sir Pulteny,) presented to Napoleon, i. 40. Takes leave of him, 76. Returns from the Cape, 136. Interview with Napoleon, 191, 224, 284. Defends Sir Hudson Lowe, ii. 324, 56. Sails for England, 59.
Malcolm, lady, i. 284, ii. 66, 69.
Malouet, i. 326.
Malta, i. 231.
Mamelukes, ii. 79.
Manning, Mr., ii. 43.
Mantua, siege of, ii. 65.
Manuscrit venu de Ste. Helene, ii. 116, 121.
Maresca, ii. 176.
Maret, i. 257, ii. 94.
Maria transport arrives at St. Helena, ii. 101.
Marie Antoinette, ii. 96.
Marie Louise, i. 287, ii. 87, 130, 217.
Marchand, i. 145, 181.
Marlborough, ii. 132.
Marmont, his treachery, ii. 87.
Marriage, (Napoleon's), particulars of it, ii. 218.
Marriage, Napoleon's opinion, i. 37.
Marseilloise, characterized by Napoleon, i. 316.
Massena, his character, i. 148, 238, 302 ; ii. 201.
Masseria, i. 158.
Maxwell, captain, Murray, ii. 61.
Meade, general, i. 71, 72.
Mehee, de la Touche, i. 276.
Menou, i. 270, ii. 269.
Merry, Mr., ii. 65.
Metternich, i. 307.
Meuron, i. 78.
Mœurs et Coutumes des Corses, ii. 323.
Meynell, (captain,) presented to Napoleon, i. 40. The emperor's anxiety on account of his illness, ii. 328.
Ministry, the English, i. 271, 291, 297, 307, 326 ; ii. 5, 13, 23, 84, 138.
Miot, i. 202.
Moira, lord, ii. 134.
Money, raised in London for Napoleon's expedition from Elba, i. 326.
Money, Napoleon's, seized by **, ii. 132.
Monks, Napoleon's aversion to them, i. 300.
Montchenu, (marquis of,) his arrival at St. Helena, i. 39. His manners, 135. Comes to guard, not to dine with Napoleon, 265. His imbecility, 292. His indecent language, 312.
Montholon, general, i. 187, 236, 323 ; ii. 121.
Montholon, Madame, i. 280.
Moore, (Sir John,) his character, i. 34.
Moreau, his character, i. 146. His share in George's conspiracy, 169. His death, 169

Privy to Pichegru's conspiracy, 277. His character, ii. 9. Anecdote of his death, 11
His conduct towards Pichegru, 12. His celebrated retreat condemned, 13.
Moreau, Madame, anecdote of, ii. 9.
Moscow, conflagration of, i. 120. Napoleon's retreat from, i. 323.
Mouton, Duvernet, i. 238.
Murat, death of, i. 15. His character, 15. His bad conduct, 127. His official papers
falsified, 298. His expedition to Cicily, 319. His declaration respecting the battle
of Waterloo, ii. 47. Napoleon's intention of dethroning him, 52. His bravery, 215.
Mussey, i. 276.

NABOBS, ii. 135.
Naples, descent upon, by Sir J. Stewart, ii. 193.
Narbonne, his character, ii. 88. His birth, 88.
National debt, (English,) Napoleon's mode of paying it, i. 218, 243.
National spirit, greater in England than in France, i. 217, 295.
Neapolitans, character of, i. 127, ii. 54.
Nelson, lord, i. 190.
Newspapers, (English,) editors of, in pay of the Bourbons, i. 250.
Ney, his promise to bring back Napoleon in an iron cage, i. 238.
Ney, his conduct at Fontainbleau, i. 275.

OATH, Napoleons's, at his coronation, i. 296.
Ocean, her arrival at St. Helena, ii. 34.
Officers of the 53d, their camp at Deadwood, i. 12. Introduced to Napoleon, 14. Re
ceive hints from Sir H. Lowe, that their visits to Madame Bertrand were not agree?
ble to him, 23.
O'Hara, general, i. 126.
O'Meara, Mr. Barry, his first interview, with Napoleon, i. 2. His certificate from Captain Maitland, 4. Questioned by Sir H? Lowe respecting Napoleon, 24. Questioned
by Napoleon as to his precise situation in regard to himself, 26. His reply, 26. Singular interview with Napoleon, 70. Offers to resign, 91. Assists Count Bertrand in
translating the new restrictions, 92. Dines with the commissioners, 104. Attacked
by the liver complaint, 143. Attention of Bonaparte to him, 144. Endeavors to effect
a reconciliation between Napoleon and Sir H. Lowe, 178. Is presented with a snuff
box by Napoleon, 187. Defends the character of the English ladies against Pillet, 201.
Is requested by Sir H. Lowe to report Napoleon's conversations, 241. Receives a letter from young Las Cases, 242. Gives Napoleon his opinion of himself, 249. More fit
to write about Napoleon than any one, 264. Defends the practice of medicine in a
conversation with Bonaparte, 314. Disputes with Sir H. Lowe, ii. 6. Disputes with
Sir H. Lowe respecting the newspapers, 26. Dines with Lord Amherst, 60. Interrogated by Sir H. Lowe in presence of Sir T. Reade, 73. Ordered by Sir H. Lowe tc
hold no conversation with Napoleon except on medical subjects, 90. Refuses to betray Napoleon's confidence, 91. Rallied by Napoleon on his supposed attachment for
Miss * *, 125. Reproached by Sir H. Lowe for not having defended himself and the
English ministry against Napoleon, 140. Has a long conversation with Bertrand respecting the bulletins of health, 159. Violently abused by Sir Hudson Lowe, 165.
Disputes with Sir H. Lowe, 174. Ordered to quit the governor's house, 175. Censured
by Sir H. Lowe for buying goods for the French at Longwood, 197. Refuses to go
again to Plantation House, 204. Is informed by Sir H. Lowe that he is only tolerated
to visit Napoleon, ii. 207. Interrogated by the governor respecting his conversations
with Napoleon, 209. Farther disputes with Sir H. Lowe, 213. Refuses to give up his

rights as an English officer, 221. Recounts to the emperor the manner of his treatment by Sir H. Lowe, 227. Is informed that he is not to pass out of Longwood, 235. Tenders his resignation in consequence. 236. Has an audience of Napoleon, 236. Is released, 237. Is requested by the colonel of the 66th to withdraw from the mess, 241 Letter from the colonel, 242. Letter in reply, 242. Dismissed from attending on Napoleon by the British government, 245. Receives a snuff-box and a statue of Napoleon from the emperor himself, 247. His parting from the emperor, 247. His letter to Lord Keith, 263. To Colonel Lascelles, 290.
Ordener, colonel, i. 279.
Oudinot, i. 238.

Palm, his arrest and death, i. 266.
Paoli, i. 155.
Paul, Emperor of Russia, i. 232. His assassination, 233. His intended invasion of India, 234. Idem, ii. 21.
Pauline, i. 130, ii. 292.
Peltier, i. 237, 250, 266.
Pepin, colonel, ii. 213.
Peraldi, i. 191.
Phaeton, frigate, her arrival at St. Helena, i. 17.
Philadelphi, society, formed against Napoleon, i. 208.
Phillipeaux, i. 129.
Piccioli, ii. 189.
Pichegru, his character, i. 148. Proofs that he committed suicide, 206. His conspiracy, 276. Betrayed by D'Intraigues, ii. 10. Napoleon's intentions towards him, 24
Pichon, i. 280, 286.
Pillet, i. 198, 201 ; ii. 4.
Piontkowski, i. 104.
Pitt, i. 109, 281.
Plague, i. 290, ii. 67.
Plampin, admiral, ii. 58, 111.
Plate, (Napoleon's,) broken up for sale, i. 74. Sold, 93, 185.
Podargus, ii. 56.
Poles, their attachment to Napoleon, i. 118. In cold weather, better soldiers than the French, 118.
Policy of Napoleon in case of landing in England, ii. 223.
Polignac, i. 278.
Poniatowsky, Napoleon's intention of making him king, i. 118.
Pontons, i. 199. ii. 4, 115.
Pope, (the,) ii. 51.
Poppleton, captain, i. 103, 117, 134, 170, 224, 265, 266, 271, 318. ii. 46.
Port regulations at St. Helena, ii 286.
Post-office, (London,) all letters opened there, ii. 109.
Poussilguere, ii. 79.
Pozzo di Borgo, i. 179, 190. ii. 179.
Pradt, Abbe de, ii. 119.
Predestination, Napoleon's belief in, i. 123, 230, 315, 316. ii. 130, 149.
Presents, Napoleon's, to Mr. O'Meara, i. 187. ii. 247.
Presents, Mr. Elphinstone's, to the emperor, ii. 61.
Prisoner, Napoleon nearly made one by the Uhlans, i. 263. At the close of the battle of Waterloo, ii. 89.

Prisoners, French, how treated by the English, i. 200, 325. ii. 9.
Prisoners, Turkish, at Jaffa, i. 202, 256.
Prize-essay, by Napoleon, ii. 94.
Proclamation, Sir H Lowe, ii. 238, 289, 296.
Protest, (Napoleon's,) against Sir H. Lowe's conduct, i. 182. Against his being made a prisoner, ii. 285.
Provisions scantily supplied to Napoleon, ii. 42. Indifferent quality, 46, 57.
Prussia, king of, his character, i. 63, 140, 306. ii. 18.
Prussia, queen of, her character, ii. 82.

RACES at Deadwood, i. 311. ii. 121.
Rails (iron) to surround Napoleon's house, i. 241, 272.
Rainsford, Mr., his death, i. 312.
Rapp, i. 287.
Rats, numerous at Longwood, i. 303.
Rats, hunting of them, i. 303, 304.
Raucour, Mademoiselle, her funeral, i. 299.
Reade, Sir Thomas, i. 57, 76, 79, 85, 142, 167, 179, 224, 240, 312, 322. ii. 55, 142, 158, 290
Real, ii. 74.
Regnier, general, ii. 17.
Religion, Napoleon's ideas of, i. 121, 273.
Resignation, tendered by Mr. O'Meara, ii. 236.
Restrictions, imposed on Napoleon's suite, ii. 264.
Restrictions on Napoleon, ii. 270.
Review, Edinburgh, ii. 117, 129.
Review, Quarterly, i. 197, 256, 286. ii. 102.
Revolution, probability of one in France, i. 168. The former one defended by Napoleon, ii. 206.
Richelieu, anecdote of, ii. 205.
Ripsley, captain, ii. 314.
Riviere, i. 276.
Robespierre, i. 160. ii. 94.
Romanzoff, ii. 88
Rome, capture of, by the French, ii. 208
Rosey, captain, i. 279.
Rovigo, duke of, ii. 74.
Rousseau, i. 103
Russians, dangerous to the rest of Europe, i. 236. ii. 21, 31.

SAINTS, patron, ii. 43.
St. Denis, i. 143, 245.
St Helena, Napoleon's arrival at, i. 5. Description of, 6. Its poverty, 86. ii. 114. Further description of, 251, 263. Its port regulations, 286.
St. Hilaire, i. 276.
St. Priest, general, his death, i. 170.
St. Regent, one of the contrivers of the infernal machine, i. 210
St. Roque, the curate of, i. 300.
St. Victor, i. 276
Saliceti, ii. 176.
Santini, i. 104. ii. 35, 46. His intention of shooting Sir H. Lowe, 230.

INDEX. 321

Savary, his character, i. 101. His pamphlet respecting Wright, 102.
Saxe, Marechal, ii. 32.
Saxony, king of, his character, i. 141.
Schoenbrun, i. 212.
Scott, released from prison, i. 230.
Schwartzenbergh, his character, i. 126.
Seamen, American, superior to the English, i. 110.
Seamen, English, Napoleon's opinion of them, i. 310. Their friendship for him, 293. His esteem for them, 310. Assist him in forming a bridge of boats over the Meuse, 310. Form his guard at Elba, 311. Compared with the French, ii. 17. Anecdote of the escape of two from Verdun, ii. 80.
Sections, their attack on the convention, ii. 212.
Shipwrights, not sent to Algiers or Tunis by Napoleon, i. 308.
Sicily, Murat's expedition to, i. 319. Plot to drive the English out of it, 320.
Sieges, English mode of carrying them on, ii. 110.
Sieyes, anecdote of, ii. 96, 145.
Skelton, colonel, i. 145.
Skelton, Mrs., i. 280.
Smith, sir Sidney, his character, i. 129. His conduct at Acre, 129. Challenges Napoleon, 130. His conduct towards Kleber, 129.
Smithers, Mr., ii. 89.
Smugglers, English, i. 55, 326.
Snuff-box presented by Napoleon to Mr. O'Meara, i. 187. ii. 247.
Soldiers, English, i. 107, 124. ii. 19.
Soult, his character, i. 65, 237, 303. His conduct at Albuera, ii. 110.
Spain, Napoleon's intentions with regard to it, i. 130.
Spain, queen of, ii. 92.
Spurge, Longwood overrun with it, ii. 77.
Stael Madame de, her character, ii. 28. Not the authoress of the Manuscrit venu de Ste. Helene, 118.
Stenfell, captain, i. 284.
Statue, Napoleon's presented by himself to Mr. O'Meara, ii. 247.
Stein, Baron, i. 306.
Strange, sir Thomas, i. 166, 167.
Stuart, General, ii. 17, 193.
Sturmor, baron, i. 185, 292, 323, ii. 173.
Subsidies, English, ii. 75.
Suchet, i. 302.
Sugar made from beet-root, i. 260
Suicide, ii. 76, 93, 152 ....
Suite (Napoleon's) restrictions imposed on them, ii. 264. Document signed by them, 264.
Sunday, observation of, in England, ii. 202.
Surgeons, i. 314, ii. 144.
Surinam, Napoleon's intention of invading it, ii. 114.
Surveillers, count, ii. 247.
Suspension of arms in 1813 fatal to Napoleon, ii, 232.
Suzzarelli, ii. 17 .

TALLEYRAND, his character, i. 132. His conduct in regard to the Duke d'Enghien, 206. His treachery and corruption, 259. His triumph, the triumph of immorality, 267. His mission to Warsaw, 264. Proposes to Napoleon the assassination of the Bourbons, 318.

His character, ii. 95, 97. Defends assassination, 108. Fete given by him to Napoleon, 156. Wishes to celebrate the anniversary of the execution of Louis XVI. 156.
Talleyrand, Madame, i. 267.
Talma, ii, 173.
Title, Napoleon persists in retaining that of emperor, ii. 160
Titles, Napoleon's opinion of them, i. 101.
Tolentino, treaty of, ii. 208.
Tortoise, arrival of, i. 251.
Toulon, siege of, i. 126.
Trade, (English,) remedy for its distress, proposed by Napoleon, i. 260.
Turenne, ii. 132.
Turkey, its approaching fall, i. 231, 285.

UHLANS, i. 263.
Undaunted, (the) sailors of, fond of Napoleon, i. 293.
Usher, captain, i. 309.

VANDAMME, anecdote of, i. 77.
Varennes, Billaud de, ii. 95.
Vendemiaire, the 13th of, i. 270.
Venetians, their massacre of the French, ii. 209. Their intrigues to corrupt the direc.ory 209.
Venice, occupied by the French troops, ii. 10.
Villeneuve, admiral, Napoleon's account of his conduct and the manner of his death, i. 35.
Virion, general, i. 200.

WALCHEREN, expedition to, i. 157.
Wales, the princess of, her intention to visit Napoleon at Elba, ii. 8. Her visit to Marie Louise, 8.
Wallis, captain, ii. 124.
Warden, Napoleon's opinion of him, i. 38. His book, 256. Sent by Sir H. Lowe to Napoleon, 255. Napoleon's opinion of it, 256. His error respecting Massena, 256 ; respecting the prisoners at Jaffa, 256 ; respecting Maret, 257 ; respecting Napoleon's conversion to Mahometanism, 268 ; respecting Talleyrand, 274 ; respecting Wright, 276 ; respecting Madame Montholon, 280.
Water-company, (English) attempt to establish one at Paris, i. 255.
Waterloo, the battle of, i. 108, 284. ii. 47, 89, 227.
Webb, Mr., i. 314.
Wellington, i. 108, 284, ii. 103, 110, 132, 140.
Whitworth, lord, his interview, with Napoleon, i. 307. His character, ii. 64.
Williams, Miss, Napoleon's opinion of her "Present State of France," i. 15.
Wilson, Sir, Robert, i. 192.
Wirtembergh, queen of, ii. 220.
Wives, sale of, ii. 129.
Women, too many allowed to follow the English armies, ii. 19. Anecdote of the French 19. Their society neglected by the English for the bottle, 109. The life of conversation, 109.
Wounds, Napoleon's, ii. 131.
Wright, captain, i. 206, 256, 276, ii. 328, 102, 124.

YAMSTOCKS, i. 56.
Younghusband, Mrs., i. 311.

www.ingramcontent.com/pod-product-compliance
Lightning Source LLC
Chambersburg PA
CBHW030747230426
43667CB00007B/878